Race, Migration and Schooling

Race, Migration and Schooling

John Tierney, MA
Senior Lecturer in Sociology, New College, Durham

Peter Dickinson, MA
Senior Lecturer in Social Policy, New College, Durham

Michael Syer, PhD

Chris Mullard, PhD
Director—Race Relations Policy and Practice
Research Unit, University of London Institute of
Education

Jagdish Gundara, PhD
Co-ordinator of the Centre for Multicultural Education
University of London Institute of Education

Crispin Jones, MA
Lecturer in Comparative Education, University of
London Institute of Education

Keith Kimberley, BA
Lecturer in English, University of London Institute of
Education

HOLT, RINEHART AND WINSTON
London · New York · Sydney · Toronto

Holt, Rinehart and Winston Ltd: 1 St Anne's Road,
Eastbourne, East Sussex BN21 3UN

British Library Cataloguing in Publication Data
Race, migration and schooling.
  1. Children of immigrants—Education—
Great Britain
I. Tierney, John
371.97   LC3747.G7
ISBN 0–03–910362–5

Typeset by Phoenix Photosetting, Chatham
Printed in Great Britain by Thetford Press Ltd, Norfolk.

Last digit is print number: 9 8 7 6 5 4 3 2 1

Contents

Acknowledgements

My thanks are due to the authors of the chapters presented here, for their co-operation and commitment to the project. Mention must also be made of Helen Mackay, college editor at Holt, Rinehart and Winston, whose encouragement and support is much appreciated. Finally, thanks to my family, who put up with the disruptions and neglect entailed in getting the book together.

John Tierney
July 1981

We are grateful to the following for permission to reproduce material used in this book:

All London Teachers Against Racism and Fascism (ALTARF)
Arrow Books
Robert Brett (ALTARF)
Hazel Carby (Yale University)
Central Statistical Office
Granada Publishing
Her Majesty's Stationery Office (HMSO)
Issues in Race and Education Collective
Alex James
Lawrence & Wishart
Elizabeth Lindsay
Macmillan
Methuen Educational
Clara Mulhern (ALTARF)
National Association for Multiracial Education (NAME)
Open University Press
Irene Payne (ALTARF)
Jan Pollock (ALTARF)
Race Today Collective
Routledge and Kegan Paul
Tavistock Publications
Yale University Press

To Angela

Introduction
JOHN TIERNEY

As well as providing a critical introduction to the field of race and schooling and a sourcebook for those working in education, it is hoped that this book will help in the fight against racism and racialism. The contributors to this collection of readings are united on at least one point: that all forms of racism are to be denounced. Racism is both morally reprehensible and intellectually falacious, though the struggle against racism requires more than moral and intellectual arguments: it also requires political action. Many non-racists, and indeed anti-racists, are unwittingly caught up in institutional practices which have racialist effects, despite their own good intentions. Such effects are those which discriminate between sections of the population, which a racist would define as racially different. Such discrimination often results in the establishment or reproduction of social differences which then appear to justify racism itself. We are particularly concerned to combat the unconscious racism and the often unintended racialism that pervades our education system, as it does our society.

Primarily the book has been written for students in colleges and departments of education pursuing courses in multiracial/cultural/ethnic education, as well as practising teachers, especially those working with minority group children, though we feel strongly that the issues raised here are important for all teachers. However, as a good deal of the material presented here is of a general nature, it is hoped that it will also be useful for older students in schools and colleges of further education, as well as undergraduates taking courses in race relations in universities and polytechnics.

The book falls into three parts. It was felt important to include a certain amount of broadly based background material, thus the first part aims to provide a general introduction to the field of race, migration and race relations. Part two, which is specifically concerned with race and schooling, can therefore be read within the context of this general introduction. The final part is a resources guide.

Chapter 1 covers a very wide range of material: a theoretical discussion of racism; a discussion of the colonial background to contemporary issues and problems; a brief examination of migration into Britain; and, finally, a more detailed analysis of the position of black* people in modern British society. Concepts such as racialism,

*Following current convention we will use the term 'black' generically to refer to people from Asia, Africa and the West Indies.

prejudice, discrimination and disadvantage are discussed, and the chapter aims to illustrate the extent to which, both at the level of personal feelings and at the level of structures, racism persists as a deeply rooted feature of our society.

While the system of colonialism and its relevance to an understanding of contemporary racial issues is outlined in Chapter 1, the experiences of black and brown people as a result of Western European intrusions are looked at usually in terms of what was done *to* them, rather than in terms of what they did in response. Jagdish Gundara's chapter on black resistance redresses the balance, for here the focus is on the ways in which black people in various parts of the world, and suffering various types of oppression, have met this oppression and attempted to, or succeeded in overcoming it. The chapter stands as a challenge to orthodox versions of history which have tended to play down or even ignore struggles from below—whether on slave ships, in the colonies, or even within Britain itself. Gundara therefore repudiates those historical myths which imply that 'in the past' people behaved themselves, i.e. passively resigned themselves to oppression. The material makes important connections between resistance in history and resistance in the modern world. Events in St. Pauls, Bristol, 1980, in Brixton, London, and Toxteth, Liverpool, etc. 1981, underline the necessity for this kind of historical analysis. 'Disturbances' on English streets during the summer of 1981 have been explained away by the Home Secretary as being due to 'careless parents', and by police spokesmen as being due to a tiny clique of 'agitators' (wearing balaclavas). Chapter 2, together with Chapter 1, shows that explanations will have to go much deeper than these simplistic accounts.

Peter Dickinson's chapter, built around a framework of 'myths', examines government legislation to control black immigration into Britain, and presents some up-to-date statistical data. The chapter illustrates the racist-based nature of the immigration laws, thus underlining the fact that the policies of various governments have been racist in character. The inclusion of a section on statistics could be viewed as controversial. It is not the intention of the author to get involved in the so-called 'numbers game' over immigration figures. It is readily acknowledged that by quoting figures to show, for instance, that there are not as many black people living in Britain as many white people suggest, there is a danger of implying that something would be wrong if numbers *were* at a higher level. The numbers game has quite rightly been pointed to as a concession to racists, because it constitutes an argument set within *their* rules. It implies that the black population would be a 'problem' if it reached a certain level. On the other hand, the inclusion of some statistics is justified on the grounds that people should be aware of the reality of the situation (to the extent that statistics can do this), and therefore be in a position to argue against the myths pertaining to black people and their relationship to British society. Furthermore, such statistics are extremely relevant when we examine government legislation controlling immigration.

The second part of the book, made up of four chapters, addresses itself specifically to the question of race and education. Mike Syer presents a detailed and critical analysis of racism as a feature of Britain's education system. Developing his argument around the notion of 'atomistic' and 'deterministic' thinking, he suggests that there are tendencies within education to promote ways of thinking which make racism and racialism more likely. Syer argues that these often unconscious tendencies need to be recognized by teachers in order for racism and racialism to be eradicated.

The notion of 'multicultural education' has gained wide currency in the literature, both in Britain and in the United States, though its meaning is not always made clear. In Chapter 5 Jagdish Gundara examines the major approaches to multicultural education showing the ways in which the various approaches have been translated into actual educational practices. While there is general acceptance of Gundara's point that in Britain and in societies generally the category of race is an important aspect of diversity, he shows how different individuals and groups have developed quite different views on how best to approach racial diversity. At the level of theory and practice, Gundara, importantly, argues that educational and other social policies have avoided the real issues—such as structural inequality and institutional racism—in favour of a relatively superficial liberal reformism.

Taking models of multiracial education as his framework, Chris Mullard presents a critical analysis of the various phases of government policy *vis à vis* black children and their education. He suggests that since the early fifties there have been in essence three analytically distinct phases/models: assimilationist, integrationist and (a revised version of the latter) cultural pluralism. His crucial argument is that the various models evolved over the years, and then put into practice, have 'attempted to foster the cultural subordination and political neutralization of blacks'. For the author, multiracial education has failed because it has been used as an instrument of control, a strategy which has resulted in the increasing alienation of black youth.

The chapter by Crispin Jones and Keith Kimberley focuses directly on the response of one particular local education authority—Inner London. They discuss the range of institutions, groups and individuals involved in the whole process of schooling, showing the interactions and conflicts. This entails examining such things as the relationship between the DES and the local authority and between individual teachers and anti-racist groups. Although the authority under consideration is Inner London, the problems and issues discussed in this chapter have relevance for other local authorities. Indeed, the authors argue strongly that the phenomenon of racism should be faced up to and resisted by teachers and others in all parts of the country, irrespective of the numbers of black children in the school. For Jones and Kimberley the role of the teacher, quite simply, should be to teach anti-racism.

The third and final section of the book is a resources guide. The guide includes an extensive annotated bibliography which is not restricted to the field of education, but offers comprehensive guidance to the literature in the areas of race, race relations, migration, minorities, history and racist groups. The guide also contains detailed information on many organizations and groups which we feel will be particularly useful for teachers working in multiracial schools. Periodicals and film distributors are also listed.

1

Race, Colonialism and Migration
J. TIERNEY

The aim of this chapter is to provide a general introduction to some of the issues and problems in the field of race and migration. No specialized knowledge of sociology or race relations has been assumed.

On the premise that these issues and problems can be properly understood only if they are located within a theoretical framework, the chapter begins with a theoretical discussion of racism. Racism as a concept is approached developmentally, in the sense of building up from a relatively simple and often used definition to a more complex and, it will be argued, satisfactory definition. No grandiose attempt has been made to cover the entire range of possibilities, the aim is simply to provide a starting point.

The need to situate contemporary racial issues within a historical context is also recognized as being of crucial importance, thus the section outlining some of the features of colonialism attempts to make these connections between the past and the present.

The rest of the chapter examines migration into Britain, and the present position of black people within British society. Certain themes developed during the discussion of racism and colonialism will be reintroduced in these last two sections.

In spite of the obvious danger of oversimplification in writing an 'overview' chapter such as this, it was felt important to include a general chapter in order to provide a backcloth against which the rest of the book may be read.

RACISM

While many writers would agree that racism exists throughout the world, the massive literature available on the theme of race and race relations contains no consensus regarding a definition of the term racism. As one writer puts it: 'There exist as many definitions in the literature as there do specialists and experts in the field'.[1]

Many writers working in this field have utilized a concept of racism based upon the notion of racial prejudice existing at the level of personal feelings. In this formulation a definition of racism involves two elements. There is, first of all, a belief that the world is composed of different 'races', in the sense that human populations can be compartmentalized into different types on the basis of some immutable biological characteristics transmitted genetically from one generation to the next. Historically colour of skin has been taken as the crucial biological characteristic. Secondly, there is the belief that some of these 'races' are biologically inferior to others, this inferiority being manifested in intellectual performance, moral qualities, or forms of social behaviour. In other words that one's potential as a human being is biologically determined according to one's racial membership.

Race

Taking the first of these elements—the idea that races exist and that they can be readily classified—it is true that at the level of common sense the argument has been, and still is, a persuasive one. Such discussions of race have entered into day-to-day conversation to the extent that there is often an implicit assumption that races exist as easily measurable entities. For this reason anthropologists have in recent years gone to great lengths to stress the problematic nature of all discussions of race. The point made by the anthropologist Ashley Montagu in 1942 still stands:

> All but a few persons take it completely for granted that scientists have established the 'facts' about 'race' and that they have long ago recognized and classified the 'races' of mankind . . . It is not difficult to see, therefore, why most of us continue to believe that 'race' really corresponds to something which exists.[2]

Montagu's argument is an important one. It is that while no-one disputes the existence of physical, genetically determined differences among human beings, the actual classification of people on this basis is a *social* endeavour. It is social in that 'races' are created by theorizers processing empirically gathered data relating to physical differences into some sort of classificatory scheme. A race is a human population so defined.

One major problem facing the would-be classifier is that of deciding which biological characteristics to use as a basis for classification. Historically, scientists and laypeople alike have used what are called phenotypes; a term describing types of individuals who share certain external physical characteristics, such as skin colour or body shape. Given that different phenotypes do exist in the world, the obvious question to ask is which of the external physical characteristics should one use for classification into so-called races? Why should colour of skin, for instance, be viewed as the significant variable, and how does one measure scientifically differences in skin colour anyway? Clearly, the use of skin colour as a basis for classification has arisen socially, rather than as a result of some biological fact inherent in the enterprise. Fundamentally it has arisen out of the social fact of the domination of black/brown peoples by whites.

Modern-day anthropologists have moved away from the anachronistic reliance on phenotypes towards the use of genotypes. These are, in the words of one anthropologist, types of individuals 'which are described in terms of composition of genes and chromosomes in their cells.'[3] And he goes on to say:

> Physical anthropologists are fast forsaking the phenotypes and becoming qualified geneticists. To do otherwise would be to reduce their science to the level of alchemy.[4]

However, whether using phenotypes or genotypes, the researcher still has to contend with the fact that human populations cannot be sectioned off into neat, discrete categories. Genetic combinations have never been stable; over the centuries they have been subject to genetic drift, mutation, migration and selection. Put simply, one so-called race has blended into another across the globe. For this reason, it is quite inappropriate to speak of 'pure' races—though the notion is obviously a powerful generator of political capital. In the words of the anthropologist Raymond Firth:

> Hence to embark on the discussion regarding the intermixture of a number of hypothetical pure stocks is unprofitable, and there is no direct evidence whatever for the existence of 'pure' racial populations. To claim any purity of stock for a living European group is therefore ludicrous.[5]

Thus a whole range of factors outside of simple biology—geographical, social, political, economic—has been at work for thousands of years.

The final point I wish to make on the question of race is, I think, the most fundamental, and arises out of the observation that the classification of 'races' is a social process. Such classifications take place within specific sorts of society at specific stages of development, thus political and economic pressures have to be taken into consideration. In any discussion of race and racial types it is important to know *why* someone should want to classify people into races:

> If one has no purpose for classification, the number of races can be multiplied almost indefinitely, and it seems to me that the erratically varying number of races is a source of confusion to student, to layman, and to specialist. I think we should require people who propose a classification of races to state in the first place why they wish to divide the human species and to give in detail the important reasons for subdividing our species.[6]

This is not to suggest that we should censure scientific research in this field as such, but rather we should always be on guard against the politically distasteful uses to which such research has been and can be put.

Racism, Biology and Culture

We can now turn to the second element in this popular definition of racism: a belief that some 'races' are inferior to others. Here racism is viewed as a personal feeling that certain 'races' are inferior as a result of immutable biological factors. An example of racism in this form is provided by this quote from a modern-day racist:

> It is based on the simple principle of white leadership . . . while every race may

have its particular skills and qualities, the capacity to govern and lead and sustain civilisation as we understand it lies essentially with the European.[7]

The British sociologist Michael Banton argues for a definition of racism which stresses personal feelings:

> . . . the doctrine that a man's behaviour is determined by stable inherited charac-
> ters deriving from separate racial stocks having distinctive attributes and usually
> considered to stand to one another in relations of superiority and inferiority.[8]

The problem with this definition is that as it stands it is too restrictive; its power as a conceptual tool is weakened by its own narrowness. Because of the level on which it is situated it tends to ignore the structural features of racism, and concentrates instead on the psychological/ideational. Connections need to be made between racism as an ideological phenomenon, and the nature of particular societies and the treatment and position of racial minorities within those societies.

Along with other writers Banton has attempted to draw a distinction between the concepts racism and racialism, though this has not always taken them in the same direction. Of particular concern is Banton's usage of these terms. In his paper 'The Concept of Racism',[9] he refers to the 'relevant distinction' between racism and racialism made in 1957 by Margaret Nicholson: 'racism is more often applied to the doctrine, racialism to the practice of the doctrine.' From this standpoint, then, racism refers to the actual beliefs (or theories) which individuals possess, while racialism occurs when individuals (or institutions) put these beliefs into practice. Put like this the distinction is not necessarily to be criticized, and certainly, as I say above, a number of writers use these terms. John Rex, for instance, has written: 'Racism, the doctrine of racial differences between men, and racialism, the practice which derives from this doctrine.'[10] What is to be criticized, however, is the way in which the terms are taken up and used by Banton. He argues that racism as a term should be reserved for a doctrine of racial, biological inferiority, and that any doctrine that is not based on biological ideas should not be described as racism. Banton suggests that it is relatively uncommon nowadays for anyone to base their doctrines on the notion of biological inferiority. The pattern, he says, has been to supplant this archaic idea with more modern ideas based on cultural difference/inferiority. For him, those who speak of cultural difference/inferiority are the counterparts of 19th and early 20th century racists, but because they are aware of the 'scientific mistake' of racism they are not themselves racists. Banton illustrates his argument by referring to the views expressed by Enoch Powell and Peter Griffiths. The latter was a successful Conservative candidate in the 1964 General Election, winning the Smethwick constituency on the basis of what many described as a racist campaign. Banton writes:

> Some commentators have spoken of the 'changing nature of racism', but this is
> justified only if one defines it in terms of its functions. I argue that if we label the
> new culturally based doctrines 'racist' we may mislead people. To call them
> racialist is much preferable, but not an ideal solution. In my view these new
> arguments and sentiments are more accurately classified as forms of ethno-
> centrism.[11,12]

Thus, for Banton, the views expressed by politicians such as Powell are not racist because they supposedly do not make reference to the idea of biological inferiority. It is more preferable to call Powell's views racialist, and best of all to call them ethno-centric.[13]

This approach poses a number of immediate problems. Firstly, if he sees the policies of certain politicians as not racist but 'racialist', how is it possible to differentiate between racialism and other political policies? Secondly, if racism only has reality at the level of biological ideas, in Banton's terms, then it would follow that as soon as those involved ceased to believe in such ideas the problem of racism would disappear.[14] Thirdly, if racialism is the practice informed by a non-racist doctrine, then what should we call the practice that is informed by a racist doctrine, given that Banton seems to agree with the racism/racialism distinction on the basis of doctrine/practice?

Two basic issues have emerged in the above discussion. These we can now develop further, and in the process point to an alternative approach to racism, an approach which rejects an analysis of racism pitched simply at the level of racial prejudice and ideas. Here the focus is on the structural features of racism within the context of a capitalist society.

Firstly, is Banton correct when he says that we should only see racism as existing when there is a doctrine based upon the notion of biological inferiority in crude 19th century terms? And is he also correct in saying that nowadays politicians and others (being better informed than their 19th century counterparts) have ceased to hold these views, and exhibit doctrines based on negative evaluations of other *cultures* rather than on biologically based racial inferiority?

Secondly, just how adequate is a basic definition of racism situated at the level of psychological ideas, that is, as an astructural feature of society?

Biology and Cutlure

Taking the first of these, and for the moment arguing simply at the level at which Banton is arguing, it would be naive to assume that in modern Britain there has been a widespread appreciation of the 'scientific mistake' of racism. Most obviously racism in the form of a belief in the immutable biological inferiority of black and brown people is in strong evidence within the ranks of certain right-wing groups such as the National Front and the British Movement. Furthermore, this crude and obvious form of racism is arguably not uncommon among sections of the general public today, even though it is clearly impossible to measure this accurately. Neither can there be a guarantee of immunity from racism, as defined by Banton, among certain members of the Conserva-tive Party and its associations. In 1971 the chairman of the Sussex Monday Club told the *Daily Mirror*:

> I accept I am a racialist. If you read *Mein Kampf* you will see it has been wrongly derided. I personally am an admirer of Hitler.[15]

In this context the 'scientific racism' in the work of Putnam, Shuey, Jensen, Eysenck and others might also be mentioned.[16] Here an attempt has been made to 'scientifically' show that apparent differences in measured IQ between blacks and whites in America are the result of genetic factors. This work has produced a mass of criticisms from all quarters. In particular, scholars have criticized the IQ tests and their administration, the validity of the data produced, the uses to which the material has been put as political propaganda, and the failure of the researchers to take properly into consideration a range of historical and social factors, such as 400 years of slavery and oppression of the black people in America.[17]

However, this still leaves Banton's argument that culturally based doctrines should not be viewed as racist. Let us state the argument in its simplest form. It is that there are many white people in modern Britain (e.g. some politicians) who do not believe that black people are biologically inferior, yet are unhappy about their presence because, as white Britains, they see black cultures as alien and unacceptable. There is a negative view of black cultures. They may acknowledge that some black groups may be good at some activities, e.g. singing the Blues, but they are inferior to whites at other activities, e.g. writing pastoral sonnets, or whatever.

Even if we work within Banton's definition of racism as ideas, such apparently culturally based doctrines have to be seen as racist. This is because all such doctrines are essentially based on biology, though not always in obvious ways. One problem is that it is difficult to know with certainty just what connections are being made on the part of, say, a politician, between biology and culture. Basically what Banton means by a 'culturally based' doctrine is a variant on the 'culture of poverty' concept.[18] Black culture is seen as being different/inferior not as a result of genetically determined characteristics, but as a result of members of that racial group being socialized into specific cultural patterns. Black people thus generate their own different/inferior culture, and any negative features of this culture can therefore be blamed on black people themselves. In the same way the culture of poverty concept postulates that poverty can be blamed on the poor. Having said this, it should be noted that sometimes, although not made explicit, there is a tacit belief in a biological basis for these differences. For instance, what did Enoch Powell really mean when he made this statement in 1968?

> The West Indian or Asian does not, by being born in England, become an Englishman. In law he becomes a United Kingdom citizen by birth, in fact he is a West Indian or an Asian still.[19]

Let us take what is from Banton's point of view the most obviously non-racist doctrine: where there is a feeling of antipathy towards black culture(s), though this different/inferior culture is not viewed as being biologically determined, but simply the result of socialization processes. In this situation biology is still involved because the doctrine is formulated in terms of identifiable racial categories;[20] it is directed specifically at black people and black culture. Even if the dimension of cultural inferiority is missing, with the emphasis just on 'difference', this difference is still based on racial categories. The doctrine posits the existence of distinct racial groups, and ascribes to these racial groups particular cultural characteristics, and in this way the biology of racial membership, over a particular span of time, is linked to specific cultural patterns.

Remember that we are here discussing those who hold feelings of antipathy towards black people, and thus it is an antipathy built upon a belief in unacceptable cultural differences specifically identified with black people, and there is often, if not usually, assumed to be a biological base anyway. Furthermore, and very importantly, this ascription of negatively valued cultural characteristics on the part of what Banton calls 'racialists' or 'ethnocentrics' has actual, and potential, consequences for the groups involved. Thus these culturally based doctrines, so-called, need to be linked to the position of black people in society, and their treatment by that society. When Enoch Powell makes a speech on race it can be as powerful in its consequences as far as black people are concerned as speeches coming from what Banton would describe as more old fashioned racists. More powerful, perhaps, in that Powell, as a Westminster MP, has a certain level of status which will act to make more legitimate the sentiments being expressed. At the same time some of his audience will be unaware or unaccepting of the 'scientific mistake' of racism, and will therefore incorporate what he is saying within their total, racist, world view.

Racism as a Structural Feature of British Society

We can now discuss the second issue to emerge in the earlier discussion of Banton's work: the adequacy of a psychological/ideational definition of racism.

An adequate definition of racism has, at the very least, to recognize the ways in which racism as a doctrine constitutes a justification, or rationale, for the unequal treatment of certain groups conceived of as distinct racial categories and manifesting distinct, and negatively valued, cultures. We thus leave behind the constraints imposed by Banton's definition of racism, and move towards approaches to racism which cannot be seen simply in terms of personal feelings more or less detached from social structure. An improvement on Banton's approach is provided by the American sociologists Hodge, Struckman and Trost. They argue for a definition of racism which goes beyond 'prejudice'. What is required, they say, is a definition which embodies a condition whereby those defining themselves as superior also believe that they should put this belief into practice, and so create and sustain a set of relationships based on domination and subordination. This approach has the virtue of situating racial practices within a framework of institutional power relationships:

> The harm occurs when a group not only believes that this superiority entitles it to rule and control . . . [it is] the predication of decisions and policies on considerations of race for the purpose of *subordinating* a racial group and maintaining control over that group. The problem of racism, then, is not prejudice, but domination.[21]

However, this only provides a partial understanding of racism, and a development of this discussion now involves a brief exploration of Marxist-informed approaches to racism.

Racism as Ideology

While Marxist accounts of racism are sometimes in danger of drifting into a crude form of functionalism, or a simplistic economic determinism, it is important that analyses of racism pay attention to the connections between ideology and economic structure stressed by Marxism. There is a strong argument that racism did not originate in capitalism, and yet capitalist systems have sustained and benefited considerably—from colonialism to the present day—from the existence of racism. Race and class cannot be conflated into one entity, and yet analyses of racism which fail to include class structure and class relationships can only be inadequate. The form and content of ideology is totally determined by economic imperatives in only the crudest reading of Marx, and yet we cannot ignore the economic when looking at the historical development and present constitution of racist ideology within capitalist society.

Colonialism and its relations of domination and subordination, together with an attendant racist ideology, are discussed later on in this chapter. In modern societies such as Britain we have seen a reproduction of these relations, now in a metropolitan setting. Not only did Britain's colonial past lead to the creation of the ex-colonies of the Third World from which to draw labour in the post war period, it also ensured that the labour recruited was directed to the lower paid, more menial jobs vacated by a white working class. As Rex says:

> In the metropolitan societies there develops a set of unwanted economic and social positions which can most readily be staffed by colonial or immigrant workers. Within this context of power, authority, status, oppression and exploitation, men work and live their social lives.[22]

Thus, at the outset, it is important to appreciate that black workers have entered, or have been born into, a society already differentiated on the basis of power and wealth: class divisions, inequalities and discrimination are built into the structures of capitalism. Racism is a feature of this system in that particular, identifiable (because of colour) sections of society are ascribed economic and social roles based on subordination within the social structure. The black worker is thus caught up in the most vicious of vicious circles, in that his subordination serves to confirm racist ideology, and racist ideology justifies his subordination.

It is also important to recognize that the social and economic system of capitalism has benefited from the presence of racism in that it has ensured a supply of cheap labour, depressed wage levels and weakened the potential for working-class solidarity. In other words, capitalism, via discrimination and disadvantage has benefited from the existence of racism as ideology.

What follows is an attempt to indicate how we can draw together both the structural features of racism, and the notion of racism as a subjective understanding of the world, as an element of consciousness. In order to accomplish this we have to begin with the central observation that racism is a form of ideology, and then examine the ways in which this, and indeed ideology in general, is interconnected with other aspects of a capitalist system.

For Marx an ideological superstructure—within which will be located the media, religion, education and other institutions for the production and dissemination of ideas—may be separated out for the purposes of analysis from what he calls the economic base or structure, the 'mode of production of material life'. In all societies there will be some correspondence between the economic structure and the ideological superstructure. Put another way, within capitalist society the nature of the economic will give rise to certain kinds of ideologies which will represent belief systems tending, in varying degrees and in various ways, to support what goes on in the economic sphere. It should be stressed that Marx is not suggesting that ideology is *determined* by the economic structure, though he has been criticized by some writers for what they see as economic determinism. The French Marxist Louis Althusser has argued for what he calls the 'relative autonomy' of the superstructure,[23] and it will be argued here that the ideological superstructure has a degree of independence from the economic and its 'requirements'.

Consciousness and ideology are, for Marx, inextricably bound together. Ideologies, for instance, legal, moral, metaphysical, and their corresponding forms of consciousness, are not seen as having autonomous existences, transcending material life. On the contrary, they are seen as developing out of the material lives of individuals. Consciousness and ideology are manifestations of material conditions and experiences:

> The production of ideas, conceptions, and consciousness is at first directly inter-woven with the material activity and the material intercourse of men, the language of real life.[24]

'Material' here refers to more than concrete physical objects; it also includes social interaction and the institutional forms that ideologies take, e.g. a system of schooling. The ideological superstructure, then, is composed of both material conditions and experiences, and consciousness of these conditions and experiences. It is important to see that in Marx's writing the so-called economic base and the ideological superstructure together form, in reality, a whole, a unity: they are not separate worlds, having independent existence. The relations of production constituting the economic base of society contain, and indeed are sustained by, a co-existing ideology. Right at the point of commodity production these relations will reflect a dominant ideology. This is a long way from saying that everything that happens in society is directly determined by the economic; a point that Engels made some time after Marx's death:

> Marx and I are ourselves partly to blame for the fact that the younger people sometimes lay more stress on the economic side than is due to it.[25]

And again, in another of his letters:

> Political, juridical, philosophical, religious, literary, artistic, etc. development is based on economic development. But all these react upon one another and also upon the economic basis. It is not that the economic situation is *cause, solely active,* while everything else is only passive effect. There is, rather, interaction on the basis of economic necessity, which *ultimately* always asserts itself.[26]

Marx did not view ideas, e.g. about other 'races', as independent forms of mental activity, arising ahistorically simply as a result of autonomous reflection by human beings. Furthermore, as all modes of production up to and including a capitalist one (apart, that is, from 'primitive communism') have been characterized by the existence of a ruling class, so the dominant ideas are linked to the interests of that class:

> The ideas of the ruling class are, in every age, the ruling ideas: i.e. the class which is the dominant *material* force in society is at the same time its dominant *intellectual* force.[27]

Such ideas, then, are not interest-free, neutral things, but rather function as ideological supports for relationships organized on the basis of domination and subordination. Racism can be seen to provide this kind of support. This has implications for those whose work is based upon the analysis and dissemination of ideas, e.g. sociologists, economists and political scientists. As Paul Walton and Andrew Gamble put it:

> The intellectual can therefore choose whether to become an abstraction of alienated man establishing himself as a measure of that alienation, or a philosopher of the ruling class, who makes it his 'chief source of livelihood to develop and perfect the illusions of the class itself'. The former will be acting as a *dereifying agent,* the latter as an *ideologist.*[28]

In terms of the ideology of racism, the 'intelligentsia' has in essence a straight choice to make between exposing the 'illusions' of racism in all its guises, or acting as an agent in the perpetuation of the ideology. It is always time to stand up and be counted.

Ideologies arise out of material conditions and provide types of explanation regarding phenomenal reality: the social world as it is experienced and known. They are, therefore, versions of reality, and find their expression in people's consciousness. Phenomenal reality and the ideological explanations available are analysed by Marx within a framework of social relations. From this standpoint the phenomenal world is composed not of things, but of relations. Put another way, the things that people experience as social reality are social-historical crystallizations of relations. Using this reasoning, phenomenal reality is conceived of by Marx as material social relations, and the dominant ideology exists as a false account or interpretation of these relations:

> If in all ideology men and their circumstances appear upside down as in a camera obscura, this phenomenon arises from their historical life process just as the inversion of objects on the retina does from their physical life processes.[29]

However, this does not mean that he believed that people simply 'soaked up' as propaganda ideological accounts; the process is seen as a dialectical one, which does not allow man/woman to be separated from society. Man is given an active creative role both in the present and, importantly, in a potential future, when ideologies will be 'unmasked'. In order to survive at all ideologies must make sense, that is, ideologies must offer accounts and interpretations which correspond to people's material experiences, otherwise ideologies lose their power. Ideologies do not simply distort what people experience. If we take a principal defining feature of capitalism—the extraction and appropriation of surplus value by the owners of the means of production, by the bourgeoisie—we are faced with a process which is generally interpreted (by bourgeoisie and workers alike) only on the basis of surface appearances. The internal relations of production are concealed by the apparent fairness of free wage labour being paid an agreed wage for hours worked. The outward appearance of this relationship constitutes its phenomenal form—it *is* reality—though behind this phenomenal reality lies a more fundamental structure of relations based upon exploitation. Ideological accounts of the relationship between capital and labour confirm outward appearances, and thus in this way ideology corresponds to material reality. Thus ideology functions as a conceptual trap. The task, as Marx saw it, was to change accounts at the mental level *and* the reality corresponding to these accounts. For him the potency of ideology begins to atrophy when ideological accounts fail to correspond to the phenomenal form taken by social relations. Therefore, Marxian analysis is not just aimed at exposing the falsity of ideology, it is also aimed at the falsity of reality itself as constituted in a capitalist system.

We can perhaps clarify what has been said by focusing specifically on racist ideology. Racist ideology is not simply propaganda or justification for the way that things are. In order to be effective it must in some way correspond to the real world that people experience. This is how ideologies have force; they offer beliefs that work. Thus ideologies can be seen as interpretations or accounts of the world as experienced by people, but they exist as false interpretations. If racist interpretations are to have credibility then they must *appear* correct according to the individual's own experiences of black people. These experiences may be direct (living in a neighbourhood containing black families, working with black people), or indirect (stories from friends, newspaper reports, history lessons). Take as an example the over-representation of black children in ESN schools in comparison with white children. From a crude racist standpoint the explanation of this is simple: it is due to the natural intellectual inferiority of black children. This interpretation is confirmed by direct or indirect experiences—the racist's interpretation corresponds to the facts as s/he understands them, and appears to account for them. The task for the anti-racist, say, a teacher, is to debunk such interpretations by offering alternatives, and, importantly, to work to alter the reality of the situation itself. In this case one would need to understand how black children are treated by the education system (undervaluation of their language and culture, self-fulfilling prophecies, modes of assessment, etc.) and their treatment by the wider society (housing problems, poverty, etc.).

Building on the deep-seated racist attitudes that stem from Britain's colonial past, it is at times of economic recession that racist ideology can break out in its most virulent form. As we have seen, unemployment, bad housing, problems with the National Health Service, inner-city decay, and so on, have all been blamed on black people by groups such as the National Front. The point is that these are real problems experienced by both black and white working-class people in Britain. Racist ideology is able to exist and grow precisely because it offers a simplistic, yet credible interpretation of these problems. The task is to challenge both the interpretations and their inherent falseness, and the material conditions which help to sustain them.

The above discussion has focused on the interaction between individual consciousness and the wider social structure, to show how the ideological superstructure and corresponding forms of consciousness, together with the economic 'base', make up a totality.

While capitalism has certainly benefited from the existence of racism as ideology, whether a capitalist mode of production 'needs' racism (as a permanent feature) is a moot point. Many writers within the Marxist tradition have tended to emphasize the 'requirements' of capitalism *vis à vis* racism in terms of economic/political exigencies. Oliver Cromwell Cox, for instance, suggests that different types of exploitation (feudal, capitalist) require different types of social attitudes.[30] For Cox, racism arose with capitalism because it provided a belief system appropriate to the new forms of exploitation on which capitalism was based. Other writers, for example, Eugene Genovese,[31] have criticized this kind of approach, arguing that it represents a brand of economic determinism.[32] Chris Mullard has argued strongly against deterministic accounts of racism; he emphasizes the 'relative autonomy' of racist ideology. By this he means that racist ideology is relatively independent from the 'needs' of a specifically capitalist mode of production. Mullard argues that racism did not originate with capitalism, and that we should recognize the 'quasi-independent existence of competing belief and meaning systems'.[33] A further implication of this is that while a black and white working class shares the same relationship to the means of production, and therefore shares a common class position, the categories of race and class cannot be conflated into one entity. The structural position of black people in society has been strongly influenced by racial differences as perceived by white people.

André Gorz has argued that the functions fulfilled by immigration have been advantageous for the capitalist class: he sees these advantages as economic and political. The economic advantages are to do with the fact that through immigration capitalist societies in Western Europe are able to import a 'ready-made' labour force from poorer regions, a labour force that is at the height of its productive powers. The cost of raising this workforce has been borne by the country of origin. This argument is developed more fully by Stephen Castles and Godula Kosack.[34] The political advantages are, for Gorz, even more important. Put simply, he suggests that immigrants are a weak and unorganized sector of the labour market who function to dilute the solidarity of the working class as a whole.

We can incorporate into Gorz's argument the notion of racist ideology, in that the ideology can be seen to provide a necessary support for what is happening. Racist ideology, for instance, helps to shape white working-class attitudes which are based on separation from, and antagonism towards, their black fellow-workers; clearly this works against the development of working-class consciousness.

Thus a range of structures and processes interact at particular moments in history, within a particular kind of society. Economic and political benefits accrue to capitalism through the use of migrant labour; a racist ideology (laid down during the colonial period) is, as it were, available, and is reproduced within the institutions of the ideological superstructure—schools, mass media, etc.; this is part of a process whereby corresponding forms of consciousness arise. The ideology serves to confirm and sustain the exploitation of migrant labour, and the effects of this exploitation serve to justify the ideology, because the forms of consciousness corresponding to the ideology are continuously reproduced through the material conditions and experiences of the individuals concerned.

THE COLONIAL BACKGROUND

Only by placing the relationship between white majorities and black and brown minorities into an historical context, and specifically into the context of colonialism, can we begin to understand that relationship. Modern so-called race relations have not simply arisen out of the blue, but have their historical roots in the development of Western capitalism and colonialism. In particular, we can relate contemporary examples of racism to the historical fact of colonialism and its long-term pervading influence on social relationships. As Rex has written:

> Racial discrimination and racial prejudice are phenomena of colonialism. It was as a result of the conquest of poor and relatively underdeveloped countries by the technologically advanced nations during the nineteenth century, that new kinds of economy, new forms of social relations of production involving both conqueror and conquered, were brought into being. The inequalities between men of different nations, ethnic groups, or religions, or between men of different skin colours, which resulted, were often justified in biological racist theories or some functional equivalent.[35]

This is not to suggest that racism is only present in those societies which have at some time been colonial powers; it is quite possible for racism to be present in a society that has had no direct involvement in colonialism—though most of the countries of Western Europe have made imperialist intrusions into other lands at some time in history. The point is that colonialism was based upon the *white* European domination of black and brown populations, and thus there developed over a period of time a set of collective feelings regarding white superiority; intellectual, moral and cultural. By the late 19th century various 'scientific' theories purporting to prove the biological superiority of white Europeans had influenced the way that Europeans viewed the indigenous populations of the colonies: the 'natives' or 'lesser breeds'.

Pre-colonial Civilizations

From the time of the Renaissance, technological, scientific and economic developments in Western Europe had facilitated the growth of colonialism. Such things as ships capable of sailing around the world, efficient means of navigation, weaponry capable of subduing a native population and economic surpluses for the financing of voyages of exploration and discovery provided the necessary conditions for European expansion. The result was that more and more countries were to come under the domination of the countries of Western Europe. In turn, and very importantly, this colonial expansion itself facilitated the economic development of Europe. The consequence was that by the end of the 19th century power and wealth was firmly concentrated in those countries that were mainly white.

This is not to say, however, that all important knowledge, technical inventions, or cultural movements originated in Western Europe or North America. The movement of ideas across the world has never been one way; indeed Europe owes a great (though usually unacknowledged) debt to civilizations in other parts of the world. As examples, arithmetic, trigonometry and algebra were learnt from Arab mathematicians; the numeral system used in Europe is Arabic; it was the Arabs who first discovered that coffee beans could be used to make a drink; and for centuries physicians in Western Europe relied upon a medical book written by an Arab, Ibn Sina. Glass was invented by the ancient Egyptians; porcelain and paper by the Chinese. India was the first country to domesticate cotton, and use sugar as a sweetener. The domestication of cows began in Asia Minor; and butter was originally used as a cosmetic in the near East.

It is also important to note that prior to the advent of European colonialism there had existed in various parts of the non-European world many large and important civilizations. In the Old World there were the civilizations of ancient Egypt, Sumer and Mesopotamia, for instance, and in the New World the civilizations of Middle America and Peru. When the Spanish began their conquest of the New World they met a civilization that was still flourishing and developing, though this was to be brutally cut short. The civilizations of South America possessed large urban centres and complex social institutions such as class stratification, political and religious hierarchies, a complex division of labour, written records, scientific knowledge and prediction, administrative officials, and so on.

Although pre-colonial Africa south of the Sahara was largely composed of small-scale, simple societies, large important empires also arose. Graham Hancock in a recent article on underdevelopment in Africa discusses the pre-colonial empires which existed in Africa south of the Sahara.[36] The great Ghanaian empire spanned the fifth and thirteenth centuries, reaching a peak between the ninth and eleventh centuries. In the eleventh century the University of Sankore in Ghana exchanged professors with the University of Cordoba in Spain. Also at this time Ghana traded extensively with Portugal, Spain and other countries, exporting such things as gold, ivory and kola nuts. Following the decline of the Ghanaian empire in the thirteenth century, the country of Mali rose to prominence, becoming very wealthy, and well known in Africa and other parts of the world as a centre of learning. The University of Timbucktu in particular was widely respected for its scholarship. When Mali declined in the fifteenth century the state of Songhay rose in importance. Thus in the Middle Ages parts of Africa possessed advanced forms of state organization, often more sophisticated and efficient than those found in many parts of Europe.

Having said this, I must stress that I am not suggesting that non-European civilization should be judged according to European criteria; cultural differences between nations can be evaluated on the basis of a variety of criteria. Small-scale societies, for example, in Africa, possessed cultural patterns—relating to such things as family life, child-rearing, attitudes towards property—which were evaluated by European colonizers according to their own particular value system. Clearly the latter should not be seen as having superiority in any absolute sense, and the worth of a society should not be assessed according to how closely it approximates to one's own.

The Phases of Colonialism

Western European expansion took a number of forms and passed through different stages. And as we shall see, the four centuries of colonialism involved a great deal of violence; in some cases leading to the extermination of large populations.

To begin with there were the early voyages of exploration and plunder. Passing around the Cape of Good Hope, the Portuguese explored the East African coast in the fifteenth century—a region that had already experienced Arab slave traders—and in the process destroyed many flourishing ports in an effort to establish a trading monopoly. In South America the violent plundering of the Spanish conquistadors is well documented, though here the straightforward forcible extraction of precious metals for export soon gave way to more formalized systems of production based upon the exploitation of local labour.

Colonialism as an Extension of the Mother Country

Following on from the early expeditions such as these, colonialism basically went through two phases. Prior to the 19th century, Europeans set up colonies as extensions of the mother country; these lands were to be new white colonies, populated by European settlers. The fact that the lands were already populated by an indigenous people was irrelevant. Indeed, North America, Australia and New Zealand were officially described as 'empty', though Indians, Aborigines and Maoris were living there. Eventually, after becoming part of the British Empire, Canada, Australia and New Zealand became the Old Commonwealth, that is, the white Commonwealth. The native populations, however, could not be ignored, for as the white settlers increased their territorial hold on a country so they met with resistance. Those who resisted—and sometimes those who did not—were frequently slaughtered, and the remainder placed on reservations. In North America the Indians found themselves being pushed further and further back from their homelands, finally to be settled on reservations. The final irony was that in some cases mineral deposits were discovered on the reservations, so the Indians would find themselves being moved on yet again. There was a great deal of resistance, and the Indians enjoyed significant military victories, such as the famous one at Little Big Horn (though the whites gained savage retribution for this defeat when they slaughtered Indian men, women and children at Wounded Knee). However, in military terms the Indians were no match for the whites in the long run. It is estimated that the Indian population of North America just prior to the advent of white settlers was two million; by the end of the 19th century, as a result of warfare, disease and starvation—partly due to the decimation of the buffalo by settlers—the population was less than a quarter of a million.[37]

Nineteenth century attitudes towards the Indians are well represented by this extract from a book by a professor at Yale University published in the late 19th century:

> There is no doubt that the Indians were sly, suspicious . . . Their worst trait was the spirit of revenge, and the merciless cruelty which made them delight in indiscriminate slaughter, and in inflicting tortures on their enemies and captives. To count up as many scalps as possible was the ambition of the Indian youth.[38]

To the Indians, and especially those who came into contact with 'soldier blue', it was the white settlers who were cruel, who carried out unprovoked attacks on peaceful encampments, and who showed a cynical disregard for treaties that were made. And it was the early white settlers who first introduced the art of scalping to North America.

In Australia the extermination of Aborigines was carried out on an even more spectacular scale. When Cook arrived there in the 18th century the black population of Australia was about 300 000; by the 1930s it had been reduced to around 60 000.[39] Even as late as the 1920s Aborigines were being hunted as sport by whites.

As was the case in other parts of the world, the traditional way of life of the indigenous people came into conflict with the European values imported into the country by white settlers. Chris Forsyth and Dexter Tiranti describe how the Aboriginal way of life and technology had developed to fit in with the imperatives of a fragile ecology, and how a clash of cultures was inevitable:

> They had to travel light therefore they had few material possessions. But undoubtedly in the cultural and spiritual sense their lives were complex and rich. They established a close relationship with nature, and had a strong spiritual link with the land ... the tribes had no chiefs, everyone engaged in decision making ... Obviously the strong hierarchial and materialist society of the European settlers, whose comprehension of land being 'used' was only if it was farmed or mined, found difficulty in understanding a people who lived by such values.[40]

In Tasmania an Aboriginal population of perhaps 4000 at the time of the first white settlers had been reduced to extinction by the 20th century.

The 17th century saw the growth of the plantation system in North and South America and the West Indies. In order to make commercial use of the land and other resources that had been captured it was necessary to find ways of exploiting whatever labour was available. In the beginning the colonizers relied upon local native labour. Eventually, however, the huge amounts of labour demanded by the plantations could not be met from local sources, consequently the plantations began to introduce slave labour from Africa. The Spanish tried a number of alternatives before introducing slaves. There was, for example, a system of indenture where tribute was extracted from Indian workers. Ensuring that such systems worked in an orderly manner, in other words ensuring that the Indians did not rebel, led to the use of extreme forms of violence by the Spanish settlers. The extent of this violence can be measured by the fact that during the 16th century the population of what is now Mexico was reduced by half.

Slavery

The first Africans were transported to America in 1619, though in these early years they were not officially described as slaves. Indeed, taking the American continent as a whole, there were always degrees of unfreeness; the most extreme forms being found in North America.

The African slave trade was enacted on such a scale that it is difficult for the 20th century mind to grasp the violence and dehumanization it entailed. We will never know exactly how many Africans were forcibly removed from their continent, but most estimates put the figure somewhere between 15 and 60 million; some estimates, though, go as high as 150 million. About two-thirds of the slaves died en route to the Americas as a result of ill treatment and disease. The barbarity of slavery can be traced through the various traumas to be endured before the slave, if he survives, begins working on the plantation. He is captured, rounded up and chained together with others who seem fit and strong, just like an animal. Then there is the long march to the coast, which many will not survive. At the coast he is sold and stowed away on board ship; like cargo, human beings are packed one on top of the other. And then comes the long journey across the Atlantic—the 'middle passage'—which over the 300 years of the slave trade killed millions. If he is still alive when he reaches the New World, he is sold again, to the plantation owner. Then follows the 'settling in' period, when he has to eradicate from his mind all notions of dignity and freedom; he must surrender himself completely to his master and his master's social system.

Slavery was finally abolished in the British Empire in 1834, with the government softening the blow for the slave owners by paying them £20 million in compensation. The United States abolished slavery in 1865, and the French in 1848, though with the French a system very similar to slavery—*engagés forces*—was in existence until 1872. Slavery in Puerto Rico was abolished by the Spanish in 1872, and in Cuba in 1898. Slavery in Brazil ended in 1898. In terms of world history, then, slavery is a relatively recent phenomenon.

Clearly, in order for slavery as a system to be sustained there must have been a powerful ideology at work justifying the treatment of blacks. This justification was provided by various types of racist ideology. Blacks were classified as sub-human, as the biological inferiors of white 'races', thus it was morally acceptable for them to be owned by white people, to be deprived of all freedoms, and for slavery to be a socially inherited status. Consider, for instance, this observation by the philosopher Hume made in the middle of the 18th century:

> I am apt to suspect the Negroes, and in general all the other species of men . . . to be naturally inferior to the whites. There never was a civilized nation of any complexion than white, nor even any individual eminent in action or speculation. No ingenious manufactures amongst them, no arts, no sciences.[41]

Before we leave slavery, one final point is worth making. The *development* of Western Europe has been accompanied by the *underdevelopment* of the Third World countries who in various ways experienced European imperialism. In the case of slavery, not only did the system obviously provide a steady flow of non-wage labour for the colonies, and callously trample on African culture, it also, for three centuries, deprived Africa of its most productive labour—an important factor as far as Africa's economic and social development has been concerned.

Colonial Occupation

With the second phase of European colonial exploitation there was less emphasis on the plantation system. The aim in this phase was not the establishment of a 'white man's country', as an extension of the mother country, but rather to intrude into a country in order to extract mineral resources or grow cash crops for export to Europe. Unlike North America or Australia these countries were not declared 'empty'—a difficult declaration even for colonialists to make in a country such as India—but in a variety of ways came under the control of the European nations. During this phase vast areas of Africa and Asia were annexed by the Western powers, and commercial exploitation was placed in the hands of European companies, such as the East India Company, or private individuals. Labour was provided by the native populations, being cheap and available in quantity. Among the imperial powers it was firmly believed that it was Destiny for them to manage these lands, to be their trustees, so that the natives might be guided along the road to civilization. In the words of Lord Rosebery:

What is Empire but the predominance of Race? How marvellous it all is! Do we
not hail, in this, no less the energy and fortune of a race than the supreme direction of the Almighty?[42]

There were, of course, certain economic benefits to be derived. Put more sharply, the
European domination of two-thirds of the world was the foundation upon which
Western capitalism was built. Colonialism provided for the countries of Western
Europe three fundamental economic benefits: the colonies were a source of raw
materials; they provided a source of cheap labour; and they developed into important
markets for manufactured goods. Those countries coming under British domination
during this phase—in Asia and parts of Africa—were in time (together with the West
Indies) to become the New Commonwealth, that is, the black Commonwealth.

The colonizing nations also gained an important ideological benefit. In Britain people
were socialized into accepting a picture of the world in which *Great* Britain was a
dominant, unassailable power engaged in the glorious task of bringing civilization to the
'natives' of the Empire; a task that was nothing less than her Destiny. Such a picture,
based as it was upon the supposed inferiority of native populations, helped to promote
feelings of solidarity among the British people, whatever their position in the hierarchy.
For countless schoolchildren the broad expanse of Imperial Red on their classroom map
of the world was visual confirmation of Britain's position as a world power, and thus, by
implication, proof of her inherent quality of leadership so generously bestowed upon
her people by Providence. Today this is the kind of sentiment that groups such as the
National Front would like to exploit; stirring memories as Britain nosedives in the order
of world powers.

Using the example of slavery I have already suggested that European development
and Third World underdevelopment are two sides of the same coin. As far as an
understanding of modern racism and race relations is concerned this is a crucial point,
and one that cannot be emphasized enough. As a result of the direct or indirect rule of a
European power, colonized countries were directed to concentrate on the growing of
one or perhaps two cash crops for export, whereas previously they were in many cases
agriculturally self-sufficient. The result of this was that instead of growing a range of
crops for their own consumption, they became increasingly dependent on one crop; this
is a major problem in the Third World today. The colonies, then, were thrust into a
world commodity market that was dominated by the European powers, and became
dependent on the income received. However, the European nations were able to fix
their own prices; consequently they got the products they required for their domestic
economies, at a price that suited them. In the modern world the underdeveloped
nations still face the problem of a reliance on one cash crop and a commodity market
largely controlled by the richer nations. If we take the case of India, there was a conflict
of interest between Britain and India over the manufacture of cotton material. At the
end of the 18th century the industry accounted for over half of India's export trade;
however, this competed with the Lancashire cotton industry, and so Britain prevented
the Indians from manufacturing their own cloth. A new system was introduced whereby
cotton growing was expanded and the raw cotton shipped to Britain to be made up into
material; some of this would then be exported back to India.

In the long term the effect of the underdevelopment of the Third World has been the creation of a pool of cheap and 'willing' workers who could be used in the postwar development of the European economies.

Depending on general conditions, a number of strategies were employed by the Europeans to maintain a hold on a country. It was impossible for the white nations to establish direct control of *all* non-white societies, and so alternative forms of domination were used. Some societies were designated as 'protectorates'; here members of the indigenous population were allowed to 'rule' their society, but under the strict guidance of an agent from the metropolitan country. Sometimes a European nation created a 'zone of influence', meaning that it had some form of responsibility for that region. In some instances this guardianship of a region was shared out among the European powers; this happened, for instance, in China and Thailand.

From the middle of the 19th century there began a period of intense colonial activity, when the countries of Europe competed with each other for territorial control of Africa and Asia. In 1884 all of the colonial powers met in Berlin literally to carve up the African continent among themselves. No attempt was made to take into consideration the wishes of the people living there, or traditional boundaries based on tribal or ethnic groupings. The result was a re-mapping of the African continent, with quite arbitrary divisions drawn across the land. In places such as South Africa and Kenya the planters formed a 'boss class', taking over vast areas of land, and developing systems of rule which guaranteed their superiority and domination over native populations. The end result was that the whites gained possession of the best land, while the blacks were forced onto reservations or the least fertile backlands.

In the 1870s King Leopold of Belgium took over the Congo basin, an area rich in mineral deposits, and ran it as a private estate. Eventually this region was taken off the king by the Belgian government following a world outcry at the discovery that the systematic torture of Africans was taking place. When the Herero tribe in South West Africa rebelled against the German colonizers following the seizure of their lands, General Von Trotha reacted by ordering that the tribe be exterminated. The order was eventually countermanded by the Kaiser, though not before 75 000 Africans had been slaughtered.

The 20th century has seen the gradual disappearance of such forms of colonialism, though in some parts of the world more sophisticated forms of neo-colonialism have developed. In a number of ways the consequences of colonialism have continued through to the present day, and the rest of this chapter addresses itself to these consequences.

MIGRATION INTO BRITAIN

The growth of Western capitalism has been dependent upon the movement, sometimes forcible, of large numbers of workers. From rural areas into the towns during the early stages of capitalism; from Europe out to the colonies; and, more recently, from the ex-colonies and poorer parts of the Mediterranean into the richer European nations. The migration of labour into Britain is by no means a recent phenomenon.

Indeed, black people first arrived in this country at the time of Elizabeth the First.

In the 19th century over one million Irish workers entered Britain, their labour being used for the building of the railways and canals. In the early 19th century Irishmen came into Britain for seasonal farm work, then returned home when the harvest was completed, though as industrialization proceeded Irish workers increasingly became a permanent feature of the industrial towns. At the end of the century there was such a shortage of clerical staff in London that thousands of German clerks had to be brought over to make up the deficit. During the 19th century immigration was more than offset by the emigration of British people, to the United States and overseas colonies. In each decade between the mid 19th century and the First World War Britain lost a minimum of 100 000 people through overseas migration; at its highest the figure was 800 000.[43]

Immediately following the Second World War thousands of workers were recruited from the enormous pool of refugees created by the war in Europe. And it was in the postwar period, beginning with the 1950s, that the migration of black labour from the ex-colonies to Britain began on a significant scale. The economic boom following the period of postwar austerity had created a situation where there was an acute shortage of labour, especially in the lower-paid sectors of industry. British capitalism was, therefore, compelled to recruit labour from overseas, and the ex-colonies, with their vast and cheap sources of labour, were an attractive proposition.

It is important to recognize that black people did not simply foist themselves on British society, but entered the country in response to economic demands generated by what turned out to be a relatively short-lived period of rapid economic growth. While the economic demand for labour in the metropolitan society is a crucial factor, it cannot be looked at in isolation from a range of other factors facilitating labour migration. The fact that the ex-colonies were, and are, underdeveloped societies is of enormous importance; the extreme poverty in the Third World was such that many of those living there were willing to travel halfway around the world to settle as British citizens in what had been described to them as the 'mother country'. In the West Indies as a whole, immediately following the Second World War there was a deterioration in economic conditions, and in 1952 the McCarran Act more or less stopped West Indian immigration to the United States. Thus, given the demand for labour, West Indians increasingly looked towards Britain. On the Indian sub-continent the partition of the Punjab, which resulted from India becoming independent in 1947, meant that millions of people had to move from India into Pakistan and vice versa. The acute shortages of land for farming created by the entrance of four million or so refugees into the Eastern Punjab acted to increase pressure for emigration to Britain.

The view of Britain as the mother country is still held by many black people in the Commonwealth. Consider this comment from a Ghanaian speaker at a recent 'inter-racial' meeting:

> We think of Britain as our mother country, the head of the Commonwealth. So we always felt that if we came we would be received as a mother receives a child.[44]

Unfortunately, in reality Britain did not always measure up to this cosy image of motherhood projected by the speaker. Indeed, instances of baby-battering have not been uncommon. On the other hand, the metaphor may not be altogether irrelevant when one considers the maternalistic (or paternalistic) way in which some groups have viewed and treated black people.

Public and private organizations set up job centres in the New Commonwealth, or employed agents to organize recruitment drives. The National Health Service, for example, established job centres in the West Indies in order to attract nursing staff for British hospitals. Interestingly enough, while he was Minister of Health between 1960 and 1963 recruitment of this type of labour was strongly encouraged by Enoch Powell. It is important to appreciate the economic role earmarked for New Commonwealth immigrants. In general they became a replacement labour force, taking the low-paid, menial jobs being vacated by white workers, or being created as a result of new forms of industrial production. No provisions were made by governments to meet their social needs. Pushed as they were into the already decaying areas of inner cities, they found themselves increasingly in competition with a white working class for a range of scarce resources such as housing. In this situation it was inevitable that immigrants came to be seen as the cause, rather than the victims of inner-city decay. Racist ideology is confirmed by the material experiences of the white working class.

Hostility

From the 19th century to the present day migrant workers in Britain (and other European countries) have frequently had to contend with widespread hostility in the so-called 'host society'. The verbal and physical excesses of contemporary right-wing groups represent only the more recent examples of a long and inglorious line of racist reaction.

The hostility encountered by migrant workers from Ireland during the 19th century provides a good example. In fact a number of important parallels can be drawn between the 19th century Irish immigrants and the black immigrants entering in the second half of the 20th century. Both came from societies that had experienced the status of a British colony—though for the Irish, of course, their country was still a colony. Frederick Engels makes frequent reference to Irish migrant workers in his *The Condition of the Working Class in England*, which he wrote in 1844/45. The Irish worked at the lowest paid jobs, and as a consequence tended to live in the very poorest parts of the large towns and cities. It was widely believed that Irish folk could be easily recognized, though not simply because of their life-style, but because of supposed racial traits which led them to have particular physical features quite different from those of the English. Consider this extract from an observation made by Thomas Carlyle:

> The wild Milesian features, looking false, ingenuity, restlessness, unreason, misery, and mockery . . . He is the sorest evil this country has to strive with. In his rags and laughing savagery, he is there to undertake all work that can be done by mere strength of hand and back—for wages that will purchase him potatoes. He lodges to his mind in any pig-hutch or dog-hutch, roosts in outhouses, and wears a suit of tatters . . . The uncivilized Irishman . . .There abides he, in his squalor and unreason, in his falsity and drunken violence, as the readymade nucleus of degradation and disorder.[45]

Engels' comment on this is:

> If we accept his exaggerated and one-sided condemnation of the Irish national character, Carlyle is perfectly right.[46]

Engels then continues:

> What does such a race want with high wages? The worst quarters of all the large towns are inhabited by Irishmen. Whenever a district is distinguished for especial filth and especial ruinousness, the explorer may safely count upon meeting chiefly those Celtic faces which one recognises at the first glance as different from the Saxon physiognomy of the native, and singing, aspirate brogue which the true Irishman never loses.[47]

There was, then, also a language difference which further helped to demarcate the Irish from the English.

The Irish temperament is seen by Engels as being quite different from that of the English, and 'in part by a mixture of the races, and in part by the ordinary contact of life', he believed that what he saw as the English temperament was being altered. Irish immigration had contributed because of:

> the passionate, mercurial temperament, which it imports into England and into the English working class. The Irish and English are to each other much as the French and the Germans.[48]

This mixing, however, is for Engels a good thing, in that it hastens a working-class confrontation with the bourgeoisie:

> the mixing of the more facile, excitable, fiery Irish temperament with the stable, reasoning, persevering English must, in the long run, be productive only of good for both.[49]

Thus, as is the case with New Commonwealth immigrants, an exploitative relationship developed through colonialism was reproduced in the metropolitan society, with the exploited constituting a lower stratum within the working class, and being viewed by the host society as racially inferior.

Bearing in mind the earlier discussion of the political benefits to capitalism of migrant workers, Marx noted the following with respect to the Irish:

> Every industrial and commercial centre in England now possesses a working class *divided* into two *hostile* camps, English proletarians and Irish proletarians. The ordinary English worker hates the Irish worker as a competitor who lowers his standard of life. In relation to the Irish worker he feels himself a member of the *ruling* nation . . . This antagonism is artificially kept alive and intensified by the press, the pulpit, the comic papers, in short, by all the means at the disposal of the ruling classes.[50]

Those living in the society into which migrant labour enters will be especially susceptible to racist propaganda during times of economic recession, when immigrants can be pointed to as being responsible for job shortages. In this respect it is interesting to compare New Commonwealth immigrants in Britain with migrants working as contract labour in the rich European countries—in the 'Golden Triangle'. With the latter system workers are taken on when there are labour shortages, then returned home when demand for labour slackens off. The European system of contract labour thus creates a relatively easily dismissed reserve army of labour. In Germany, for example, Turkish 'guestworkers' are exposed to this kind of treatment. Although both Britain's 'immigrants' and contract labour from the poorer parts of the Mediterranean frequently experience hostility, those from the New Commonwealth (as well as those born in this country—now over 40 per cent) occupy what is an even more vulnerable position in terms of racial/ethnic scapegoating. Apart from having to contend with attitudes and relationships stemming from colonialism itself, they have also consituted a more or less permanent feature of the labour market in Britain. This is because New Commonwealth citizens were allowed to settle in Britain as British citizens and bring in dependents. Consequently, during periods of rising unemployment, although they are likely to be laid off in proportionately greater numbers than are white workers, they are not dismissed from the country. Thus in the distorted imaginings of right-wing racist groups it is their very presence which provides proof of their responsibility for, or role in, economic recession. On top of this, black immigrants will find themselves exposed to further criticisms for being unemployed social security scroungers.

Looked at in economic terms, it is clear that contract labour provides a better deal for the host society than does immigration that allows for rights of settlement. Contract labour frees that society from the responsibility of providing state support for those workers made unemployed, and for providing state support for their families. Furthermore, contract labour means that the cost of reproducing labour is borne by the society from which the migrant comes. In other words, as has been discussed previously, the host society gets a ready-made worker at the peak of his productive powers, while all social provisions from the time of his birth have been generously met by his native country. One can understand Castles and Kosack's mordant comment that migrant labour is a form of aid given by the poor countries to the rich. Seen in this context the chapter on immigration controls makes interesting reading, for the trend in Britain has been more and more towards the European system of contract labour, with a progressive run-down in immigration from the New Commonwealth. And since the 1971 Immigration Act came into force in 1973 New Commonwealth workers have come into this country not as settlers, but as migrants.

BLACK PEOPLE IN CONTEMPORARY BRITAIN

I want now to turn to what we can call the major contextual factors that should be taken into consideration when analysing the problems faced by black people in contemporary British society. These are:

1. Racist ideology and racial prejudice.
2. Discrimination.
3. Economic position and social disadvantage.

4. Colour and culture.
5. The Third World.
6. Government controls.
7. Economic recession.

Of course, many of these problems are faced, or have been faced, by other minority groups—for example, gypsies, Irish, Italians—in fact one can go further and say that the working class as a whole experience a range of common problems. It has been argued earlier in this chapter that inequality and discrimination are built into the fabric of British capitalist society, and have an impact on people in various ways whatever their colour of skin or ethnic origins. However, to lump together all problems of race with problems of class, so that, for instance, relationships and ideologies stemming from the colonial past become unimportant, leads to a very inadequate type of analysis. While it is crucially important to take into account the class position of black people, it is also important to take into account the racially specific ways in which they experience and are treated by society. Thus certain contextual factors need to be identified and their impact on black people taken into consideration. My argument here is that when compared to other minority, or majority, groups in modern Britain, black workers are in a particularly vulnerable position when viewed in terms of these factors, for these may be seen as converging on the situation of black people in such a way as to produce an extremely powerful problem-creating and problem-sustaining set of conditions.

Racist Ideology and Racial Prejudice

Racist ideology may be conceived of as a belief system which provides a picture of the world in which individuals are classified as inferior/superior in terms of moral, intellectual or cultural worth, these being deterministically based on what are seen as racial origins. Contemporary forms of racist ideology have their roots in colonialism. For generations of British people the fact of colonialism—supported by various forms of racist ideology—confirmed their (white) superiority. It is not too difficult to see how contemporary beliefs, attitudes and stereotypes have grown out of accumulations of colonial experience. At the centre has been the notion that blacks and natives are somehow inferior: coons, wogs, niggers—a whole range of labels exist to stress this inferiority. Evidence of the inferiority of 'native' populations, in both earlier and more recent times, is supposedly provided by their social and economic subordination to the white 'races'. But it functions as more than evidence. Racist ideology represents a world view which serves to justify this subordination, and to make it necessary and inevitable; the most civilized should lead the least civilized. And, as indicated earlier, it is at times of economic and social tension within the metropolitan society that these beliefs and stereotypes can readily be rejuvenated.

Following the earlier discussion of racism as ideology, we can now examine in more detail some actual examples from the mass media and children's literature which illustrate the ways in which racist ideology manifests itself. This is followed by a look at a number of studies which have attempted to measure the extent of racial prejudice in Britain. Racial prejudice may be defined as a negative and harmful opinion regarding people belonging to what are thought to be other racial groups. As such it exists as an aspect of racist ideology.

A number of studies have examined the role played by the mass media and the education system in the formation and perpetuation of such beliefs in modern society. Hugo Young of The *Sunday Times* has pointed out how vitally important is the manner in which newspapers deal with racial issues:

> It is clear to students of race relations that there is a strong connection between race reporting and racial attitudes among the public; that the newspaper treatment of race relations has an important bearing on the quality of race relations on the ground; hence that newspapers, when dealing with race, have a particularly delicate responsibility.[51]

Paul Hartmann and Charles Husband provide a detailed analysis of the mass media and their treatment of race.[52] They discuss, for example, the strong tradition of racial and ethnic stereotyping in newspaper cartoon jokes. Obviously the cartoon is, by definition, dealing in stereotypes. A shared knowledge of such stereotypes among members of society allows a cartoonist great economy in presentation. Thus we are all familiar with characters such as the mother-in-law of truly enormous proportions, the weedy man and the shapely girl thrown together by fate and a shipwreck on the desert island, the unwashed hippy smoking pot, the Irishman in wellies and donkey jacket, and so on. When 'natives' are called for the cartoonist can fall back on a string of well-worn stereotypes: turban headgear, bed of nails, snakecharmer, the missionary boiling in the tribal cooking pot. They are so much part of our daily lives that they pass by almost unnoticed, and clearly in themselves they are not of crucial importance, except that cumulatively they do constitute part of the total image-building process whereby certain kinds of common-sense knowledge gets stored up. In fact it is the triviality of such examples which perhaps contributes to their long-term potency. The play 'Ten Little Nigger Boys' became 'Ten Little Indians', but the odd cartoon involving a racial stereotype, or a little golliwog on the side of one's morning marmalade jar, do not always leap out as being, in themselves, such glaring examples of harmful imagery. In this respect there is, over the years, a quiet process at work whereby tacit understandings of other people are formed.

What is more serious though, as Hartmann and Husband point out, is when these stereotypes are applied to events in the real world, events involving real people. They illustrate this with numerous examples. For instance, the cartoon in the *Daily Mirror* in 1970 which represented a comment on the discovery of 40 illegal immigrants in a cellar in Bradford. The cartoon showed two lovers on a beach, one of whom was saying: 'I thought you said this was a quiet beach?' The beach meanwhile was being overrun by what were meant to be illegal immigrants. They were all dressed in turbans, one sat astride an elephant, one carried a bed of nails, and one was carrying a snake all ready for charming. The perceptive reader might wonder how long Bradford has been one of Yorkshire's coastal resorts.

Other newspapers dealt with the illegal immigrants story in their own inimitable way. Evoking a suitable colonial image, the *Daily Express* headed its report: 'Police find 40 Indians in "Black Hole" ', while the *Sun* had a cartoon showing an 'illegal' immigrant addressing a white man as 'sahib' when asking for directions (to the beach at Bradford perhaps?)

A particularly good, and more recent example, was provided by the *Sun* in 1976, when there appeared a cartoon relating to the appeal by the then head of the Metropolitan police force, Robert Mark, for more black men and women to enter the police. The *Sun,* with all the sensitivity of a handgrenade, printed the cartoon on the day after they had carried the large advertisement from the police headed, 'Is Racial Prejudice Keeping You Out of the Metropolitan Police?' The cartoon showed a burly English police sergeant behind his station desk speaking into a telephone: 'Ask Sir Robert if he'd mind scrapping the minimum height regulation . . .' At the same time, waddling into the police station was a line of grass-skirted, grinning pygmies, wearing rings through their noses and waving spears in the air.

The transmission of racist ideology to children through the literature that they are exposed to is especially disturbing. Even in these supposedly more enlightened days a great deal of material published for children is still presenting harmful images and stereotypes. Sometimes the stress is on white initiative and leadership, and black superstition and treachery; sometimes the only time that a non-white character appears it is associated with fear; and sometimes the black character is presented as a figure of fun, to be treated in a patronizing manner. As one writer put it in the first edition of *Dragon's Teeth*—a journal concerned with the question of racism in children's books:

> Third World people invariably play secondary roles; they clean, cook, serve, are sex objects, brute figures or figures of fun. They are objects of pity, lack drive or are vague and indecisive. All of these stereotypes are reinforced by the press, television and radio. These stereotypes presented over and over again gradually destroy our children's perceptions until the stereotypes as well as the myths about whole groups of people become accepted as a reality, sometimes even by the subjects themselves.[53]

The Biggles books by W. E. Johns provide a rich source of material for the student of colonial imagery. In *Biggles and the Black Raider,* for instance, Biggles says he will take the job:

> On the understanding that there's no interference by bureaucrats. I want no bleating in the House of Commons about a poor innocent native being shot . . . Nobody says a word if fifty British Tommies are bumped off; but let one poor benighted heathen get the works and the balloon goes up. Then people wonder why things are going to pot.[54]

On the theme of racist images in children's books, Bob Dixon provides a useful discussion in his *Catching Them Young.* In the books (there are two volumes) he examines a range of literature still found on the shelves in classrooms and children's libraries. At one point he discusses a school in London where the white children habitually called the black children names such as 'blackie' and 'wog'. The teachers put some posters up showing 'Little Black Sambo'. Dixon writes:

> If the school had been using the Adventures in Reading Series, published by the

Oxford University Press, the pupils might possibly have read two stories by Gertrude Keir, The Old Mill and the Circus, where a monkey called Sambo appears . . . It's not difficult to imagine what fun this linking of events could have given rise to amongst the children. 'Ifs and ans', you might think, but isn't it by the constant and maybe sometimes chance assembling of hosts of such details that racist attitudes are built up? Sambo is a name normally applied to people of African race: here, it's applied to a monkey. What kind of psychological association do we expect children to form? If, later, the same children had seen some of the programmes in the television series, Love Thy Neighbour they would have seen the same kind of name-calling presented as entertainment. And on the table at breakfast or tea-time, these same children might well notice a jar of Robertson's jam or marmalade with the usual golliwog grinning at them. Some people like to think that such things have no significance but it's an increasingly hard line to defend.[55,56]

On the question of stereotypes, in his study of 'paki-bashing' in a Lancashire town, Geoff Pearson has neatly summed up the stereotypical Pakistani—the so-called 'paki' (as distinct from the real thing):

The stereotype of the 'paki', which is as contradictory as many stereotypes, finds him sitting down at home (where he lives in filth with at least a dozen others) to a meal of tinned cat-food or dog meat, weary from his day of labour at the dole office. He is dirty and promiscuous and cheeky, but he also keeps himself to himself and does not mix at all. He is also a 'homo', but is nevertheless always sneaking up to white girls in search of 'jig-a-jig'. He is a layabout and an idler who threatens to put other men out of work. Working every hour that he isn't sleeping (and when he isn't sleeping another 'paki' is sleeping in his bed) and with more money than sense, the 'paki' is always, inevitably, out of work and scrounging on social security. In short, he is a thrifty spendthrift, a secretive show-off, a ramp-antly heterosexual homosexual, a social security scrounger on the night shift in the spinning room, a randy man with an exotic religion which forbids sexuality, a workshy layabout with the strength of a horse who is only too happy to take the lowest, butt-end jobs which a whiteman would only laugh at. How can he encom-pass all these conflicting projects? Quite simply, because he is not an ordinary man but a 'paki'—that is to say, a figment of the collective imagination.[57]

Obviously it is extremely difficult to sort out the different ways in which white people experience and perceive black people, and in some cases feel what is usually referred to as racial prejudice. In Lancashire, for example, many people will frequently refer to Pakistanis as 'pakis', though no racism at all is necessarily involved. Studies which have attempted to measure the extent and nature of racial prejudice have faced a very real problem when it comes to interpretation and quantification of data. In the workplace, for instance, a kind of peaceful co-existence may be in evidence between white and black workers, while beneath the surface attitudes and relationships are less than amicable. Brooks in his study of London Transport found that on one level West Indian workers were integrated into the organization, and yet on another level had to contend with a significant amount of hostility.[58]

In E. J. B. Rose et al's study for the Institute of Race Relations, published in 1969, it was suggested that on the basis of questionnaires 10 per cent of Britain's white population is strongly prejudiced, 17 per cent prejudiced-inclined, 38 per cent tolerant-inclined and 35 per cent tolerant.[59] The study also indicated that prejudice is less likely to be found among women than men, and among young people than older people, especially those educated to sixth-form level.

Compared with the results obtained in a Gallup Poll ten years earlier some improvements had apparently occurred, though this was not the case in all respects, for as Rose and his colleagues pointed out: 'when respondents were asked to consider the situations in which they are personally concerned they have been inclined over the past 10 years to express less favourable views'. Their study, however, has not escaped criticism, the main one being that it underestimates the extent of racial prejudice in Britain. Certainly there are some anomalies in the results; for instance, although only a minority of 27 per cent appear to be prejudiced or prejudiced-inclined, three-quarters of those in the survey said they agreed with the views of Enoch Powell.

This study and a study published in 1968 by Mark Abrams have been re-analysed by Chris Bagley in the light of his own examination of prejudice in five English boroughs with relatively high concentrations of immigrants.[60] His conclusion is that a significant amount of hostility on the part of white people exists. For example, in answer to the question: 'Do you think the majority of coloured people in Britain are superior, equal or inferior to you?' 52 per cent of respondents said that coloured people are inferior. This finding has relevance for the discussion of the definition and extent of racism at the beginning of this chapter. On the basis of this argument, whether these 52 per cent of respondents believe that the inferiority is based on immutable genetic endowment or on cultural patterns, the viewpoint still represents an example of racism. Bagley did suggest, however, that lower levels of prejudice are found among white people who have black neighbours living in close proximity. This was one of the findings in Rose et al's study, and reinforces an earlier piece of research carried out by C. S. Hill and published in 1967,[61] where it was shown that in the three London boroughs studied, there was more racial prejudice in those areas of the lowest immigration. This optimistic reading of the situation has to be viewed with a little caution though, as a number of broader considerations need to be taken into account. The degree of prejudice in any area will be tied in with a range of locally based issues and problems, for example, competition over resources. Competition over housing was a crucial factor explaining racial prejudice among the white working class in Rex's and Moore's study of Sparkbrook in Birmingham.[62] The general social and economic climate will also influence levels of prejudice; the effects of economic recession will be particularly important. Furthermore, immediate issues, and the way in which they are treated by the mass media will influence people's attitudes.

Discrimination

In the literature racial discrimination is conceived of in terms of unfavourable treatment in respect of access to resources, employment and rights. From the evidence of this literature a substantial amount of such discrimination exists in Britain—in spite of legislation aimed at its control. There is another way in which discrimination works, though, which involves the problem of *easy* access, rather than barriers to access. I will return to this below.

The 1975 government White Paper, Racial Discrimination, making reference to the race relations legislation noted:

> Legislation is not and never can be a sufficient condition for effective progress towards equality.

It must be hastily pointed out that 'equality' here does not have the same meaning that it has for some other people. It is not referring, say, to equality in the sense of an equal distribution of wealth. Rather it refers to equality of opportunity for minorities seen in terms of access to employment, education, etc. Certainly we have to agree that government legislation alone cannot eradicate racial prejudice and discrimination, thereby creating 'equal opportunities'. Racism and its consequences cannot be destroyed simply by the threat of legal sanctions. However, even the legislation that exists has not been allowed to make any real impact on discriminatory practices.

A great number of studies show that racial discrimination is still an important feature of social and economic life in this country. Of pivotal importance here is discrimination in the field of employment, for one's occupation obviously has a crucial bearing on one's whole way of life. Having said this though, discrimination in other areas of life is also of enormous importance. In 1979, for instance, out of the 1894 people arrested under the 'sus' law, 767 were black. Tony Bunyan has pointed out how in the 1970s official figures seemed to show significant increases in 'black crime', and that this was a decade when black unemployment was growing at a much faster rate than white unemployment, with black communities already living in the most deprived areas of London. He goes on:

> Not only were these areas defined by the police themselves as 'high crime areas' which required the full employment of fire-brigade policing techniques, like the continued introduction of the Special Patrol Group, but black people in general and young black people in particular were seen by the police on the streets as a 'criminal' class. Young black people became 'targets' for special attention and the rise in the numbers arrested, not just for 'mugging' but for 'sus' and other street offences, is hardly surprising.[63]

To return to employment, even in those cases where applicants for jobs are not personally seen by the employer there is a strong tendency for those with names usually belonging to black minority groups to be discriminated against. As with sex discrimination it is often very difficult to prove in law that discrimination has actually taken place.

David Smith found that West Indian and Asian workers experienced discrimination in 46 per cent of their job applications. At higher qualification levels this discrimination is shown by the fact that only 31 per cent of men belonging to ethnic minorities and qualified to degree level are in professional or managerial positions; the figure for white men is 79 per cent.[64] As a confirmation of the findings of Smith, Roger Ballard and Bronwen Holden found that even black applicants with British qualifications had to make far more applications for positions than did their white counterparts. In their research the black sample was completely made up of people who were born in this country.[65] Neil McIntosh and David Smith found that in 30 per cent of all applications for jobs, black people were discriminated against at the recruitment stage.[66] The same figure was arrived at in a survey carried out in Liverpool in 1975 by the Community Relations Commission.

All studies point to the fact that the most important variable, from the point of view of the applicant's physical characteristics, influencing the degree of discrimination is colour of skin. Sheila Patterson has shown how those with lighter shades of skin colour experience less discrimination than those with darker shades.[67] Patterson found that the incidence of rejection is greater for West Indians than Asians, and greater for Asians than it is for Cypriots. This situation is reflected in surveys which have asked those from minority groups the extent to which they have been personally discriminated against in job applications. In W. W. Daniel's study the respondents were asked to answer the question: 'Do you believe that employers do discriminate?' The percentages answering 'yes' were as follows: West Indians 87 per cent; Indians 73 per cent; Pakistanis 58 per cent; Cypriots 38 per cent.[68]

When discussing the incidence of reported discrimination Smith argues that the decrease indicated by a comparison of data from the 1967 and 1974 Political and Economic Planning (PEP) reports shows that the 1968 Race Relations Act has had some success. However, as John Lea has pointed out, we should be careful here.[69] Smith himself is aware that we should be cautious when interpreting data relating to racial discrimination because, as he puts it: 'the victims of discrimination are not usually aware of it', thus his optimism is only supported by the data if it is assumed that the same proportion of unknown discrimination was present in 1967 and in 1974. As well as this Lea highlights a number of other considerations when interpreting such data. A decrease in the amount of reported discrimination is, he points out, quite compatible with a decrease *or* an increase in equality of opportunity. In other words, reported discrimination tells us little about the extent of social mobility among black groups, given that equal opportunities to be socially mobile is a professed aim of the anti-discrimination legislation. This is because, firstly, increasing concentrations of black people in some localities may mean that they have less contact with white people, and therefore there will be less competition for jobs and housing, leading to a decline in reported discrimination. Secondly, there seems to be a tendency for black workers to apply for jobs only when there is a good, known chance of being taken on. And thirdly, a decline in discrimination may simply mean that more opportunities exist for immigrants, but these are opportunities in low-paid jobs with unsocial hours.

This takes us back to the point mentioned at the beginning of this section: that discrimination can work in two directions. On the one hand, as it is usually understood, a lack of access into certain types of employment, and on the other, easy access, though into jobs of the worst type. This is connected to the willingness of immigrant workers, partly because of their experience or knowledge of discrimination when applying for better jobs, to take these low-paid jobs. In this way discrimination for some black workers may actually decrease, and yet social mobility based on equality of opportunity may show no improvement at all. The section below on economic role indicates that for the bulk of black workers this is probably the case. An end to reported discrimination, then, is not necessarily a cause for celebration.

The Race Relations Act introduced in 1968 has been described as a 'liberal *quid pro quo* for immigration restrictions',[70] following as it did in the wake of legislation controlling immigration into this country. The fundamental philosophy behind the Act was that for 'racial harmony' to prevail it was necessary to both control black immigration, via the Immigration Acts, so that those already here could more easily be integrated into the community, and ensure by legislation that discriminatory practices did not subvert this integration. What we have here is a policy of integration based, on the one hand, on discrimination against black people at the level of the state, and on the other, on anti-discrimination legislation within society.

Enforcement of the Act was to be through a Race Relations Board, backed up by a Community Relations Commission, the latter concerning itself with co-ordinating the work of various voluntary organizations. In reality, though, the Act was largely ineffective. In particular the Race Relations Board lacked the powers of enforcement necessary for anything like a real attack on racial discrimination in public places, housing and employment. Another problem was that victims of discrimination could not, under the terms of the Act, take their cases to court. The lack of effectiveness of the 1968 Act is well illustrated by the assessment of discrimination in Smith's 1973 and 1977 studies for PEP. In the latter study Smith argues that, assuming that actor tests are fairly accurate reflections of discriminatory practices, there will be about 6000 cases of discrimination in the field of unskilled work alone every year. Actor tests are carried out to assess levels and types of racial discrimination on the part of employers. They involve a number of people ('actors') of different colour/ethnic background, all with the same qualifications, applying for the same job. If Smith's estimate is fairly accurate, it is sobering to consider the fact that in 1973 the Race Relations Board dealt with only 150 cases of racial discrimination.

The 1976 Race Relations Act was introduced to make the anti-discrimination laws more effective. These laws, however, are still subject to many limitations when it comes to their implementation.[71] Under this Act the Race Relations Board and the Community Relations Commission ceased to exist, their work being gathered together under the newly created Commission for Racial Equality; the Commission itself was given stronger powers. The Act allowed an individual to bring a complaint of racial discrimination to the courts: in the field of employment to an Industrial Tribunal, and in other matters to a County Court. In spite of these changes, only a small proportion of cases of racial discrimination appear to reach the Industrial Tribunals. Between June 1978 and June 1979, for example, the Tribunals dealt with only 394 applications, and only 58 of these were upheld. As Bowers and Franks say: 'This low level may reflect an educated view of the likely chances of success.'[72]

A report by the Runnymede Trust published in 1978 argues that racial discrimination in employment occurs on a massive scale, and that even companies working on government contracts, who are supposed to conform with a clause prohibiting racial discrimination, are heavily involved in this discrimination. One major problem, argues the Trust's report, is that the 1976 Act does not obligate employers to actively prevent racial discrimination within their company. The result is that no real mechanism exists which can effectively work towards an equal employment policy. As the report states:

> The political will of central government to eradicate racial discrimination and disadvantage appears to be weak; statutory penalties under the Race Relations Act are so small that most employers could budget for the risk and hardly notice

the difference; the Commission for Racial Equality, with its potentially powerful legal armoury, has done virtually nothing in its first year.[73]

If discriminatory practices on the part of employers were to decline significantly—and governments could strive for this goal with much more vigour than they have done—there is still the problem that this does not guarantee less racial prejudice and racial conflict. This is because if discrimination did decline significantly it might mean that white workers felt even more threatened by black workers, especially if there is a no-growth economy with high levels of unemployment.

I have already pointed out that racial discrimination not only operates to stop black workers getting certain jobs, it also operates to ensure that those workers are available for employment in other jobs, jobs within the low-wage sector of the economy, a sector that has been dependent on this type of labour. The implications of this have been well argued by Lea:

> The mechanism of discrimination comprises a combination of refusal of access to employment, etc. in some areas and an acceptance of immigrants in others. These two aspects are interdependent. Acceptance of immigrants is associated in a large number of cases with their 'willingness' to accept wages and conditions of work that native workers would reject. This 'willingness' is a product of their exclusion from other areas of employment, coupled with an ability of employers to deny immigrants access to effective trade union rights.[74]

Because of this there exists a fundamental contradiction lying at the core of government policies, oriented as they are around the idea of equality of opportunity. As Lea puts it:

> Specifically, we are presented with the problem of how low-wage sectors of employment previously dependent upon immigrants are to retain their labour force in the absence of racial discrimination against immigrants in higher paid jobs, given that racial discrimination has been a major mechanism serving to guarantee the availability of immigrants as a pool of cheap labour.[75]

In order to try to achieve a degree of racial integration and thus, they speculate, lessen the possibility of public disorder, British governments have introduced anti-discrimination legislation. This, though, is in conflict with the needs of the low-wage sector of the economy. If Britain's economy had continued to expand beyond the 1960s, then upward mobility among black workers could have taken place, and providing that a replacement low-wage labour force based on new migrant workers was introduced, then these structural problems would for a time have been accommodated. This expansion, however, did not take place.

Economic Position and Social Disadvantage

This factor is of crucial importance for an understanding of modern race relations and racial problems. Black workers entering Britain in the postwar period, and their children who were born here, have been incorporated into already existing structures of wealth and power. Entering primarily as replacement labour for jobs being vacated by native workers, they have generally found themselves employed in the lowest paid jobs with unsocial hours. Explanations of problems associated with race which ignore this structural dimension—for example, the 'cultural strangeness' hypothesis, which seeks to explain problems simply in terms of (psychological) white prejudice—are unsatisfactory. Whether or not a minority group within a host society is viewed as inferior by the indigenous population will depend upon the relationship of that minority group to the overall system of power and wealth. Even those black people who hold higher qualifications are, when compared to white people with the same qualifications, proportionately under-represented in those positions commensurate with that standard of education. In postwar Britain, then, we have seen a reproduction, in a changed form, of the earlier colonial relationship based on domination and subordination; though in contemporary society the groups meet as fellow-workers and citizens. Rex has argued[76] that this places a severe strain on that relationship. Furthermore, there will be an intensification of conflict arising from the fact that conflict is inherent in a capitalist system anyway—conflict between labour and capital over the distribution of company income, conflict over housing, jobs, status and so on.

The lowly position occupied by black workers in the economic system has been confirmed by a large body of research. Smith shows how they are proportionately over-represented in unskilled and semi-skilled work.[77] According to Smith, 18 per cent of white men are employed in unskilled and semi-skilled work, while the figures for other groups are:

> Pakistanis/Bangladeshis 58%
> Indians 36%
> West Indians 32%
> East African Asians 26%

And while 40 per cent of the white population are employed in professional/managerial/white-collar work, the figures for other groups are:

> East African Asians 30%
> Indians 20%
> West Indians 8%
> Pakistanis/Bangladeshis 8%

There are very heavy concentrations of black workers in certain industrial sectors, for example, the low-paid end of the service industry and the National Health Service, transport, and as labourers in foundries and textile factories. Stuart Hall et al[78] point out that black labour is generally associated with three types of work, and particularly so if Asians are included:

1. Sweat-shop type work involving small-scale production. Such employment being characterized by low piece-work rates and low levels of unionization.
2. Work in the service and catering industries, where hours are long and unsocial, and the work frequently involves large-scale 'massified' labour, for example, in catering and office-cleaning.
3. Assembly-line industries: these being highly capitalized, and using low levels of skill and a great deal of shift work. In fact, currently, over one-third of black workers work shifts, this is twice the figure for whites.

As far as earnings are concerned, Smith has shown that at all skill levels, from professional to unskilled, white men enjoy higher weekly earnings than do men from minority groups.[79] He also found that even when allowance was made for possible differences in educational standards between Britain and Asia, the job levels occupied by Asian men are significantly lower than those occupied by their white counterparts.

Nowadays we cannot discuss work without also considering unemployment, and the same pattern of inequality shows itself here. Figures from the Department of Employment show that unemployment rates for black workers have always been higher than the national average. If we separate out the various groups we find that West Indians in particular come out badly, especially West Indian women; up to fairly recently the figures for Asians approximated more closely to the national average, however, there is a trend away from this now. Between 1973 and 1975 unemployment, for the first time since the war, reached one million, and doubled. There were four times as many black unemployed people in 1975 as there were in 1973. At the moment the unemployment rate for black school-leavers is four times the national average, and in some inner-city areas more than 60 per cent of black school-leavers are unemployed.

Latest figures show that between August 1979 and August 1980 unemployment in general rose by 38 per cent, the figure for minority workers was 48 per cent—from a level that was already higher than that of the white population anyway. Pakistanis and Bangladeshis are concentrated in manufacturing and manual labour, and these industrial sectors are particularly vulnerable to the economic recession. For these, unemployment increased by 61 per cent between August 1979 and August 1980. Apart from racial discrimination playing a part, minority groups will also be particularly prone to unemployment because a high proportion of them are young, and because so many are living in the inner-city areas where job opportunities are rapidly declining.[80]

It is clear from the research that in terms of housing black families are worse off than are white families. The 1971 census showed that while four per cent of all households in Britain live in shared dwellings, the figure for households where the chief breadwinner was born in the New Commonwealth was 21 per cent. Smith found that 22 per cent of Asian and 30 per cent of West Indian households were living in shared dwellings.[81] He also found that black minorities were 10 times as likely to be sharing baths and six times as likely to be sharing a toilet. They were also over represented in older, terraced property. Thus, using a range of indicators, black families in contemporary Britain, when compared with white families, find themselves living in housing conditions that are significantly inferior.

These inequalities are also apparent when we examine council house estates. The 1975 Runnymede Trust report, Race and Council Housing in Britain, shows that in the inner-London boroughs black tenants are over-represented on the pre-war, high density estates, when compared to white tenants; while 22 per cent of general council house tenants live on these estates, the figure for New Commonwealth tenants is 52 per cent. Conversely, black tenants are under-represented on the estates built since 1961. Only 0.6 per cent of the more recent suburban cottage estates are tenanted by black families, and even in recent inner area estates they occupy only a little over three per cent of houses. The present government's commitment to the sale of council houses will exacerbate these inequalities.[82]

As education forms a major part of this book, there is no need for me to enter into a detailed discussion of it here, though a few general points may be made.

In many ways black children share the same problems as white working-class children within the education system. However, there is a racial dimension to how the black child experiences and is treated by schooling. Although individual teachers and administrators may be committed to racial equality, a complex of racially specific factors is at play acting on the black child and shaping his treatment by the education system. The end result is a strong tendency (albeit unwitting) for schools to prepare black children for the lower grade, less well-paid jobs—or no jobs at all. Examples of racially specific factors are stereotyping within the school, or even in some cases racist feelings on the part of staff. The content of the syllabus is often biased in favour of certain types of white interpretations of events, to the extent that history may be misrepresented, and black culture, even in schools with high proportions of black pupils, may remain unrecognized and undervalued. Furthermore, the black child not only carries with him or her into the school a working-class culture derived from family and neighbourhood, but at the same time a *black* working-class culture. Thus in a school system geared to a white middle-class culture the black child can experience severe problems of adjustment. A West Indian derived language style, for instance, being a crucial component of that culture, is often undervalued and written off as 'substandard' speech.

One of the most powerful phrases available in the liberal-reformist phrasebook is 'equality of opportunity'. Capturing as it does the full potency of all that is desirable in a welfare-oriented, humane capitalist future, who, apart from the most reactionary elements, would dare to criticize it? Especially in the field of education the concept of equality of opportunity has been given pride of place. All of the major political parties are, in their own particular ways, publicly committed to its attainment. Students of the sociology of education will have noticed that up to quite recently this specialism was really the sociology of equality of opportunity, or more correctly, lack of opportunity.

One problem with the concept is that above the level of a very broad and vague definition, there is no consensus among its users regarding what it means. Perhaps it is this vagueness, combined with its quality of immediately sounding impressive, which has helped to strengthen its ideological usefulness. At the most general level—where it sounds most platitudinous—it is commonly taken to mean that all children, regardless of background, should have an equal chance to show what they can do and achieve in the education system.

The notion of equality of opportunity is predicated on the assumption that society will be based upon class differentiation; what is being argued for is a system which gives all children an equal chance to be 'successful', first of all in education, but ultimately in terms of their eventual position in the class structure. Thus to support a policy of equal opportunity to be successful is, at the same time, to support a policy of equal opportunity to be a failure. The implicit assumption is that 'failure' constitutes a permanent feature of social life. In other words, the concept posits the continued existence in British society of badly paid, low-status, yet necessary, jobs; a society based, therefore, on inequality, though people should have an equal chance to be unequal. If society is differentiated on the basis of power, wealth and education, then how can children coming into the education system from various parts of that differentiated society, ever, as it were, line up equally? This is the central contradiction. From the point of view of governments there is a need to identify those reforms necessary for equality of opportunity in education, yet at the same time, in order to give this idea any meaning it is also necessary to preserve the structural inequalities which prevent it from being realized, for these inequalities represent the success/failure rewards on which equality of opportunity is based.

Successive governments have used equality of opportunity as an organizing philosophy for the solutions to what they see as problems of race relations. While on the one hand controlling immigration into Britain, they have on the other introduced legislation aimed at controlling discriminatory practices on the part of employers, etc. Through the race relations legislation it is hoped that black people may eventually enjoy equality of opportunity in society. The intended end result is a more harmonious, more integrated society; the results so far are not encouraging. As we have seen, there is a great deal of evidence to show that racial discrimination still occurs on a massive scale, and there is also evidence to suggest that upward social mobility among black workers is not taking place. This continuing concentration of black workers in certain lower grade jobs, and certain types of job, will also influence their concentrations in certain poorer areas and poorer types of housing. Smith found that rather than dispersal taking place, there is in some areas a tendency towards even greater concentrations.[83] He also points out that as far as occupational mobility is concerned, if this was taking place on any significant scale we would expect to find that those who have been in this country the longest are in general further up the scale; in fact Smith found no correlation in this respect.

As is the case with education, an approach to race relations based upon a philosophy of equality of opportunity contains certain inherent weaknesses and limitations. Essentially, such an approach directs attention away from those structures in society which create and sustain inequality, and towards the individuals within those structures. The approach allows the structures of inequality to remain intact, and yet still gives the impression of 'doing something' about the issue. The race relations legislation treats the problem in terms of discriminatory practices, so that the emphasis is on trying to prevent white people from discriminating against blacks, which will in turn create more black social mobility and less racial prejudice, because whites will realize that black people are just as capable as they are. The central contradiction, in the field of education and race relations, arises from the fact that equality of opportunity cannot be achieved in a society that is fundamentally unequal: a society where people (working class/black working class) start off from positions of inequality *vis à vis* the structures of power and wealth.

The notion of equality of opportunity as it is applied to black children in the school system, as well as black people in general in British society, has to be criticized in that it focuses on the individual and his failings/prejudices rather than on the inequalities rooted in a capitalist social structure. The economic and political benefits accruing to British capitalism from the presence of immigrant groups (in particular in the low-wage sector) and the perpetuation of the structural inequalities experienced by black people, function to limit severely the opportunities open to them. It is true that in the field of education certain equality of opportunity linked reforms, such as fewer racist textbooks, more resources for multiracial education, more enlightened teachers, can make an important and welcome impact on the performance of individual black schoolchildren, and thereby create a more representative 'racial balance' at all stages and levels of education. The significance of such reforms should not be underestimated; greater opportunities for black children are obviously to be welcomed. However, we also need to recognize the limitations in reforms such as these. Eventually they need to be linked to a more fundamental struggle against racism and racial inequality in the social structure, for it is here that the real sources of educational inequality have their roots. No amount of state-sponsored tinkering with the education system can 'compensate' for the inequalities existing in the wider social structure.

Colour and Culture

Black minority groups in Britain whose roots lie in the West Indies, Asia or Africa, are obviously easily recognizable, though geographical and ethnic accuracy cannot always be guaranteed in the classifications made by white people. At the same time certain cultural characteristics, such as language, will also be used to make racial distinctions, though, again, confused, uninformed opinions are quite common here. Having said this, it has to be stressed that these differences are in themselves not that important; what is important is the historical and social context within which these differences exist and are perceived. In the 19th century, Irish migrants in Britain were believed to be recognizable because of their facial features—the 'wild Milesian features', as Carlyle put it—and they were also believed to possess an inferior culture (standards of behaviour, attitudes, etc.)

Modern-day racists will often attack black people on the basis of the supposed inferiority of their cultures, and counterpose these 'alien' cultures against white culture. Apart from the obvious fact that such arguments totally misrepresent West Indian, Asian and African cultures, there is also the misleading invocation of some monolithic 'British culture'—usually under the banner of the 'British Way of Life'—when in reality so-called white culture is composed of all kinds of culturally differentiated groups and classes.

The Third World

The relationship between the development of Western capitalism and the underdevelopment of the Third World has already been discussed. In the modern world the dominant image of the underdeveloped nations among those living in the technologically advanced nations is made up of a mixture of fact and fiction. Colonial stereotypes still abound, whereby the poverty of the Third World is explained in terms of a lack of initiative or basic laziness on the part of the people living there. This is then seen as being reflected in their less 'civilized' cultural patterns. Black people in Britain, including those born here, will frequently have to contend with these negative images and stereotypes as a corollary to their familial roots being in one of the poorer parts of the world.

Government Controls

By the introduction of a succession of controls on *black* immigration since the 1962 Act, governments in this country have assisted splendidly in fostering the idea that black people are a problem. By specifically earmarking black people, that is focusing on colour, and seeing the problem in terms of numbers (backed up by speeches on the 'swamping' theme), the legislation implicitly gives support to the racist ideology which allocates blame for such things as urban decay to the presence of black immigrants. A neat point is made in an article in The *Sunday Times* in 1978 written by a New Zealand Maori. The article gives 'sympathetic' support to the 'swamping argument' used by the Prime Minister, Margaret Thatcher. Referring to the determination of Mrs Thatcher to preserve Britain's cultural heritage in the face of threats from other cultures, the writer of the article does express surprise 'that she should feel that less than 5 per cent of the population is a cause for concern'. The writer then goes on to offer encouragement:

> Perhaps it would comfort the British to know that we Maoris have managed to keep our language and some of our traditions alive in spite of being overwhelmed 10 to 1 by British immigrants over the last 150 years—and that in spite of a determined attack upon our culture by the immigrant majority which lasted for over a century.

Economic Recession

This has become a crucially important factor. There are a number of ways in which economic recession will have a particularly damaging impact on black people. These have been discussed in detail in various parts of this chapter and may be summarized as follows:

1. A no-growth economy means that there will be a lack of upward mobility, which will tend to maintain the concentration of black workers in the lower paid jobs.
2. Competition for jobs will increase, thus discriminatory practices will lead to fewer job opportunities for black workers, creating even greater unemployment among this group. Black school-leavers, for example, will find it increasingly difficult to obtain employment, which in the long term will further worsen their position, for there will be a lack of skills and work experience.
3. Given their concentration in the lower socio-economic strata, black people will be particularly affected by cuts in public expenditure and a continuing process of inner-city decay.
4. Economic recession also increases the likelihood of black people being treated as scapegoats, as the cause of unemployment, lack of houses, etc.

In conclusion, it is true that black and white working-class people share a range of similar problems, but what I have tried to show above is that we also need to take into consideration a number of racially specific factors. These problem-creating and problem-sustaining 'contextual factors' converge on black people living in Britain. The task facing those who are committed to fighting racism and racialism is to remove forever these contextual factors. To paraphrase the words of another contributor to this volume: the aim has to be the replacement of a society containing black and white working-class people with a society containing people.

NOTES AND REFERENCES

1. Mullard, C. (1980) *Racism in Society and Schools: History, Policy and Practice*, p. 4. Occasional Paper No. 1. Centre for Multicultural Education, University of London Institute of Education.

2. Montagu, A. (1952) *Man's Most Dangerous Myth*, p. 1. 3rd Edition London: Harper and Row.

3. Bohannan, P. (1966) *Social Anthropology*, p. 192. New York: Holt, Rinehart and Winston.

4. *Ibid.,* p. 192.

5. Firth, R. (1958) *Human Types*, p. 23. New York: Mentor.

6. Washburn, S. L. (1966) The study of race. In Jennings, J. D. and Hoebel, E. A. (Eds.) *Readings in Anthropology,* p. 116. New York: McGraw-Hill.

7. John Tyndall, quoted in Walker, M. (1977) *The National Front*, p. 81. London: Fontana.

8. Banton, M. (1970) The concept of racism. In Zubaida, S. (Ed.) *Race and Racialism*, p. 18. London: Tavistock.

9. *Ibid.*

10. Rex, J. (1973) *Race, Colonialism and the City*, p. 191. London: RKP.

11. *Op. cit.,* p. 31.

12. There is an inconsistency in Banton's work in that while he at one point supports the distinction between racism as doctrine and racialism as practice, later on he says that: 'if we label the new culturally based *doctrines* "racist" we may mislead people. To call them racialist is much preferable'. (My emphasis.) Racialism here is related to doctrine.

13. Ethnocentrism is usually taken to mean a condition whereby one group feels that another group or culture is inferior, without the idea of racial categories necessarily being involved.

14. These points are made by Rex, J. (1970) The concept of race in sociological theory. In Zubaida, S. (1970) *op. cit.*

15. Quoted in Walker, M. (1977) *op. cit.,* p. 125.

16. Putnam, C. (1961) *Race and Reason.* Washington D. C.: Public Affairs Press.
Shuey, A. (1966) *The Testing of Negro Intelligence.* New York: Social and Economic Press.
Jensen, A. (1973) *Educability and Group Differences.* London: Methuen.
Eysenck, H. (1971) *Race, Intelligence and Education,* London: Temple Smith.
Eysenck, H. (1973) *The Inequality of Man.* London: Temple Smith.

17. For a useful discussion of scientific racism see: Bagley, C. (1975) On the intellectual equality of races. In Verma, G. K. and Bagley, C. (Eds.) *Race and Education Across Cultures.* London: Heinemann.

18. The 'culture of poverty' idea was introduced by the American anthropologist Oscar Lewis in the late 1950s:
    Lewis, O. (1959) *Five Families.* New York: Basic Books.
    Lewis, O. (1961) *The Children of Sanchez.* New York: Random House.
    Lewis, O. (1966) *La Vida.* New York: Random House.

19. Quoted in Walker, M. (1977) *op. cit.*

20. This is from the point of view of those doing the labelling, and, theoretically, any physiological characteristics could be used.

21. Hodge, J. J., Struckmann, D. K. and Trost, L. D. (1975) *Cultural Bases of Racism and Group Oppression.* Berkeley, Calif.: Two Riders Press.

22. Rex, J. (1973) *op. cit.,* p. 202.

23. Althusser, L. (1972) Ideology and ideological state apparatuses. In Cosin, B. R. (Ed.) *Education: Structure and Society.* London: Penguin.

24. Marx, K. and Engels, F. (1965) *The German Ideology,* p. 37. London: Lawrence and Wishart.

25. Engels, F. (1970) Letter to J. Bloch. In Marx, K. and Engels, F., *Selected Works,* p. 683. London: Lawrence and Wishart.

26. *Ibid.,* p. 694.

27. Marx, K. and Engels, F. (1965) *op. cit.,* p. 61.

28. Walton, P. and Gamble, A. (1972) *From Alienation to Surplus Value,* p. 18. London: Sheed and Ward.

29. Marx, K. and Engels, F. (1965) *op. cit.,* p. 37.

30. Cox, O. C. (1959) *Caste, Class and Race: A Study in Social Dynamics,* New York: Monthly Review Press.

31. Genovese, E. D. (1972) *In Red and Black: Marxian Explorations in Southern and Afro-American History.* London: Allen Lane.
    Genovese, E. D. (1974) *Roll Jordan Roll: The World the Slaves Made.* London: André Deutsch.

32. For a detailed discussion of this issue see: Gabriel, J. and Ben-Tovim, G. (1978) Marxism and the concept of racism. *Economy and Society,* **7,** 2, May.

33. Mullard, C. (1980) *op. cit.,* p. 7.

34. Gorz, A. (1970) Immigrant Labour. *New Left Review,* 61, May/June.
    Castles, S. and Kosack, G. (1973) *Immigrant Workers and Class Structure in Western Europe,* London: Institute of Race Relations/Oxford University Press.

35. Rex, J. (1973) *op cit.,* p. 75.

36. Hancock, G. (1979) Why is Africa poor? *New Internationalist,* 71, January.

37. For an excellent and readable account of the events surrounding the massacre at Wounded Knee see:
    Brown, D. (1971) *Bury My Heart at Wounded Knee: An Indian History of the American West.* London: Picador.

38. Fisher, G. P. (1892) *The Colonial Era in America*, pp. 10–11. London: Sampson Low, Marston and Co.

39. Well worth reading on Aboriginal history is:
    Roberts, J. (1978) *From Massacres to Mining: The Colonization of Aboriginal Australia.* London: War on Want/CIMRA.
    Roberts, J. (Ed.) (1975) *The Mapoon Story by the Mapoon People.* Victoria, Aust.: International Development Action.

40. Forsyth, C. and Tiranti, D. (1979) Aborigines and mining: the conflict. *New Internationalist,* 77, July, p. 5.

41. Quoted by Hartmann, P. and Husband, C. (1974) *Racism and the Mass Media,* p. 24. London: Davis-Poynter.

42. Quoted by Tinker, H. (1977) *Race, Conflict and the International Order: From Empire to United Nations,* p. 17. London: Macmillan.

43. Stern, W. M. (1963) *Britain Yesterday and Today.* London: Longman.

44. *Durham Advertiser,* Friday, 17 April, 1981.

45. Quoted by Engels, F. (1969) *The Condition of the Working Class in England,* p. 122. London: Panther.

46. *Ibid.* p. 123.

47. *Ibid.* p. 123.

48. *Ibid.* p. 153.

49. *Ibid.* p. 153.

50. Quoted by Castles, S. and Kosack, G. (1973) *op. cit.*

51. Quoted by Hartmann, P. and Husband, C. (1974) *op. cit.,* pp. 163–164.

52. *Ibid.*

53. Kuya, D. (1979) Racial bias in children's books. *Dragon's Teeth,* **1**, 1, p. 3.

54. Quoted by Hartmann, P. and Husband, C. (1974) *op. cit.,* p. 30.

55. Dixon, B. (1977) *Catching Them Young 1: Sex, Race and Class in Children's Fiction,* p. 103. London: RKP.

56. Dummett, A. (1973) *A Portrait of English Racism*. London: Penguin.
    Husband, C. (Ed.) (1975) *White Media and Black Britain*. London: Arrow Books.
    Proctor, C. (1975) *Racist Textbooks*. London: National Union of Students.

57. Pearson, G. (1976) Cotton town: A case study and its history. In Mungham, G. and Pearson, G. (Eds.) *Working Class Youth Culture*. London: RKP.

58. Brooks, D. (1975) *Race and Labour in London Transport*. Oxford: Oxford University Press.

59. Rose, E. J. B. et al (1969) *Colour and Citizenship: A Report on British Race Relations*. London: Oxford University Press.

60. Bagley, C. (1970) *Social Structure and Prejudice in Five English Boroughs*. London: Institute of Race Relations.

61. Hill, C. S. (1967) *How Colour Prejudiced is Britain?* London: Panther.

62. Rex, J. and Moore, R. (1967) *Race, Community and Conflict*. London: Institute of Race Relations/Oxford University Press.

63. Bunyan, T. (1981) Review of: 'Mugging as a Social Problem'. *Race and Class*, **22**, 4, Spring.

64. Smith, D. J. (1974) *Racial Disadvantage in Employment*. London: PEP.

65. Ballard, R. and Holden, B. (1975) The employment of coloured graduates in Britain. *New Community*, **IV**, No. 3.

66. McIntosh, N. and Smith, D. J. (1974) *The Extent of Racial Discrimination*. London: PEP.

67. Patterson, S. (1968) *Immigrants in Industry*. Oxford: Oxford University Press.

68. Daniel, W. W. (1968) *Racial Discrimination in England*. London: Penguin.

69. Lea, J. (1980) The contradictions of the sixties race relations legislation. In National Deviancy Conference (Eds.) *Permissiveness and Control*. London: Macmillan.

70. Bowers, J. and Franks, S. (1980) *Race and Affirmative Action*. London: Fabian Tract, 471, 3.

71. For a detailed discussion of this legislation see *ibid*.

72. *Ibid*.

73. The Runnymede Trust (1978) *Beyond Tokenism: Equal Employment Opportunity Policies*. London: Runnymede Trust.

74. Lea, J. (1980) *op. cit.*, p. 133.

75. *Ibid.*, p. 134.

76. Rex, J. (1973) *op. cit.*

77. Smith, D. J. (1977) *Racial Disadvantage in Britain*. London: Penguin.

78. Hall, S., Critchley, C., Jefferson, A., Clarke, S. and Roberts, B. (1978) *Policing the Crisis*, London: Macmillan.

79. Smith, D. J. (1974) *op. cit.*

80. Home Office Research Bulletin, No. 11 (1981).

81. Smith, D. J. (1977) *op. cit.*

82. Burney, E. (1967) *Housing on Trial*. Oxford: Oxford University Press.
    Smith, D. J. and Whalley, A. (1975) *Racial Minorities and Public Housing*. London: PEP.
    Cross, C. (1978) *Ethnic Minorities in the Inner City*. London: Commission for Racial Equality.
    Rex, J. and Tomlinson, S. (1979) *Colonial Immigrants in a British City*. London: RKP.
    See also various Runnymede Trust reports.

83. Smith, D. J. (1977) *op. cit.*

2

Lessons from History for Black Resistance in Britain

J. GUNDARA

By 1900, British colonies and dependencies exceeded 13 million square miles, with an estimated population of over 366 million.[1] The passing of that Empire is still viewed with considerable nostalgia. European colonialism, on a scale hitherto unknown, expropriated the wealth of the third world and in the process exploited and enslaved its peoples, sometimes even committing genocide—in Kiernan's words, 'whole healthy races were wiped out'.[2] It is a story of insatiable greed, combined with gross inhumanity. But Europe chooses to remember its colonial venture differently, seeing it, above all else, as a civilizing mission to the world, essentially welcomed by the colonial peoples. The belief that colonialism was, on balance, beneficial remains strongly persistent in European thought.

Imperialist history will teach the black child to be grateful that Europe allowed its religion, culture, institutions and technology to be transplanted to all the corners of the globe. The liberal version will be tempered by the admission that in the process great suffering was also inflicted upon the recipients of this beneficence. The view of the Empire expressed in terms of the 'white man's burden' must, of course, be challenged. But as a counter, it is insufficient simply to chronicle the enormity of the injustices perpetrated. Colonialism needs to be explained in economic and political terms and colonial history recorded from the perspective of the oppressed. Resistance to colonial domination and control occurred virtually everywhere, yet it is largely ignored in popular historical accounts. This chapter briefly sketches examples taken from a wide variety of colonial situations of resistance and struggle against European domination.

These examples have been selected to suggest to teachers that colonial resistance to oppression has links with today's resistance of blacks in Britain. White youth, in particular, has assimilated attitudes developed when Britain was an imperial power; attitudes which have not been counteracted by a study of history in terms of society's elite. For a true understanding of contemporary British society, historical discussion must be widened to include Britain's long involvement in the slave trade, colonialism and now neo-colonialism. This is as important for white youth as it is for black because of the way colonialism has shaped and reinforced the bourgeois institutions and government of British society. Colonialism cannot be equated with civilization. As Cesaire and Fanon explain, it decivilizes and brutalizes the colonizer as much as the colonized.[3]

The presence of the black minority in Britain is a result of long colonization. As Sivanandan has said 'We are here because you were there'. The struggle by this token is both there and here and the connections between the struggles in the colonies and the resistance here in Britain today are real.

The historical heritage of the black community in Britain arises from its longstanding experience of oppression by the West and from the awareness of the resistance of successive generations. The consciousness of the oppressed is derived from an amalgam of failures and successes in the struggle. For blacks in Britain their cultural history is based on the experiences of the generations who lived on the slave plantations or worked as indentured labour in the colonies. The experiences gained during the lifetime of grandparents in the Middle passage, the Atlantic System and the Monsoon System in the Indian Ocean of the 17th and 18th centuries are retained and transmitted and should be given a contemporary dimension in the classroom discussion. As Gramsci writes,

> In the accumulation of ideas transmitted to us by a millenium of work and thought there are elements which have eternal value, which cannot and must not perish. The loss of consciousness of these values is one of the most serious signs of degradation brought about by the bourgeois regime; to them everything becomes an object of trade and a weapon of war.[4]

The resistance to this domination has taken place and continues to take place not only in the third world but also in the exploitative North.[5] It is not only relevant to the blacks but also the Scots, Welsh and Irish,[6] and not least the English working class. 'The history of the local working-class militancy is frequently forgotten . . . the working class must preserve its heritage.'[7]

It is not always true that the oppressed willingly accept their situation. Although the history of colonial resistance is still to be fully recorded, there are many examples of struggles against the ruling power ranging from full-scale armed struggle, to isolated skirmishes, passive resistance and individual acts of defiance. The following section illustrates this point by selecting examples from slavery, wars of liberation in Haiti, Aboriginal resistance in Australia, the 1857 uprising in India, opposition to the scramble and examples of contemporary resistance in Britain. Other examples could equally well have included the Innuets in Canada, the Opium Wars in China and the early Namibian struggles against the Germans.

SLAVE RESISTANCE IN THE AMERICAS

Slave resistance in the New World started on board the transportation ships. Slaves contested their enslavement in every possible way, and the sailors on these ships had to keep a wary eye for fear of attacks. Nets were erected around the decks to prevent captives from jumping overboard: it seems slaves frequently preferred to commit themselves to the sharks rather than to submit to slavery. This mode of autodestruction can be illustrated by the example of a slave who was brought on the deck of a ship to be killed and who jumped overboard. An officer on the ship said,

> The slave, perceiving that he was going to be caught immediately, dived under the water, and by that means made his escape, and came up again some few yards from the vessel, and made signs which it is impossible for me to describe in words, expressive of the happiness he had in escaping from us. He again went down and we saw him no more.[8]

This is a case of individual defiance which must be distinguished from suicide since it illustrates vividly the significance of liberation from the oppression and degradation of slavery.

Time and time again there were rebellions against transportation. In 1839 the Spanish schooner *Amistad,* sailing from Havana to the Cuban port of Principe with 54 African slaves on board, was seized by the slaves led by a man called Cinque. After two months of fruitlessly trying to force the Spanish crew to sail the schooner back to Africa, Cinque and his men put into a US port for supplies and were seized by the US naval authorities. An historic court case developed from this incident. The Spaniards claimed that the ship and slaves were their property, while the American defence held that the slaves had simply been acknowledging their right to fight for their freedom on the high seas.[9] Eventually the US Supreme Court, in the same way as Lord Mansfield in England in 1772, came out in favour of the captives, and in 1842, three years after their revolt, they were sent back to Africa. The *Amistad* revolt was not exceptional: one American historian calculated that at least 55 ship revolts had taken place on the American trade route alone between 1699 and 1845.[10]

'The docility of the Negro slave is a myth'[11] which is perhaps best illustrated by the Jamaican Maroons (from the Spanish term *cimarron* meaning 'wild, untamed') who escaped into the hills, forests and remote areas. Another similar example is provided by the Djukas of Surinam.[12]

These were groups of slaves who had escaped early in the history of their respective colonies; the Maroons moving to the mountains of Jamaica and the Djukas into the swamps, dense jungle area and rural basins of Guyana. These two groups were cut off from direct European influence and from the plantation economy, pursuing a life of freedom (though they had to defend it constantly), living as closely as possible to their traditional African ways and evolving an African-type society in the New World.[13]

Maroons were found wherever there was slavery in the New World. There were groups in the mountains of Dominica, St. Vincent and St. Lucia, many of whom had mixed with Carib Amerindians. They were also to be found in Hispaniola, Panama, Puerto Rico, Brazil and the United States. The most famous free settlements were at Palmares in Brazil (near the capital Palmares). These were established in 1630 and remained independent for over 60 years, increasing in that time to a population of about 20 000 people.[14] Aspects of African culture and language continue to be observed to the present day, forming part of both the black and Brazilian cultures.

The Maroons of Jamaica, although numbering only about 2000, established small and successful settlements which retained their independence for the entire 150 years of slavery in the colony. These Maroon settlements began in 1655 with the English occupation of the islands, and slaves belonging to the Spaniards joined in guerrilla warfare against the invaders. By 1720 there were two distinct groups of Maroons—one in the centre of the island, the other in the north east. The Maroon settlements involved the joint struggle of men and women, avoiding tensions based on sexual issues.

The first Maroon War started in 1731 and lasted intermittently for five years, although in fact the struggle started in 1655 and continued for 87 years. The Maroon leader, Cudjoe (an Akan name from Ghana), developed a strategy of guerrilla warfare against the British. A compromise between the Maroons and the British was drawn up by Cudjoe. Since the British could not defeat the warriors, between 1739–70 they reached an agreement with them. The Maroons were to stay in their five main towns of Accompong, Trelawny Town, Moore Town, Scots Town and Nanny Town. The latter was named after Nanny, Cudjoe's sister, who was opposed to the 1739 treaty between Cudjoe and the English. Nanny continued to rule the people till her death in the 1750s.[15]

One of the clauses in the treaty demanded that runaway slaves should not be harboured. This led to a split between the Maroons and the rest of the black population. As Cudjoe grew older he became disillusioned, but the more rebellious Trelawny Town Maroons declared a second war against the British and fought an amazing guerrilla war for five months, at the end of which they were still undefeated. After they had inflicted defeats on their enemies, they were persuaded to sign a treaty. Like Toussaint in Haiti, they were tricked and all of them, warriors, old men, women and children, were transported to the cold of Nova Scotia and from there were sent to Sierra Leone several years later.[16]

Other Maroon groups who did not take part in the rebellion remained as separate groups until Jamaican independence in 1962. These struggles of resistance to the end of the 18th century were class struggles between the owner–employer class on the one hand, and the labouring slave class on the other. Such struggles also had a 'black self-determination or nationalistic aspect . . . They sought, in fact, to destroy the white superstructure and replace it, if possible on a country-wide basis with black self-determination.'[17] As Richard Hart writes, 'The Maroon Wars of 1795 and beyond; the revolts of 1815, 1823 and 1831 to 1832 in Jamaica—of 1823 in Guyana and 1816 in Barbados are evidence of the increasing tempo of slave resistance in the period.'[18] These revolts certainly made it clear that slaves would take their future into their own hands through violent and bloody confrontations which speeded the process of abolition. As a Governor of Barbados wrote in 1819 'the public mind is ever tremblingly alive to the dangers of insurrection'.[19]

Resistance by other slaves includes the actions of runaways who took jobs in towns or became fishermen and woodcutters which gave them virtual freedom from slavery. Within plantations opposition ranged from violent eruptions, the burning of cane and the poisoning of planters, to sabotage, go-slows, pretending not to understand and the development of new modes of communication unintelligible to the slave owners.

A random count of slave rebellions from 1519 to 1874 in Brazil shows some 88 examples of resistance in the New World, which must be considered the bare minimum, as, clearly, the history of the oppressed goes unrecorded. The only completely successful revolt occurred in Haiti (discussed later). The Berbice slave rebellion in Guyana in

1763 was brutally suppressed in 1764, defeated as much by internal rivalries as by the Dutch. The date of the start of the Berbice rebellion has come to be recognized as Guyana's Republic Day. Cuffy, the leader of the rebellion, is, today, Guyana's national hero.[20] The slaves outnumbered the planters by eleven to one and they were able to control the province for over a year. Instead of going deep into the forests like the Djukas, they decided on a direct confrontation with the enemy. Since the Berbice population was small, and Cuffy's forces were not large, the Dutch refused to accept terms and in 1764 brought in reinforcements from Holland. Issues were further complicated because of quarrels within rebel ranks and Cuffy eventually shot himself. The new leaders could not retain control of the area and began to retreat. Of the hundreds of rebellions, Berbice was only one during the period of slavery in the New World. Large-scale rebellions took place in Martinique, Guadeloupe, Jamaica, at the same time as the Haitian revolt; these were later followed by others in Barbados (1816) and Jamaica (1831).

The American rebellions were smaller in number, partially because estates were smaller and there were higher proportions of locally born rather than African-born slaves. Slave revolts in New York in 1712 and Stone, South Carolina, in 1739 anticipated those of the Maroon communities in Florida, Virginia and Carolina. In the final 70 years of the 18th century, there were over 1300 advertisements for runaway slaves in Virginia newspapers.[21] The revolts of Gabriel in 1800 and Denmark Vesey in 1822 were relatively small affairs and were easily suppressed. Perhaps the best known of the American rebellions was that led by Nat Turner in 1831. Turner was born in Virginia in 1800 as a house slave. He was extremely intelligent and was taught to read and write by the family which 'owned' him. As a preacher he moved freely amongst slaves and began planning a rebellion. When he was about to be sold from the Virginia estate to the harsher conditions of the Deep South in 1831 he felt the hour was at hand. With the aid of seven others, he captured the armoury of the county capital, Jerusalem, and escaped to Dismal Swamp, 30 miles to the east. Nat Turner's talents for secrecy, surprise, planning and swift and ruthless action resulted in a large measure of success. The slaves killed the family that owned them, burned and destroyed everything on the way to Jerusalem. Fifty-five Southerners were killed on the route. A few miles short of the capital, confronted by armed militia and planters, they were defeated and seventeen rebels, including Turner, were executed. The Negro spiritual referring to Jerusalem is primarily a reference to Nat Turner's revolt.[22] As Toynbee has said, the blues are the slave's response to the challenge of oppression. Most of the slave rebellions took place where they found space to mobilize themselves and implement alternative forms of community to replace those imposed by the dominant class.

THE HAITIAN REVOLT

The Haitian Revolt—the most celebrated of all—is eloquently described by C. L. R. James in his classic work *The Black Jacobins*.[23] The French possession of San Domingo had, by 1770, become a flourishing colony based on slave labour. When the

French Revolution broke out there were 35 000 white colonists on the island, 22 000 free mulatto people and 450 000 slaves. The slaves had always been actively hostile to their enslavement and in 1757 François Macandal had made an extensive plan to poison all the whites, but was captured and burned alive before he could do so.

With the French Revolution, the first disturbances came from the free mulatto population, and by 1798 a complex series of struggles between whites, mulattos and blacks ensued. By 1779 Toussaint had become the undisputed master of the colony, moulding the slaves into a formidable fighting force. As Governor General of the island, he defeated the mulattos, the English and the Spaniards. The French Republican Army chose to negotiate with him. Toussaint was known as 'The Centaur of the Savannas' because he was such a perfect horseman. His father was reputed to be an African chief although Toussaint was born a slave. He learnt some French, Latin and Mathematics from his godfather Pierre Baptiste, another slave. His father taught him about his African heritage, including herbalism and folk medicine. Toussaint started as a cattle herdsman, later becoming a coachman and finally a steward of livestock. As leader of the rebellion he proved that house slaves were neither docile nor servile. Similarly, no easy generalizations can be made about field slaves because many slave rebellions were initiated by them. Toussaint joined the slave rebellion one month after it began, leading to ultimate control over San Domingo.

Toussaint resisted and subverted French culture and developed a Haitian alternative. Napoleon Bonaparte did not approve of this 'gilded African' in what was considered a French colony. Napoleon used his brother-in-law Victor Leclerc to trick the black revolutionaries to sign an oath of allegiance and lay down their arms. Toussaint, however, was not swayed and the French decided to use 20 000 troops to suppress the revolutionaries. Toussaint, and his generals Christophe and Dessalines, conducted a series of brilliant campaigns and by April 1802 brought the French to the brink of disaster.[24] Toussaint miscalculated in deciding to make peace with Leclerc and after a few months he and his family were arrested, placed aboard a warship and imprisoned high up in the Jura mountains in France where he died on 7 of April 1803. This betrayal of Toussaint resulted in massive revolts all over Haiti. Leclerc died in 1802 and Haiti was blockaded by the British during the war with the French. The freedom fighters gained an upper hand but during this period the population had diminished from 500 000 to 350 000. Haiti became a symbol for the slaves in the New World, although a major-power embargo on the Haitian economy left it crippled. There were also civil wars between mulattos and blacks which further compounded problems.

THE ABORIGINAL RESISTANCE IN AUSTRALIA

The oppression of the Aborigines in Australia has been largely ignored as has been their resistance. Attempts at reconstructing Aboriginal resistance have been far fewer than for the Caribbean, Africa and Asia. At the present time, the overseas mining companies would like to suppress the Aboriginal's militant past so as to prevent a militant future where their traditional ownership of Aboriginal lands might be threatened.

According to writers like Fergus Robinson and Barry York, the regional struggles of the Aborigines have given them a national (Pan Australian) character and created a national consciousness. The numerical and technical inferiority of the Aborigines *vis à vis* that of the colonial enemy made guerrilla warfare their most effective weapon. As a testimony to the efficacy of their strategy they continued fighting into the 20th century in Western Australia, Queensland and the Northern Territory. The Aborigines had no private means of production or private property and no class divisions; thus their struggles were markedly different from those of peoples with more complex social structures like the Zulus of South Africa who for so long successfully fought both the British and the Boers.[25] The Aboriginal headmen were nothing more than the heads of families, and in contrast to the British, had no standing army, no full-time police, courts or bureaucracy.

The Aborigines faced two stark choices. On the one hand, not to resist meant physical survival but cultural death. On the other, to resist meant partial liquidation but cultural survival and they took the latter choice. The strategy involved passing information during walkabouts or 'dream time' from one tribe to another. By inflicting minor defeats on the enemy, they were able to observe their strengths and weaknesses, thereby avoiding the total wrath of the Europeans and their own total annihilation. By striking against the explorers when they were extremely weary, the enemy was taught a lesson, and their habits were observed for future reference.

Aborigines were recruited by the British for the local police and when half this native police force was demobilized in 1855, many of them joined Aboriginal tribes and attacks on settlers' homesteads increased. There were instances of white convicts, also suffering under colonial oppression, joining forces with the Aborigines. In the context of neo-colonialism in Australia, black resistance to the instruments of white control continues. At another level, the poor settler and Aborigines have jointly expressed their feelings in the Land Rights demonstrations in various Australian cities. The militant Aborigines are in the forefront of keeping both the American corporate structure and the Soviets out of their land.[26]

THE 1857 UPRISING IN INDIA

To the British, India may have been the 'Jewel of the Empire', but to the Indians, colonial rule signified foreign subjugation. The history of the British Raj is marked by frequent and bitter struggles and among the most important is the bloody 1857 uprising. Despite the fact that the Bengal, Madras and Bombay Presidencies did not join the 1857 revolt, the scale of the conflict is startling; it encompassed 150 000 square miles and involved 45 million people at a time when Britain's 90 000 square miles were inhabited by 28 million people.[27]

One of the causes of revolt was that while the British mercantile bourgeoisie remained free from direct taxation, the average proportion of land tax in India was extremely high. It made up 61 per cent of the state income of British India between 1840 and 1857, while in the north-west provinces, where resistance was extremely strong, it reached 80 per cent reducing the peasantry to bare subsistence. Marx wrote in 1858 that 'taxation crushes the mass of the Indian people to the dust, and that its exaction necessitates a resort to such infamies as torture'.[28] The village system had been broken up and the ancient co-parcenary system of property ownership was undermined. As late as the 1890s Baden Powell admitted 'the destruction of the ancient land system had a direct bearing in turning the 1857 uprising into a social war, a war of the rural classes against new land grabbers'.[29] Most Indian soldiers and their families were personally dispossessed of land and were exceedingly dissatisfied with the state of things in the villages. Hence the connection between the social conditions in Oudh and the North-West Frontier had the sympathy of the soldiers. Marx further pointed out that after the conquest of India, the soldiers were required to maintain it:

> From soldiers they were converted to policemen; 200 000 000 natives being curbed by an army of 200 000 soldiers officered by Englishmen and that native army in turn being kept in check by an English army numbering only 40 000. On first view it is evident that the allegiance of the Indian people rests on the fidelity of the native army, in creating which the British rule simultaneously organized the first general centre of resistance which the Indian people ever possessed.[30]

When the British army insisted that the Indian soldiers use rifle cartridges greased with pig fat—an instruction which offended the religious sensibilities of both Muslim and Hindu— the sepoys felt compelled to rise and the way was paved for an upsurge of the people. Hindu and Muslim masses came together and the 1857–1859 uprising of the people was a 'national uprising'. It fits Lenin's definition: 'For what is a national uprising? It is an uprising aimed at the achievement of political independence of the oppressed nation . . .'[31]

The future nationalist movement in India was determined by this uprising. However, Gandhi's passive resistance in the 20th century comprised a category of non-violent revolt which was also secular in its orientation. This movement identified with the suffering masses and, like the Pan-African movement, the Gandhian movement transcended narrow ethnicities.

RESISTANCE DURING THE SCRAMBLE FOR AFRICA

From 1880 it took the European powers a quarter of a century to complete their conquest of West Africa and their political control was not fully established until 1905 because of the strength of African resistance. Parts of the Ivory Coast, Mali, Niger and Eastern Nigeria were not 'pacified' until the second decade of the 20th century. As Michael Crowder states:

> Not only was resistance bitter, it was often skilful and not only provided by a few states with well developed armies like Dahomey or Ashanti but by a very wide range of peoples. Indeed, it is rarely appreciated that a good majority of the states of West Africa, large and small, as well as most of the people living in segmentary societies opposed European occupation with force.[32]

While Europe might have overcome Africa with superior weapons, their occupation was only slowly achieved. The Ashanti, with their better knowledge of the forest, attacked the British flanks where they were most vulnerable. However, one of the major problems was to obtain supplies of European arms. Tactical problems were compounded by the Africans having to use inferior weapons discarded by the European armies. The Hausa-Fulanis used swords, spears, lances, and bows and arrows, but these were ineffective and merely acted as irritants. In addition, the ruthlessness of the Europeans in using such methods as burning villages and shooting the wounded, as in the case of the Hausa-Fulani, had a cumulative effect in undermining resistance.

The Europeans also used local allies which divided the African forces. Thus, for example, the British allied with the Tanti against the Ashanti; the Frence with the Yoruba against Dahomey; the British with Ibadan against Ijebu; the French with Bambara and other groups against Tukolor;[33] the French with the Tukolor against Mahmadon Lamine. Hence diplomacy was used to forge military alliances. The major weakness of African resistance was that it was undertaken state by state. Alliances between African states, even if they had not defeated the Europeans, would have put the cost of the conquest higher than the metropolitan powers might have been prepared to pay.

The French Chamber of Deputies criticized the high cost of the campaigns against Sudan in 1891 and 1893, and the fiasco of the British expedition against the Ashanti in 1863 was responsible for a decision in 1865 by the Parliamentary Select Committee to limit British commitments on the West Coast. While Europeans followed policies of divide and conquer, the African leaders followed a policy of divide and survive. However, European rivalry did not manifest itself in colonial ventures. In spite of competition 'when it came to serious colonial upheaval', Kiernan writes, 'white men felt their kinship and Europe drew together'.[34] The Europeans won Africa in conventional wars because of superior weaponry but found difficulty in contending with guerrilla tactics. For example, the Nana of Ebrohimi[35] used his superior knowledge of the creeks through which the British sailed to reach Ebrohimi to attack them. Bai Burah appreciated that once he picked off the European leaders their African levies would become immobilized.

However, continued guerrilla warfare could only have staved off the inevitable. West African agricultural societies had to cope with industrialized Europe with its infinite resources. It was unfortunate for Africa that instead of the Europeans turning their sophisticated weapons against each other in the scramble for Africa, they used their might to crush African states.[36]

THE CONTEMPORARY STRUGGLE

As African nationalism grew in response to colonial rule, the nationalist movements learnt from the past. The struggles for liberation in Guinea-Bissau, Mozambique and Angola had traumatic political consequences for both the colonizing power, Portugal, and the foundations of revolutionary change in these African countries. The ZANU/

ZAPU victories in Zimbabwe demonstrate their political and military sophistication in defeating a powerful Western-backed settler regime.

In Southern Africa the struggle of SWAPO continues alongside that of the Azanian people in fighting the last stronghold of white domination. A new generation of black revolutionaries emerged during the Soweto uprising. The growth of the Black Consciousness Movement and the organization of black students into an effective body of resistance are similar indicators of the struggle against oppression.

In third-world countries where political independence was gained without changing Western economic domination, the people are regrouping to fight against the oppression of their national bourgeois elites who are supported by Western and Soviet imperialism. The struggles of the Workers Party in Guyana, those of the Indian masses against the oppression in that country, and the fight against various corrupt regimes in Africa, Latin America and the Caribbean, demonstrate this resistance. The murder of Walter Rodney in 1980 by the repressive Burnham Government has not dampened the collective struggle of the Guyanese people.

Another dimension to the contemporary struggles of colonized peoples is their effects upon the colonizing power. The struggles of national liberation are directly linked to the structures and politics of the metropole. Thus the impact of Algerian independence on France and the Vietnamese resistance on America matched the changes that occurred in the Portuguese political and social system following the independence of Guinea-Bissau, Mozambique and Angola.

In order to set up modes of production advantageous to the colonizing power, the existing bases of communal life and means of production were dismantled to the detriment of the colonized peoples. Through the consciousness of historical resistance to this destructive colonization, black people in Britain are as aware of this form of oppression as their cousins in the Third World. Therefore, to label as ethnic the resistance of people whose forbears and Third World contemparies have been through, or are engaging in, struggles against their brutal exploitation is to brush aside their basic rights as people.

In Britain there are numerous manifestations of resistance by black people in schools and society generally. In the previous colonial period, in Trinidad, the oppressive forces of authority felt that the carnival constituted a threat to the colonial apparatus. Similarly, the local state apparatus in Notting Hill Gate might consider that its carnival can be used to articulate resistance.[37]

This resistance in cultural and political terms is further highlighted by the growth of Rastafarianism among the younger generation of the black community. This section of the community rejects both the neo-colonial aspects of control in Jamaica, as well as informing and strengthening the 'culture of resistance' in Britain.[38] The struggles in this respect are firmly embedded in the structures of the black community as it has developed in the metropolitan context. The younger generation discard, adapt and transform their parents' struggles to suit their changed position in society. This is done without in any sense becoming alienated or separated from the older generation. Given the dynamic nature of this struggle, neither the Rastas nor their community struggles can be stereotyped or co-opted by the state. The structures of community relations, community policing and social policy can neither acquire the sophistication nor the means to control these processes because they are not amenable to being either stereotyped or understood by the existing sociological frames of reference.

The struggles of black workers, primarily the women, demonstrate how a supposedly traditional and passive section of the community cannot in fact be stereotyped. The Mansfield Hosiery Strike, Loughborough (1972), Imperial Typewriters, Leicester (1974), Grunwick Film Processing, London (1976), Chix, Slough (1980), were mainly based on the resistance of women. The supposed generation gap between the older and younger women from the Indian sub-continent and East Africa proved irrelevant in the context of their larger unity. This struggle at the workplace was not sustained by sympathetic co-workers but by the support accorded by the home and community.

The most widespread evidence of a stand against the repression of the police and the fascist groups was manifested in open rebellion. The resistance of blacks in April 1980 in Bristol became the battle cry of blacks in Brixton in April 1981. These were, however, not isolated incidents but reflected the collective historical memory of shared experiences and contemporary struggle against racism. The uprising in British cities in July 1981 demonstrated this larger unity since it started in Southall against the presence of fascists and had reverberations in at least thirty British cities in the span of about a week (see the coverage of these events in the *New York Times,* 5 July 1981 to 16 July 1981).

The police had continually failed to defend the black community; there were reports of at least forty racially motivated murders in the last five years, attacks on black people, their homes, shops and community institutions. Instead the police have turned a blind eye and assumed the role of an occupying force in the black areas of British cities. The black community has increasingly had to cope with further racism in legal, institutional and structural terms.[39]

The discriminatory immigration legislation has been supplemented by the 1981 Nationality Act which has strengthened a system of external and internal control over the black British population. Families were kept apart by placing hurdles in the path of attempts to reunite husbands with wives and parents with children. The cases of Anwar Ditta (Rochdale), Jaswinder Kaur (Leeds), Nasira Begum (Manchester) illustrate the opposition of women and whole communities to repressive legislation. Their names are now part of the consciousness of the community. These individual cases only highlight the wider opposition to racist immigration legislation (1962–1971) and the Nationality Act (1981). The Joint Council for the Welfare of Immigrants in the opening sentence of their Annual Report (1980/81) state:

> It is not a coincidence that the year which has seen the most serious disturbances in some of Britain's multiracial inner-city areas has also been the year in which nationality and immigration law struck more deeply than ever before into the security of Britain's black community.[40]

The black community is a settled and permanent part of British society. Attempts by the state, the police and the fascist groups to abrogate their fundamental rights will only lead to a greater resolve on their part not to allow these rights to be further encroached upon and diminished. In fact, as the above events demonstrate collectively, black resistance is widespread and will arise when and where it is least expected. These events show that while the strategies of struggle will differ in Grenada from those in Brixton, consciousness is not necessarily different. It is not easy to suppress or direct any of these struggles because they are neither hierarchial nor specific. They relate to all oppression and oppressed masses, and though small failures may appear to impede the struggle, the heightened consciousness can only enhance the ultimate victory.

In addition, resistance takes varying forms. It may be of a cultural nature or involve political organizations. It may be passive resistance or based on violence. The rise in the consciousness of women, particularly against patriarchal exploitation and the state apparatus, lends a new dimension and strength to this struggle.

The historical incidents related above demonstrate that when people are subjugated, resistance and revolt are inevitable. 'Unlikely oppositions (India, Algeria, Vietnam, Guinea-Bissau, Iran, Mozambique)'[41] develop. Black resistance to their oppressors is markedly less violent when compared to the massive terror employed by the ruling classes. These seeds of resistance within the oppressed are part of their culture and cannot be obliterated by any means by the oppressors.

Schools and classrooms in Britain similarly contain elements of resistance to 'schooling'. Black youth does not accept the negative stereotypes, the low level of teacher expectations and the perpetuation of their low socio-economic role in society. The resistance takes the shape of distinctive linguistic and cultural modes which reject the standard norms expected by society.[42]

The role of teachers in this context is to help consolidate the lessons gleaned from the history of struggle and attempt to unify the different sub-groups of the oppressed. By adopting this positive stance, teachers would shift from 'schooling' children to the role of 'educating' in the widest sense of the word.[43] 'Educating' children provides history teachers with a positive framework for developing an area of work which is largely neglected at the present time. History, as a subject, is particularly deficient in providing a space in which students can learn about the resistance of peoples to domination.

NOTES AND REFERENCES

1. Hobson, J. A. (1968) *Imperialism: A Study*, p. 20. London: Allen and Unwin.

2. Kiernan, V. G. (1969) *The Lords of Human Kind*, p. 311. London: Weidenfeld & Nicholson.

3. Fanon, F. (1967) A Dying Colonialism, p. 65. *Monthly Review Press.*
   Fanon, F. (1968) *The Wretched of the Earth*, pp. 52, 57, 86. *Monthly Review Press.*

4. Gramsci, A. (1968) *The Modern Prince and Other Writings*, p. 20. New York: International Publishers.

5. Rodney, W. (1972) *How Europe Underdeveloped Africa.* Dar-es-Salaam and London: Tanzania Publishing House.

6. Hechter, M. (1975) Internal Colonialism: The Celtic Fringe in British National Development 1536–1966. London: Routledge & Kegan Paul.

7. Jacobs, S. (1976) *The Right to a Decent House*, p. vii. London: Routledge & Kegan Paul.

8. *The Parliamentary Papers, Accounts and Papers,* (1790–1791). Vol. **92** (34). London: HMSO.

9. Martin, C. (1979) *The Amistad Affair.* New York: Abelard-Schuman.

10. Sterne, E. G. (1968) *The Long Black Schooner.* Chicago: Follett.

11. Williams, E. (1964) *Capitalism and Slavery*, p. 33. London: André Deutsch.

12. *Ibid,* pp. 202–208.

13. Kopytoff, B. (April 1978) The Early Political Development of Jamaica Maroon Societies. *William and Mary Quarterly,* Vol. **XXXV**, 2, p. 2.

14. Kent, R. K. (1965) Palmares, an African State in Brazil. *Journal of African History,* Vol **VI**, 2.

15. Mathurin, L. (1975) *The Rebel Women,* pp. 34–37. Kingston, Jamaica.

16. See Troper, H. and Palmer, L. (1976) *Issues in Cultural Diversity,* pp. 17–27. Toronto: Ontario Institute of Studies in Education. (A section of the black community remained in Halifax and were recently moved from 'Africville' against their will.)

17. Hart, R. (1979) *Black Jamaicans' Struggle Against Slavery,* p. 20. London: Community Education Trust.

18. *Ibid.*

19. Williams, E. (1964) *op. cit.* p. 202.

20. Jagan, C. (1966) *The West on Trial,* pp. 33–34. London: Michael Joseph.

21. Robinson, C. (June, 1980) *Coming to Terms: The Third World and the Dialectics of Imperialism,* p. 19 (mimeo) California: University of California.

22. Aptheker, H. (1978) *American Negro Slave Revolts.* New York: International Publishers (He discusses in detail the revolts of Nat Turner, Vesey, Gabriel and others. This book also contains a useful bibliography).
Elkins, S. M. (1963) *Slavery: A Problem in American Institutional and Intellectual Life,* pp. 134–139. New York: The Universal Library.

23. Detailed accounts may be found in James, C. L. R. (1963) *The Black Jacobins.* London: Vintage Books.

24. Cole, H. (1967) *Christophe: King of Haiti.* London: Eyre & Spottiswoode.

25. Davidson, B. (1964) *The African Past.* London: Longman.

26. The account of the Aboriginal struggle mainly relies on
Robinson, F. and York, B. (1977) *The Black Resistance.* (Widescope) Camberwell, Australia.
Blainey, G. (1976) *The Triumph of the Nomads: A History of Ancient Australia.* Melbourne: Macmillan.
Rowley, C. D. (1970) *Outcasts in White Australia.* London: Pelican.

27. Domin, D. (1977) *India in 1857–59,* p. 2. Berlin: Akademic Verlag.

28. Marx, K. (1858) Taxes in India. *New York Daily Tribune,* (29 June).

29. Baden Powell, B. H. (1894) *A Short Account of the Land Revenue and its Administration in British India,* p. 134. Oxford: OUP.

30. Domin D. *op. cit.* p. 2. quoting: Marx, K. and Engels, F. (no date) *The First Indian War of Independence* 1857–59, p. 41. Moscow: Progress Publishers (Marx and Engels are wrong in assuming that it was the British occupation which was central to the resistance of the Indians.)

31. Lenin, V. I. (1960) A Caricature of Marxism and Imperialist Economism. *Collected Works,* Vol. **23,** p. 62. London: Lawrence & Wishart.

32. Crowder, M. (ed.) (1971) *West African Resistance,* p. 20. London: Hutchinson.

33. *Ibid,* p. 12–14.

34. Kiernan, B. G., *op. cit.,* p. 27.

35. Ikime, O. (1972) *Nana of the Niger Delta.* London: Heinemann.

36. (Useful materials for teaching African history and resistance in schools do exist: see Crookall, R. E. (1977) *Handbook for History Teachers in Africa.* London: Evans. Sanders, P. (1973) *Moshweshwe of Lesotho.* London: Heinemann.

37. Gutzmore, C. (December, 1978), Carnival, the state and the black masses in the United Kingdom. *Black Liberator,* No. 1, pp. 8–27.

38. Gilroy, P. (1981/82) You can't fool the youths . . . race and class formation in the 1980s. *Race and Class,* **XXIII,** 2–3, 207–222.

39. Gilroy, P. (1981/82) *op. cit.* see also articles by A. Sivanandan, T. Bunyan, L. Bridges and L. Kushnick.

40. JCWI Annual Report (1980/81), p. 2.

41. Robinson, C., *op. cit.,* pp. 29–30.

42. Hall, S. and Jefferson, T. (1977) *Resistance Through Rituals: Youth Subculture in Post-war Britain,* London: Hutchinson.

43. Searle, C. (1975) *Classrooms of Resistance.* London: Writers and Readers Publishing Co-operative. The Introduction and the writing of children are an example of this type of teaching.

3

Facts and Figures: Some Myths

P. DICKINSON

'Numbers are of the essence,' said Powell in 1968[1] and for at least a decade since, immigration, rather than racism, has dominated popular discussion of issues relating to race and the black population in Britain. While rejecting the central importance of the 'numbers game'—the 'white problem' of racism as theory enshrined in official and unofficial practices is the key issue—this chapter attends to some of its assumptions, and to beliefs about the extent and characteristics of postwar immigration from the New Commonwealth and Pakistan (hereafter 'NCWP'). The aim is to provide an understanding of NCWP immigration and its contexts, in order to counteract the hysterical and apocalyptic visions that have been the currency of public debate in the last twenty years, and which have been endorsed by Mrs Thatcher in her 'swamping' imagery of recent speeches.[2]

Other and fuller analyses are, of course, widely available: on the demographic characteristics of the black population;[3] on control legislation;[4] on the operation of controls;[5] on the economic determinants of postwar NCWP immigration;[6] on the relationship between capitalism and migration;[7] on the relationship between immigration and controls;[8] and on the values implicit in the numbers game[9]. What this chapter attempts to do is provide an introduction to some aspects of NCWP immigration through the identification and examination of some of the most common myths—myths that are being perpetuated by those political leaders able to define the terms of public debate.

The examination of facts and figures to do with race and immigration is, however, a contentious exercise; two weighty objections can be lodged against it. It can be argued that the exercise is irrelevant to current problems and damaging insofar as it diverts attention from these; and that the numbers game is dangerous in that it shifts debate onto racist terrain, implicitly accepting the racist case by concentrating on the extent of immigration and the size of black communities. A few words need to be said on these before we proceed to the myths.

The argument concerning irrelevance goes something like this: why examine demographic and other aspects of immigration when Britain is a multiracial society whose black population is increasingly British born rather than immigrant? Surely, it might be added, the crucial issues are racialist attacks on the street, the racism that informs existing and proposed immigration and nationality legislation, the erosion of welfare rights for blacks, and the images of black inferiority reproduced in various cultural forms. 'Numbers', it might be argued, are no longer relevant to these issues—it was a concern of the 1960s developed by the political Right to divide the working class, and by the Labour Party to justify control measures that went against the liberal conscience,[10] but which were seen as electorally necessary.

The legislation of 1962–1971 virtually ended primary immigration but did not produce integration.[11] Black communities increasingly see themselves subject to assault, harrassment and discrimination, whether by gangs, by officials of the state, or by employers.[12] The logical consequence of the numbers game was to shift attention from potential NCWP immigrants 'out there', to the black population of the UK. It justified restrictive and racist immigration controls which in turn stigmatized the black population as not only unwanted but as a threat, thereby legitimizing attacks on them. Although racial hostility obviously has far deeper roots than misconceptions about migration flows—c.f. the legacy of the Empire and perceived competition for jobs and housing—examination of numbers can illustrate the irrationality behind such fears.

'Immigration' is the frame of reference within which public debate about Britain's black population has taken place: we hear of 'immigrant areas', 'immigrant youth' and 'immigrant births'. Thatcher's 'swamping' speech was just one more reinforcement of this problem definition. Other public figures have encouraged this also through their own utterances,[13] and through their manipulation of interviews—often aided by the interviewers' own assumptions.[14] News reporting through the 1970s consistently drew attention to immigration rather than to the rights and conditions of the black population *per se,* whether the focus was on Asian refugees from East Africa in 1972–1973, from Malawi in 1976, on the changes in the immigration rules in 1974 and 1980, on the processing of applications (Hawley Report, 1976), or on abuses in entry procedures (scandal of virginity tests at Heathrow and the subsequent Yellowlees Inquiry 1979–1980). Even cases of conflict between individuals and the Home Office, e.g. those of Anwar Ditta and Nasira Begum, direct attention to immigration rather than to rights of individuals and communities, or to the relationships between state, family and women. Such definition of issues has meant that the current Nationality Bill (1981) is popularly thought to be another measure restricting immigration. The fact that it will worsen insecurity through further endorsing harrassment and reduce rights already being eroded in welfare[15] is helped by maintaining the image of black Britons as immigrants. In turn, the existence of different standards of citizenship will facilitate the management and control of the black population by the state.

One other reason makes examination of migration relevant. Ignorance allows a sleight of hand whereby apparently neutral and technical concerns—population density and growth—become equated with keeping out blacks. Michael Dummett makes the point that 'discussion of immigration has for the most part been governed by certain assumptions which have transformed it from anything resembling a rational discussion of immigration policy . . .',[16] adding that these assumptions are that white immigration causes no problems while black immigration does and is therefore to be curtailed. Examination of migration will not of itself refute these assumptions, but it will remove the rationalizations in which they are concealed. The more the smokescreens of apparently rational concerns are blown away the better: the real question of the essentially racist assumptions can then be confronted. Examination of migration is thus a ground-clearing exercise, and one which it seems has to be repeatedly taken up, as long as those with the power to define social problems and the parameters of debate continue to talk about immigration.

The second objection is that examination of NCWP immigration which takes issue with popular misconceptions ('they're flooding the country,' etc.) attempting to show that levels of immigration are much lower than believed, that the balance of migration has usually been negative (more emigrants than immigrants), may factually refute anti-immigrant arguments while conceding the grounds on which they are based—that people from X are not desirable here, but we need not worry, the numbers have been exaggerated. Moore comments,

> Once the debate is about numbers there are no issues of principle to be discussed, only *how many?* In being drawn into this discussion, liberals allowed themselves to be drawn onto racist ground because they were unable to argue about principles but had to accept the contention that coloured people were basically the problem ... The argument about numbers is unwinnable because however many you decide upon there will always be someone to campaign for less and others for whom one is too many.[17]

Moore identifies a parallel danger encountered in discussion of economic activity: 'Similarly arguments about how much we benefited from black immigrants . . . implied that people were entitled to certain rights only because they were useful.'[18] What this does is dehumanize the people being referred to; they become units of economic activity, numbers, a problem to be feared and controlled.[19] Furthermore, the focus on numbers rather than on the class relationships determining the problems of housing and jobs leads to a variant of the 'blaming the victim' mode of interpretation.[20] Downing, commenting on the pathological characteristics of the 'analysis that black people *create* racial conflict, and that the more blacks the more racial conflict,' suggests,

> It could almost be said to be a necessary argument for a capitalist ruling class, since if Jews/Blacks/Xs do not cause hostility and conflict, the cause must be found somewhere else. And where else than in competition for scarce jobs, housing, education and other services, within and among the working class? And why are these basic resources so scarce for the majority in an affluent society?[21]

One extreme example of the tacit acceptance of NCWP immigration as a threat is provided in Paul Foot's analysis of events in the Smethwick consituency in the 1964 General Election. In an atmosphere characterized by anti-(black) immigrant hysteria, (Harold Wilson was to refer later to the unexpectedly successful Conservative candidate as a 'Parliamentary leper'), the Labour response was to accept the logic of their opponents. Thus Patrick Gordon Walker, accused of being 'soft' on immigration, accompanied his election address with the comment that 'the main flow of immigrants happened to come here in the thirteen years during which the Conservatives were in office' and an eve of poll Labour Party leaflet urged:

> Be fair: immigrants only arrived in Smethwick in large numbers during the past ten years—while the Tory Government was in power. You can't blame Labour or Gordon Walker for that.[22]

What this tells us is that the examination of immigration in isolation has its dangers; it should be a preliminary to analysing the colonial legacy, the relationships between developed and third-world economies, the class relationships determining access to, and control over, resources, and the assumption of the determination of culture by biology.

Now let us consider some common myths.

1. 'If it wasn't for the blacks there would be little immigration; stop the blacks and you stop immigration.'
2. 'Blacks and immigrants are one and the same; because blacks are immigrants they can be returned from where they came.'
3. 'Immigration is something new in British history, an unfortunate departure from our traditions.'
4. 'They're flooding the country: we're being swamped.'
5. 'Britain is an overcrowded island with a growing population, and as such can't cope with additional numbers.'
6. 'It's just as well the 1962 Act and subsequent legislation restricted NCWP immigration: they're all wanting to come in.'
7. 'Anyway there's millions of dependants.'
8. 'Even if NCWP immigration is negligible the numbers here are increasing rapidly; their birth rates will swamp us.'
9. 'They shouldn't complain about controls on immigration, these apply fairly to all immigrants.'
10. 'They've got no right to come here anyway.'

If these are seen as straw targets, artificially created and too easy to demolish, it is worth remembering that it is not just ignorant kids mouthing fascist propaganda who accept them; the metaphor of British culture 'going under', engulfed, drowned, submerged, by waves, floods and influxes of immigrants, was given the seal of approval by the current Prime Minister in her 'swamping' speech in 1978. Unfortunately, far from being a caricature of a right-wing position, these assumptions seem to be increasingly taken for granted in public debate—listen to interviewers 'questioning' Home Secretaries and race relations spokesmen—as the self-evident truths on the basis of which debate can proceed.

MYTH 1: 'IMMIGRANTS ARE BLACK'

The link between immigration and the presence of black communities in Britain is an obvious and valid one: only through the movement of people from other countries to

Britain is there a black population here. What is invalid is the implication that because black communities indicate previous population movment 'immigrant' can be equated with 'black'.

1. Black immigrants are just the latest in a long line of immigrant groups—see Myth 3.
2. In terms of net movements the period since 1870 of greatest net gain into the UK is the period 1931–1951 which saw hardly any coloured immigration.
3. More people came into the UK from the EEC (even excluding Ireland) than from India, Sri Lanka and Bangladesh combined—23 000 compared to 14 000 in 1980.[23]
4. The biggest group of foreign-born residents from any one country in Britain today are those born in the Irish Republic—709 000 in the 1971 census.[24]
5. Since 1968 more people have come to the UK each year from Canada than from the West Indies.
6. Immigration statistics produced by the OPCS from its International Passenger Survey, being based on neither 'race' nor 'colour' but rather on country of last residence are just a rough indication of ethnic origin and can be misleading: out of a total of 232 210 immigrants born in India and resident in Britain in 1966, 68 600 were white.[25]
7. 'Return' migrants are increasingly important: people moving from one country to another for a limited period as part of their career. The Migration Analysis Unit of the OPCS comments: 'thus, no fewer than one-third of the *immigrants* into the UK have been people who were born in the UK and so must have lived here previously; and this is a minimum proportion of returning residents because some immigrants who were not born in the UK will nevertheless have lived here previously.[26]
8. Immigration figures by country of last residence show that immigrants from the New Commonwealth, i.e. Commonwealth minus Australia, Canada and New Zealand, but including Pakistan, only comprise one-third of all immigrants to the UK.

	Immigrants from NCWP countries	All immigrants
1966	76 400	219 200
1970	70 400	225 600
1976	67 000	191 000
1980	59 000	174 000

Source: *Population Trends*, 1981, No. 24.

9. Figures by citizenship and last country of origin show some significant changes, e.g. in the reduction in the immigration of Commonwealth citizens from the West Indies, together with greater stability in immigration from the Indian sub-continent, reflecting the later pattern of Asian immigration.

	All immigrants	Australia	New Zealand	West Indies	Pakistan, India, Sri Lanka, Bangladesh
1970	225 600	31 200	7 500	7 400	27 500
1974	183 800	22 500	9 800	3 900	16 300
1978	187 000	18 100	8 900	4 500	37 700

Source: *CSO (1981) Annual Abstract Statistics*, 1980, HMSO.

10. There was one short period when there was a high level of immigration from the New Commonwealth—the five years 1958 to 1962. However, this was ended by the 1962 Commonwealth Immigrants Act effective from 1 July that year, and anyway had been largely a 'beat-the-ban' phenomenon.

MYTH 2: 'BLACKS ARE IMMIGRANTS'

Just as an analysis of immigration figures suggests that the typical immigrant is not black, increasingly the typical black person is not an immigrant. The OPCS estimate for the population of NCWP ethnic origin in Britain in mid 1979 was just over 2.0 million or 3.7 per cent of the toal population.[27] This includes the population of part NCWP origin, i.e. having only one parent of NCWP origin, estimated at 138 000 in mid 1976,[28] and births occurring to the British-born population of NCWP origin, estimated to total 10 000–20 000 by mid 1978.[29] The Immigrant Statistics Unit on a 1976 base estimated the population of *wholly* NCWP ethnic origin to be between 2.5 and 3 million by 1991.[30] The 1971 census gave a figure of 1 151 000 NCWP immigrants in Britain.[31] There is no incompatibility as 'immigrant' excludes those whose parents may have been born abroad but themselves are born here. Forty per cent of the NCWP population are in the position of being black and born in Britain.[32] As to identity, the term 'Black British' should not be restricted to those born here: many immigrants would regard themselves as British by virtue of their years of residence here, possession of a British passport, and the expectations inculcated by the colonial system that Britain was the 'mother' country. In addition many people, while technically immigrants, migrated as young children and have grown up here. Repatriation would not only be obscene in its racist assumptions but would also be absurd: in one sense at least, this is home.

MYTH 3: 'THERE WASN'T IMMIGRATION IN THE PAST'

Although it is true to say that Britain has traditionally been a country that has 'exported' people, it is also the case that there has been considerable immigration into Britain in the past by groups escaping starvation or persecution or providing much needed labour and skills for the economy. Over the last century the major immigrant groups have been:

1. Irish. In 1861 Irish immigrants formed 3 per cent of the population of England and Wales and 6.72 per cent of the population of Scotland; by 1966 the number of Irish-born residents in Britain was 879 000. Adding on second and third generations would give very much higher figures, but then it is part of the double standards of the numbers game that we refer to second-generation Asians or West Indians but not second-generation EEC or Irish. For the 1950s and 1960s the numbers of Irish

workers coming into the country each year have been estimated at between 30 000 and 60 000.[33] Irish immigration was both a response to the 'push' factors of poverty and starvation, particularly after the potato famine of 1846/7, and the pull factor of economic opportunities abroad, e.g. in Britain in the 1840s the railway construction boom was producing employment for a quarter of a million workers.

2. Jews. In modern times immigration occurred from 1881 onward as a result of pogroms against Jewish communities in Eastern Europe. There, attacks on Jewish property and persons were often officially inspired in attempts to provide scapegoats for social ills and deflect antagonism from the real causes of deprivation. Following these anti-semitic campaigns approximately 150 000 Jews came to Britain between 1881 and 1914.[34] Between 1931 and 1946 the Jewish population in Britain increased by 88 000 and from 1946 to 1951 by 65 000, but, as Halsey comments, it is unclear how many of these represented 'permanent' immigrants.

3. Poles. After the war many Polish refugees and servicemen who fought in the Allied forces settled in Britain. This was the biggest group of continental immigrants and by 1954 the number of Poles in Britain had stabilized at 120 000.[35]

4. European Voluntary Workers. Postwar labour shortages led to attempts to recruit workers in Europe. In the period 1946–1950 approximately 100 000 were recruited but the schemes were abandoned following criticism over workers' lack of civil rights and the inflexibility of their conditions of employment.[36] Shortage of labour in the postwar economy was met by the increased employment of married women, and, from 1948, by immigration from the New Commonwealth, initially from the West Indies.

MYTH 4: 'SWAMPED'

When Mrs Thatcher alleged in a speech in early 1978 that people were afraid that 'this country might be swamped by people of a different culture', what were the demographic facts? Certainly she could claim that in the previous year more people had come to Britain from the New Commonwealth than had left Britain for the NCWP. She could also correctly claim that this net inward movement from the NCWP had been the normal pattern for the previous 30 years. It is worth noting, however, that some changes had begun to occur: for the five years from 1970 to 1974 inclusive there were more people going to the West Indies than coming from them into the UK.

How significant though was this movement? What was the balance of migration between the UK and the NCWP, the relationship between numbers coming into the country and those leaving? What was the context in which Mrs Thatcher spoke? Had there been some sudden increase in numbers of immigrants to justify her comments?

In 1977 the NCWP net inflow was: from Pakistan, 10 100; from India, Sri Lanka and Bangladesh 6500; from the West Indies 900; the rest of the New Commonwealth provided an inflow of 1200; to the African Commonwealth there was a net outflow of 1500.[37] Altogether therefore, 1977 saw a net inward balance of NCWP migration of 17 200 in a country of 56 million—some swamping!

This only refers, of course, to net migration from some specific countries by NCWP citizenship; when we look at the balance of migration for all countries we find that 1977 showed the typical trend of more people leaving the country than entering. Excluding migration to and from the Irish Republic, there were 46 100 more emigrants than immigrants. Except for 1979 when there was a net gain to the UK of 6200 migrants, every year since the 1962 Act came into effect more people have left the UK than entered. A reversion to type was seen in 1980 when there were 174 000 immigrants to 229 000 emigrants, producing a net outward flow of 55 000.[38]

The picture is slightly different for England and Wales: net inflows occurred in the periods 1962–1963, 1963–1964, 1964–1965, 1972–1973 and 1978–1979, (mid-year to mid-year figures) due to 'immigration' from Scotland and Northern Ireland.

MYTH 5: 'BRITAIN IS AN OVERCROWDED ISLAND; WE CAN'T COPE WITH MORE IMMIGRANTS'

Thatcher on population again: 'it is not as if we have great wide open spaces or great national resources: we have not . . . so either you go on taking in 40 000 or 50 000 a year, which is far too many, or you hold out a clear end to immigration.' As we have seen, there is no overcrowding through the balance of migration—more people leave than enter the country. However, might it not be argued that overcrowding comes about because of a rapid natural increase in the population (more births than deaths) or occurs in particular areas because of the changing geographical distribution of the population, e.g. urban congestion?

Popularization of terms like 'population explosion' and the demographic experience of the last two centuries has made people think of population growth as inevitable. However, in the 20th century, fears of the consequences of a rapidly expanding population have been rare, really only occurring in the mid and late 1960s. More commonly this century, in the years before 1914 and in the 1930s, 1940s and today[39] the fear has been of underpopulation, of declining fertility with births falling below deaths and of the population failing to reproduce itself.

Although there have been fluctuations in the birth rate (number of live births per 1000 population in a given year), especially in the last forty years, the birth rate has been in long-term decline since the last quarter of the 19th century, falling from an average of 28.6 per thousand between 1900 and 1902 to 16.0 in 1971 in England and Wales.[40] Since then it has declined to the all-time low of 11.6 in 1977 with the years 1976 and 1977 showing a natural decline in the population of England and Wales—a decline made greater by the net outflow of migrants. Since 1977 the number of births has increased and the continuous decline in UK population which took place through 1974 to 1978 has been reversed. When Mrs Thatcher spoke, however, the number of births was extremely low, and still is, historically. Britain's population in mid 1979 was less than in mid 1973; and had fallen successively for four years from 1974.

England and Wales	Number of live births	Birth-rate	Number of deaths	Death-rate
1976	584 300	11.9	598 500	12.2
1977	569 300	11.6	575 900	11.7
1978	596 400	12.1	585 900	11.9
1979	638 000	13.0	593 000	12.1

Source: *Population Trends,* 1981, No. 24.

UK population	
Mid 1974	55 922 000
Mid 1975	55 901 500
Mid 1976	55 886 000
Mid 1977	55 852 000
Mid 1978	55 835 000
Mid 1979	55 883 000

Source: *Population Trends*, 1981, No. 24.

The increase in births by five per cent in 1978 and seven per cent in 1979 does not alter the picture in its essentials.

1. Fertility (number of live births to women of child-bearing age) has increased less than births. Births have gone up partly because of the increase in the number of women aged 15–44.
2. The 1978–1979 increase in births and fertility seemed to have halted by mid 1980.
3. Even after the increases the general fertility rate is still 'some 10 per cent below that necessary for the long-term replacement of the population'.[41]
4. The prospect of births reaching the high levels of the early and mid 1960s seems unlikely.
5. After 200 years of industrialization population size seems to have stabilized with low birth and death rates and little, if any, population growth.

What though of overcrowding in the cities? In the mid 1960s the fears were of urban congestion, of a totally urbanized South East and the prospect of having to build a town the size of Bristol every year to keep pace with the population growth. Within a decade the definition of the urban problem had changed. By the mid 1970s the population had begun to go into decline, with more deaths than births recorded in the first quarter of 1975. Regional population projections published in 1975[42] indicated a continuing North-South drift, but, more importantly, they predicted the greatest expansion would take place in the least industrial regions—East Anglia having the greatest expected growth over the period 1973–1991. Decentralization of population from the major conurbations was now evident. On the 1973-based projections the population of Greater London, which had been nearly 9 million in 1939 and was currently 7.35 million, would fall to under 6 million in the 1990s.[43]

Falling numbers have been greatest in the inner areas of conurbations: between 1961 and 1975 inner Manchester lost 20 per cent of its population and inner Liverpool 40 per cent.[44] Movement of the population out of inner areas has been occurring throughout the postwar years as the growth of local authority and low-cost private housing estates on the outskirts of cities provided increased housing opportunities for many working-class families. More recent decline in the manufacturing base of inner cities, with the closure of firms and failure to invest, has produced prospects of social and economic decline. The skilled and young leave, unemployment increases for those remaining—male unemployment reached 30 per cent in the central core of Liverpool in 1976[45]—the environment becomes increasingly blighted and derelict, and social capital, such as houses, schools, roads, etc., lie waste. Official recognition of 'the urban problem' can be seen in a variety of policy initiatives starting in the 1960s[46] but most emphatically in the White Paper of June 1977, Policy for the Inner Cities. Because of the initial problems of purchasing housing in the suburbs and of obtaining residence qualifications for local authority housing (amplified by the practices of sellers, estate agents, building societies, housing visitors and housing managers), NCWP groups have been forced to find accommodation in the very inner areas which the white working class were vacating—a process similar to the ghetto cycle in the US. This has meant the use of social assets which otherwise would have been increasingly wasted, and some commentators, e.g. Peter Hall,[47] have seen NCWP communities as the best hope for inner-urban regeneration.

MYTH 6: 'IT'S AS WELL THE 1962 ACT . . . RESTRICTED NCWP IMMIGRATION, THEY'RE ALL WANTING TO COME IN'

The 1962 Commonwealth Immigrants Act, since its acceptance by the incoming Labour government of 1964, has been officially interpreted as an unfortunate but necessary remedy for a desperate situation. It can, however, be seen as a self-fulfilling prophecy: based on the assumption that controls were necessary, the debates which preceded and accompanied its progress through Parliament stimulated the very immigration that was feared. The increased immigration in the 18 months prior to the Act coming into effect on 1 July 1962 then appeared to justify the controls.

Although it was 1961 before a Bill to restrict entry appeared in the Queen's Speech, there had been earlier demands for restrictions. After the Notting Hill disturbances in 1958 the Conservative Party Conference passed by a large majority a motion calling for controls. Again, from the beginning of the 1960s various organizations, especially those situated in the Midlands, began to pressure MPs for restrictions.[48] Lack of consensus within and between the major parties produced a longer period of kite-flying and debate than was to be the case with the Commonwealth Immigrants Act of 1968. As late as 1958 we can find Conservative and Labour front-bench spokesmen arguing for freedom of movement between Britain and the Commonwealth on the basis of earlier obligations and perceptions of what 'Empire' and 'Commonwealth' meant. Thus, A. Lennox Boyd, Conservative Minister at the Colonial Coffice, said:

> to me it would be a tragedy to bring to an end the traditional right of unrestricted entry into the Mother Country of Her Majesty's subjects and quite unthinkable to do so on grounds of colour.[49]

A view echoed by Arthur Bottomley, Labour front-bench spokesman in the House of Commons,

we ... are clear in our attitudes towards restricted immigration ... we are categorically against it[50]

Rising levels of net migration from the New Commonwealth in the period from 1960 to mid 1962 illustrate the extent of the movement.

Estimated net inward movement. West Indians, Indians and Pakistanis 1955–63.

							Jan– June	July– Dec	
1955	1956	1957	1958	1959	1960	1961	1962	1962	1963
35 200	37 450	34 800	25 900	20 200	58 050	115 150	75 930	6154	41 762

Source: S. Patterson (1969) *Immigration and Race Relations in Britain 1960–1967.*
Oxford: Oxford University Press.

Advantage had to be taken of unrestricted entry before controls were introduced. This and the consequent difficulties of re-entry meant potential immigrants were forced to become actual immigrants, temporary settlement became transformed into permanent settlement, and a sex imbalance with its associated problems was created in the communites expanding most rapidly. As Moore comments: 'whereas before some men in West Pakistan had migrated on a rotating basis within a family they now decided to settle and bring their families to Britain. Others who may have hoped one day to migrate, migrated to "beat-the-ban".'[51]

'Beat-the-ban' immigration was to increase the size of the NCWP population considerably—three times more migrants from Pakistan entered the country in the 18 months before the Act than in the previous five years.

Net arrivals from India, Pakistan, and West Indies 1955–62.

	India	Pakistan	Jamaica	Rest of Caribbean
1955–1960	33 070	17 120	96 180	65 270
1961–30th June 1962	42 000	50 170	62 450	35 640

Source: E. J. B. Rose et al (1969) *op. cit.*

Patterson says that not much is known about the arrivals in this 18 month period but refers to one piece of research in Huddersfield which indicated that 52 per cent of the male Pakistani population resident there in 1964 had arrived between January 1961 and June 1962.[52] Although Sikhs brought their wives to England in this period, male numerical superiority was reinforced in Pakistani communities, e.g. in Bradford the 1961 census revealed 3376 men to only 81 women,[53] meaning that future immigration would consist largely of dependants.

The other factor which contributed to the high level of NCWP immigration in 1960–1961 was the fall in unemployment.

	Total West Indian, Indian and Pakistani net inflow	*Mid-year total unemployment in UK*
1957	34 800	276 000
1958	25 900	406 000
1959	20 200	420 000
1960	58 050	326 000
1961	115 150	287 000
Jan–June 1962	75 930	406 000
July–Dec 1962	6 154	406 000

Although the historically low levels of unemployment for the 1950s and 1960s provide one context in which postwar NCWP immigration has to be seen, Peach has argued that West Indian immigration in particular was sensitive to the availablity of jobs in the UK.[54] In *West Indian Migration to Britain,* he illustrates the close connection between West Indian immigration and the number of vacancies until 1961 when 'political forces overtook those of economics in the commanding position,' and in a more recent article 'British unemployment cycles and West Indian immigration 1955–74' he extends the analysis beyond the 1962 Act commenting:

for the 20 yr. period 1955 to 1974 there is a substantial and significant inverse correlation between unemployment and net West Indian immigration . . . in other words as unemployment goes up so West Indian immigration tends to go down.[55]

Peach argues that without the 'beat-the-ban' phenomenon expected, net numbers of West Indian immigrants would have been 24 476 in 1960 instead of 49 670 and 26 816 in 1960 instead of 66 290.

Thus in both short and long terms some of the effects of the legislation were the opposite of what was intended: the level of immigration was increased and it changed from temporary to permanent settlements. Moreover, as Peach shows, the immigration that was sensitive to economic conditions would have diminished through the 1960s as unemployment increased.

Acknowledging that anti-immigration legislation did not have the same effect on Asian as on West Indian migration to the UK, Robinson has nonetheless demonstrated a similar, if less pronounced association between the former and the level of unemployment in selected industries (reflecting Asians' higher degree of industrial concentration). He comments 'the data suggest that there is a significant inverse correlation between Indian and Pakistani migration to, and unemployment within, the UK' (however) 'this correlation is neither as substantial nor as statistically significant as that for West Indian migration.'[56]

Obviously economic motivation is just one cause of migration. Other causes—more important for migrants other than West Indians—have little to do with levels of unemployment, although this may affect eventual destination.

Irish emigration provides an extreme case of population movement as a result of an inability to achieve subsistence, such that by the 1880s two-thirds of persons born in Ireland were living outside the country.[57] Jewish immigration was the result of persecution; Poles were displaced by war and the fear of return to a society dominated by Stalin's Russia; Asians were forced to leave East Africa in the 60s and early 70s by the Kenyatta and Amin regimes. The 'non-economic' migration has taken place under highly specified circumstances giving the lie to the belief that there are 'hordes out there' waiting to come in.

Immigration from the Indian sub-continent can also be partly explained by reference to the specific factors of war and consequent disruption of lives. Rose comments,

> 'One of the most striking features of migrations from both India and Pakistan is the limited extent of the areas from which they originate. When one considers the size of the two countries it is surprising that emigration has been confined to the Punjab and Gujarat and to half a dozen areas in the two wings of Pakistan.[58]

Writing in the early 1960s, Desai found that four-fifths of Indians here were Sikhs, yet Sikhs comprised only two per cent of the Indian population as a whole.[59] This extreme over-representation stemmed from the War of Partition of 1947 when some 4 million Sikhs fled from the richer western part of the Punjab (now in the new state of Pakistan) to the poorer eastern Punjab on the Indian side of the frontier. It is no coincidence that it is from the regions that have been disputed or fought over—Punjab, Mirpur, Kashmir, Bangladesh—that most immigrants have come.

MYTH 7: 'MILLIONS OF DEPENDANTS'

The 'beat-the-ban' phenomenon resulted in a net inflow especially of male Asians who would have to settle rather than rotate between, say, Pakistan and the UK, thereby creating a pool of dependants whose entry into the UK was to be on the basis of husband's/fathers' prior settlement. In 1961, for example, the sex ratio in England was 937 men per 1000 women; in the Pakistani population in Britain it was 5380 men per 1000 women.[60]

The bulk of NCWP immigration since 1962 consisted of dependants. The 1962 Act introduced a system of vouchers: 'A' and 'B' vouchers for Commonwealth citizens with a job to come to in Britain or a specific skill or qualification that was in short supply; 'C' vouchers for others on a 'first-come first-served' basis, priority being given to people who had served in the armed forces.

In August 1964 'C' vouchers were withdrawn—it could be argued that they had been merely a sop to Commonwealth governments to defuse criticism of the 1962 Act—although this was not declared policy until the White Paper, *Immigration from the Commonwealth*, appeared in 1965. The White Paper also set a maximum of 8500 vouchers to be issued in any one year. By 1968 the number of voucher-holders entering the country from the New Commonwealth was below 5000 and falling. Deakin argued that the system was

> being increasingly used to recruit highly qualified personnel from the Common-wealth to Britain. This policy was made explicit by the Minister of Labour in 1968 . . . B vouchers issued to doctors increased from 42 per cent of the total in January–May 1968 to 71 per cent in the period June–December 1968.[61]

	Total Commonwealth Immigrants	
	voucher-holders	*dependants*
1963	30 130	26 230
1964	14 705	37 460
1965	12 880	41 210
1966	5 460	42 030
1967	4 980	52 816
1968	4 691	48 650*

* inc. 4771 UK passport-holders from East Africa not included in previous figures.

Source: N. Deakin (1970) *op. cit.*

The Immigration Act 1971 came into force on 1 January 1973 and replaced the 1962 Act and the system of vouchers with rights based on patriality (close connection with the UK). Non-patrials (those who are neither UK citizens, not settled here, nor spouse or grandchild of a patrial, i.e. in practice most black Commonwealth citizens) coming for employment must have a work permit (except for a few occupations including medicine). Admissions of work-permit holders initially for twelve months from the NCWP dropped dramatically—1100 in 1973 to 2100 in 1975, to 700 in 1977, compared to 5100 work-permits going to foreign nationals in 1977.[62]

As for estimates of dependants waiting to come in, Eversley and Sukedeo produced a figure of 250 000.[63] This excluded voucher-holders (East African Asians) and so would be an underestimate on that ground although a minor one as voucher-holders have been a small minority of immigrants. They argued that the largest number of families of dependants would be from Pakistan, reflecting the later immigration from there and the imbalance in sex ratios, the majority of families from the Caribbean being nearly complete—from 1970 migration from the West Indies reversed and then stabilized. More recently, in February 1977, Alex Lyons, formerly Minister of State at the Home Office, estimated the number of dependants from India, Pakistan and Bangladesh still entitled to entry to be less than 80 000.

MYTH 8: 'SWAMPED BY HIGH BIRTH RATES'

We have seen that NCWP immigration is much less than commonly imagined and that the flow of migration overall is the opposite of what is usually believed. What though of NCWP births?

It is true that over the last few years the NCWP population in this country has grown more through natural increase, i.e. the excess of births over deaths, than through continued immigration, and that in some parts of the country, especially in some London boroughs, the percentage of births occurring to mothers born in the NCWP is very high. Baldly stated, however, these 'facts' can be misleading:

1. Extreme cases, e.g. Brent and Ealing are taken as typical.
2. Changes occurring in the oldest NCWP communities which point the way for others, e.g. the fall in West Indian births in the 1970s, are neglected.

3. Where age structures of two populations are different, birth rates cannot be compared: the crude birth rate, i.e. the number of live births per 1000 population, will appear artificially high in a population containing few older people such as the NCWP population (for 1976 it was estimated that only 12.7 per cent were aged 45 and over compared with 37 per cent for Britain as a whole, and only 1.8 per cent of the population of NCWP ethnic origin in Great Britain were aged over 65.[64]

The great importance of natural increase for growth reflects controls on NCWP migration, the ways in which these have produced a pattern of permanent settlement, the delays in re-uniting families and the fact that immigrants are overwhelmingly concentrated in the child-bearing age groups. The following is an estimate of increase in the population of NCWP ethnic origin in the UK mid-year to mid-year.

	Natural Increase Thousands			
	births	deaths	total	net migration
1969–70	+ 52	− 4	+ 48	+ 43
1971–72	+ 49	− 4	+ 45	+ 37
1973–74	+ 44	− 5	+ 39	+ 29
1975–76	+ 45	− 5	+ 40	+ 40
1977–78	+ 50	− 6	+ 44	+ 30

Source: CSO (1980) *Social Trends*, 1980.

Although people of NCWP ethnic origin constituted 3.7 per cent of the British population in mid 1979, they provided a higher percentage of births. The following information gives the percentage of live births (in England and Wales) to mothers whose country of origin are as follows:

	1969	1974	1979
UK	86.9	88.2	86.9
Irish Republic	3.1	2.3	1.5
NCWP	5.9	6.2	8.2

Source: OPCS Monitor FM1 81/1

However, what has happened is that while NCWP births have remained stable overall, the birth rate of England and Wales fell to its all-time low in 1977.

	Live births		
	1970	1978	1979
Total England and Wales	784 000	596 000	638 000
To mothers born in W. Indies	14 100	7 100	7 300
To Mothers born in India, Pakistan and Bangladesh	21 300	25 400	27 800
Total NCWP	46 000	48 000	52 200

Source: OPCS Monitor FM1 81/1.

The fall in the number of births to women born in the West Indies doubtless reflects their earlier settlement. The slight rise in the number of births to women born in India, Pakistan and Bangladesh reflects the increase in the number of young Asian women here. According to the Immigrant Statistics Unit:

the number of women of child-bearing age who were born in the Indian sub-continent rose between 1971 and 1976, probably by about 12 per cent.[65]

The above refers to births to immigrants; birthplace does not equate with 'ethnic origin'. Referring to the following breakdown of births in England and Wales by birthplace of father and mother:

	Birthplace of		
	Mother	*Father*	*1974*
(1)	NCWP	NCWP	43 100
(2)	NCWP	UK	5 900
(3)	UK	NCWP	8 900
(4)	NCWP	not known	2 200

Source: OPCS Monitor FM1 81/1.

the OPCS comments: 'not all children born to parents one of whom is NCWP born and the other UK born are children of mixed ethnic origin—categories (2) and (3) . . . in the first half of the 1970s it was estimated that in about half these cases, the NCWP-born parent and hence the children were of indigenous British origin. But, because of the increasing number of people of NCWP ethnic origin born in this country who are now reaching child-bearing age, it seems likely that an increasing proportion of children in categories (2) and (3) are of NCWP ethnic origin.'[66]

As to the distribution of births to mothers born in the NCWP, by 1977 in several London boroughs the percentage was high:

Three Highest	*To mothers born in the NCWP 1978*	
	no. of births	*% of births*
Brent	1647	45
Ealing	1676	40
Newham	1294	38

Source: OPCS Monitor FM1 80/2.

However, it must be remembered that:
1. The GLC average is much lower—22 per cent—some boroughs having few NCWP births.

Three Lowest	*To mothers born in the NCWP 1978*	
	no. of births	*% of births*
Havering	103	4
Bromley	142	4
Sutton	91	5

Source: OPCS Monitor FM1 80/2.

2. London itself is not typical, the population of NCWP ethnic origin being over-represented there: while 22 per cent of births in London in 1978 were to mothers born in the NCWP, this figure of 18 828 births was two-fifths of the total NCWP births for England and Wales (47 964).
3. Despite the over-representation of NCWP populations in conurbations, figures from some of these indicate further how uncharacteristic London is.

Merseyside, South Yorkshire, Tyne and Wear Conurbations
 (a) Total population   4 014 700   (mid 1978)
 (b) Total births   45 268   (1977)
 (c) Total births to mothers
      born in the NCWP   938   (1977)
      (c) as % of (b)   2.07%   (1977)

4. Percentages for many London boroughs can be misleading; what they frequently indicate is the process of decentralization whereby the young white middle- and skilled working-class have been moving out, thereby inflating NCWP birth figures as percentages.

5. As seen above (Myth 5), the 1977 birth rate for England was the lowest recorded and that for 1978 only very slightly higher.

What changes are likely to occur in the future? It is only to be expected that immigrants' traditional patterns of fertility will continue for a while after settlement here. Larger families in Third-World countries are a reaction to, and defence against, social conditions: in rural societies children increase family income, and where welfare provision is minimal or non-existent a large family is necessary to maintain patients in old age and sickness. How long fertility patterns characteristic of the Third World will continue in the West is debatable; it is just over half a century since England ceased to be a society characterized by high fertility rates and there is some evidence that as Third-World states industrialize and become more prosperous fertility delines. What is surprising is just how quickly the habits attitudes and expectations of the host society are picked up.

The OPCS Immigrant Statistics Unit suggests 'that total period of fertility of women born in the West Indies fell substantially between 1971 and 1976 . . . the main factor . . . (being) . . . a decrease in family size. It is estimated that by 1976 the total period fertility rate of West Indian-born women was between 2.1 and 2.2' compared to UK total period fertility of 2.3 in 1971.[67]

Fertility is as yet much higher among Asians than West Indians, reflecting the formers' later arrival, smaller proportion of working wives, greater emphasis on traditional family roles and greater isolation from host attitudes by language and religion.

High birth rates reflect the distorted age-structure of NCWP communities; high fertility reflects adjustment to the experience of migration.

The re-uniting of husband and wife could well be a factor tending to inflate period fertility rates through some 'making up' of postponed births.[68]

We can conclude with Lynne Illiffe,

It seems clear that . . . immigrant groups are gradually adopting norms which favour the voluntary control of fertility. And there is every reason to believe that the decline will continue in response to the demands of a new socio-economic environment.[69]

MYTH 9: 'CONTROLS ARE FAIR—THEY APPLY EQUALLY TO ALL'

The fact that immigration laws represent an attempt to control primarily the *black* population can be seen in several ways,

—in the context of their introduction,
—in the popular fixation upon blacks as the immigrants,
—in the response to black UK passport-holders (hereafter UKPHs) in East Africa,
—in the rationalization of the 1971 Act and subsequent attempts to produce two-tier nationality laws,
—in the procedures involved in the processing of the applications of would-be immigrants and dependants, and the way in which immigration officials use their discretionary powers.

Although 'moral panics' in the past have centred around many different immigrant groups,[70] recent concern has only been focused on immigrants with dark skins. White Australians, Americans and Germans are never defined as a problem. Controls have been developed specifically to keep blacks out. This can be seen most blatantly in the 1968 Commonwealth Immigrants Act.

Britain had encouraged migration from India to Kenya, when the latter was a colony, in order to develop commerce and act indirectly as a buffer between white administrators and native Kenyans. The Kenya Independence Act of 1963 gave Kenyan citizens (by which was understood whites) the chance of retaining UK citizenship as a means of avoiding the restrictions of the 1962 Commonwealth Immigrants Act. The post-independence government did not accept dual nationality and there followed a two-year period in which choice of final citizenship could be made. At its expiry some 100 000 Kenyan Asians retained UK citizenship. When in 1967 Africanization led to Kenyan Asians increasingly taking up their rights of entry into Britain, a campaign of scare-mongering and exaggeration was orchestrated by Sandys and Powell.[71] With indecent haste the 1968 Commonwealth Immigrants Act was rushed through Parliament to Royal Assent in three days.

The 1968 Act took away the right of free entry into the UK of Asians living in Kenya and holding British passports; only UKPHs with a 'close connection' with the UK (by birth, naturalization, parent/grandparent born in the UK) would be admitted. UKPHs without a close connection were now to be treated as though they did not have passports and were subject to the restrictions of the 1962 Act. Vouchers to admit the head of the household and dependants (assumed to be four per household) were introduced at the rate of 1500 available per annum rising to 3000 in 1971 when there was an additional 'one-off' issue of another 1500.[72] Moore and Wallace[73] give graphic illustrations of the hardship caused to the 200 000 Kenyan and Ugandan refugees by the ways in which their cases were processed.

The temporary measures of 1968 were given a rationalization in the 1971 Immigration Act which replaced the 1962 and 1968 Acts. Coming into effect on 1 January 1973, it provides the current legal framework for immigration control; under the Act, Immigration Rules govern its actual operation (changes in these took place in 1974, 1977 and 1980). To avoid the unpleasantness of acknowledging the institutionalization of racial discrimination, although this has been accepted since, for example, by Merlyn Rees,[74] the Act introduced the concepts of patriality and non-patriality. Patrials have the 'right of abode' in the UK. A patrial is a UK or Commonwealth citizen who:

1. was born in the UK;
2. has a parent born in the UK (someone with a grandparent born in the UK, not a patrial under the Act, became treated as such in the Immigration Rules following a *Daily Express* campaign);
3. has been settled in the UK and lived in the UK for five years;
4. is the spouse of a patrial.

Non-patrials can be admitted:

1. as EEC nationals, for whom there is freedom of movement, (before Ireland joined the EEC a common travel area existed with the UK);
2. on the following grounds for acceptance for settlement on arrival:
   —as NCWP wives and children of someone settled here;
   —as the husband/fiancé of a woman settled in the UK if the wife/fiancée was herself born in the UK or has a parent born in the UK;
   —as parents and grandparents aged over 65 (except for widowed mothers where there is no age limit), wholly or mainly dependent on the child/grandchild who must be willing to support them;
   —as non-patrial UKPHs subject to quota vouchers (in 1978 it was estimated there were 33 100 Asian UKPHs and dependants in East Africa).

Other immigrants are those permit-holders coming to work, a fraction of whom are from the NCWP, as well as those in the few occupations, particularly medicine, not requiring work permits. Permits can be obtained only by those with skills and professional qualifications that are in short supply in Britain. Permits are granted for one year only and permission is needed to change jobs. Each year after this the immigrant may be given further extensions providing he remains in approved employment. During this time he can be deported if the police or immigration authorities consider his presence not conducive to the 'public good'. Students and visitors are the other categories; the former must show sufficient funds and acceptance for a course of study, the latter must have funds for support and return; usually a six-month limit is imposed on visitors.

What has this got to do with discrimination?

1. The 1968 Act devalued a commitment and was specifically directed against East African Asians.
2. 'Patrial' in the vast majority of cases means a white person, and 'non-patrial', a black person.
3. Between 1962 and 1973 'Commonwealth' became an even more meaningless term:

   —some Commonwealth citizens had more rights than others (patrials *v* non-patrials);
   —a patrial could enter the country without difficulty whereas a UKPH non-patrial (if unable to get a voucher) could not;
   —non-patrial Commonwealth citizens were reduced to the level of aliens;

— the moral panics created by the immigration debate resulted in worse treatment for blacks at airports;

— legally the intending NCWP immigrant was reduced to a level lower than that of some aliens, i.e. EEC nationals who had the right to enter and work after 1973.[75]

4. Rules governing fiancés have recently been changed; the 1979 White Paper, *Proposals for a Revision of the Immigration Rules*, would have restricted fiancés and husbands entering or remaining to those whose fiancée or wife was a citizen of and born in the UK. In the rules published in February 1980 this was extended to women born of British parents working abroad, one of whose parents was born in the UK.

5. Entry certificates required by dependants are difficult to obtain, causing long periods of disruption to family life. In Pakistan in August 1977 the waiting period for a *first* interview was $14\frac{1}{2}$ months according to C. Demuth. Interviews can be unrealistic and humiliating[76] and there is a high rate of refusals.

6. People settled after 1973 must show they can support wives and children without recourse to public funds if dependants are to be allowed to join them.

How does the current Nationality Bill fit into this? The British Nationality Bill, published in January 1981 and preceded by the Labour Government's Green Paper, The British Nationality Law of 1977 and the Conservative White Paper of 1980, has been presented as a neutral measure, restricting immigration perhaps but mainly concerned with tidying up administrative confusion. The Bill proposes three classes of British citizenship: British Citizenship, Citizenship of the British Dependant Territories and British Overseas Citizenship. The latter two would go to the remaining colonies and to UKPHs respectively; only British Citizenship would give the right of entry to, and abode in, the UK. British Citizenship would be acquired by people born in the UK to a British citizen, or a person lawfully settled in the UK. Thus NCWP citizens would have no rights of entry. However, as we have seen, these rights (for non-dependants) hardly exist. Effects on immigration will be negligible.

However, two important possible consequences among the many, (e.g. the making stateless of 210 000 present citizens of the UK and Colonies) stand out. First, there is the principle laid down that UK citizenship would not automatically be obtained by birth and residence here; if neither parent was born here or was lawfully settled, then British citizenship would not be obtained. To mollify opposition, the Home Office amended this so that any child born in the UK not acquiring British citizenship at birth would have the right to become a British citizen after 10 years' continuous residence (i.e. if she/he does not leave the country for more than 90 days at any one time). However, the principle stands and it is very close to that propagated by Powell since 1968 that:

> The West Indian or Asian does not, by being born in England, become an Englishman. In law he becomes a UK citizen by birth; in fact he is a West Indian or an Asian still.[77]

This view of cultural separateness across generations can only be maintained by an implicit theory of the biological determination of culture—racism.

The second point is that two classes of citizenship are taking legal form; the Bill is 'making the huge but logical leap from immigration control to the control of immigrants once here . . . it is about reproducing in this country the status of a black colonied people.'[78] The creation of different statuses for legal and welfare rights will require increased policing and increased surveillance, a far greater role for the state, with repercussions for all.

MYTH 10 'NO RIGHT TO BE HERE'

The right of people from the NCWP to come to the UK is both a moral and a legal one.

As legal rights have been eroded by restrictive legislation, the rights once guaranteed by law become part of the moral rights of those promised, but denied, entry. Thus in the period up to the 1962 Commonwealth Immigrants Act there was freedom of entry for Commonwealth citizens wishing to come to the UK—a freedom enshrined in the British Nationality Act of 1948. During the debate in Parliament on this Bill the (Conservative) Shadow Home Secretary, Sir Maxwell Fyfe, later to become Lord Kilmuir said:

> We must maintain our great metropolitan tradition of hospitality to everyone, from every part of the Empire.[79]

This 'great metropolitan tradition' referred to by Lord Colyton in the House of Lords:

> We still take pride in the fact that a man can say *Civis Britannicus Sum* whatever his colour may be and we take pride in the fact that he wants and can come to the Mother Country.[80]

was ended by the 1962 Commonwealth Immigrants Act.

The 1962 Act replaced the imperial dream of an area of unrestricted travel with a sop to some anti-immigration organizations and a policy of selecting those immigrants with particular skills useful for Britain, which increasingly through the 1960s was to mean Asian doctors. This, of course, represents a subsidy by the poor nations to the rich (a sort of Third-World aid programme in reverse): the costs of rearing, educating and training workers is borne by those least able to do so, with the results of that expenditure benefiting others.[81] The 'C' vouchers for unskilled workers, introduced by the 1962 Act (and given on a first-come first-served basis), were little more than a sop to the NCWP to soften the operation of the Act and were withdrawn in 1964.

What are the moral arguments?

Firstly, there is the liberal belief in freedom of movement. This has existed as a central tenet of Western values, and much ideological mileage has been gained from contrasting it with East European systems. In fact the belief in Britain's traditional role as a haven for refugees is an idealized version of a frequently tawdry reality, to which the anti-semitic and anti-foreign hysteria surrounding the 1905 Aliens Act and the 1914 and 1919 Aliens Restriction Acts bears witness.

Secondly, rights have existed in the past, these being seen at the time as binding and permanent.

Thirdly, the *Civis Britannicus Sum* attitude was reinforced in the countries of the Empire, especially in the West Indies: children were taught to look to Britain as the Mother Country.

Fourthly, the right to come to Britain was not only legally promised and preached, it was also bought by the inhabitants of the colonies with the labour of their people. For two centuries and more, super-profits were extracted from the Caribbean and the Indian sub-continent. The Empire provided profits that fuelled the British Industrial Revolution, provided a buffer against world recessions and contributed to social stability ideologically and politically.

The price paid by the subject peoples was not just economic: with the destruction of the Indian economy by the early 19th century under the impact of cheap imports, the traditional Indian social structure disintegrated. In the West Indies there were the slave trade and the slave plantations.

Even in the 20th century, the costs of imperial control could be identified. The historian A. J. P. Taylor refers to the British decision to withdraw shipping from the Indian Ocean in 1943:

> . . . to sustain the Mediterranean campaign. This decision had disastrous consequences. The harvest had failed in Bengal. Imports of food were urgently needed and did not come. A million and a half Indians died of starvation for the sake of a white man's quarrel in North Africa.[82]

(In this context we might note that the total British losses in the 1939–1945 war were under 400 000.)

To the moral, legal and historical dimensions of the relationship between Britain and Commonwealth populations two further points are worth adding. One is that the initial impetus for postwar NCWP immigration did not come from the 'sending' societies. During the Second World War 7000 West Indians enlisted in the RAF were stationed in Britain.[83] After the war the greater poverty they experienced when they returned to the West Indies stimulated the first noticeable migration—the arrival of the Empire Windrush from Jamaica in mid 1948, with 400 plus migrants. Later on British employers, e.g. London Transport and the British Hotels and Restaurants Association, recruited directly in the Caribbean, in order to overcome the shortages of labour (at least for unpleasant and low paid work) in the UK.

Although direct recruitment does not seem numerically important overall—12 per cent of West Indian men taking a job definitely arranged[84]—it was significant in the early days of migration for creating a West Indian community from whom information could flow back about job vacancies.

The second point is that it is the labour performed, the taxes and insurance contributions paid and the profits created by the NCWP that give them a claim to be part of the country, and give the right of entry to these workers' dependants. In the words of an Asian commentator in a Punjabi weekly:

> It is time we asserted that our right to be in Britain is the wealth we have produced and continue to produce for this country.[85]

Because of their demographic characteristics—fewer elderly, more men than women—and economic motivation, NCWP immigrants have exhibited both higher economic activity rates (i.e. a greater percentage of the NCWP are in the labour force than is the case with the total population) and a lower use of publicly subsidized welfare services. K. Jones[86] in 1967 argued that people of NCWP ethnic origin are likely to receive only 80 per cent of what the total population receives in 'social benefit' in the form of health, education, housing, social security and local authority social services.[87]

The claim that NCWP immigrants are a drain on resources and the cause of problems in housing, health services, etc., is not just incorrect, but a vicious smear. To take but one example, the roots of the housing crisis lie elsewhere: in a system of house-building and investment for profit; in access to two-thirds of the housing stock determined by income and wealth rather than need; in the cuts in public expenditure which have meant massive reductions in council housing programmes; in higher rents at the same time that there is an open-ended subsidy to home-buyers through tax relief on mortgage interest repayments; in a sales policy which will decrease the chance, for families trapped in tower blocks, of movement to a house; in the social values that say increasingly that local authority accommodation is to be second-rate housing for the poor. None of these have anything to do with the presence of a black population in the country. At most, the presence of a black population can be used to draw attention to already existing deficiencies and problems. As the Milner Holland Report on Housing in Greater London (1965) put it:

> The plight of the immigrant is the outcome, and too often an extreme example, of London's housing difficulties; it is not their cause.

If the beliefs listed above are incorrect why are they so powerful as myths? Can it be that their significance stems only from their propagation by right-wing ideologists? While the definition, by politicians, parties and media, of problems and of the terms within which they are perceived is important, an interpretation of the world in which immigrants and blacks feature as folk-devils is not just imposed by 'society', the ruling class, etc., but has to be seen also as deriving from a set of social conditions because it is one way of making sense of the world. Even if objectively incorrect, it can explain for some their perceived experience. In other words, interests—albeit misunderstood— are involved. As Sivanandan puts it,

> the profit from immigrant labour had not benefited the whole of society but only certain sections of it . . . whereas the infrastructural 'cost' of immigrant labour had been borne by those in greatest need. That is not to say that immigrants (*qua* immigrants) had caused social problems . . . but that the *forced* concentration of immigrants in the deprived and decaying areas of the big cities highlighted (and reinforced) existing social deprivation; racism defined them as its cause. To put it crudely, the economic profit from immigration had gone to capital, the social cost had gone to labour, but the resulting conflict between the two had been mediated by a common 'ideology' of racism.[88]

Although the sources of beliefs are interconnected, it is crucial to see racism and ethnocentrism not just as false ideas, mental aberrations, but as rooted, in part at least, in material circumstances. Criticism which misses this concentrates on symptoms rather than causes and so misses the point. As a Victorian immigrant and political refugee remarked in another context: 'the call to abandon their illusions about their condition is a call to abandon a condition which requires illusions.'[89]

NOTES AND REFERENCES

1. Birmingham speech 20 April 1968 in Smithies, B. and Fiddick, P. (1969) *Enoch Powell on Immigration*. London: Sphere Books.

2. C. f. Powell's 'like the Roman, I seem to see "the River Tiber foaming with much blood" ', *ibid*. For a general account of political hostility c.f. Foot, P. (1965) *Immigration and Race in British Politics*. London: Penguin.

3. C.f. Runnymede Trust/Radical Statistics Race Group (1980) *Britain's Black Population*. London: Heinemann.

4. *Ibid*. and c.f. also Demuth, C. (1978) *Immigration: A Brief Guide to the Numbers Game*. London: Runnymede Trust.

5. Moore, R. and Wallace, T. (1975) *Slamming the Door: The Administration of Immigration Control*. Oxford: Martin Robertson.

6. C.f. Peach, C. (1968) *West Indian Migration to Britain:* Oxford: Oxford University Press. Peach, C. (1978/1979) British unemployment cycles and West Indian immigration 1955–1974. *New Community*, **7** (1). Robinson, V. (1980) Correlates of Asian immigration: 1959–1974. *New Community*, **8** (1 & 2).

7. Castles, S. and Kosack, G. (1973) *Immigrant Workers and Class Structure in Western Europe*. Oxford: Oxford University Press.

8. Rose, E. J. B. et al (1969) *Colour and Citizenship: A Report on British Race Relations*. Oxford: Oxford University Press.

9. Moore, R. (1975) *Racism and Black Resistance in Britain*. London: Pluto Press.

10. C.f. Hattersley's aphorism: 'without integration, limitation is inexcusable; without limitation, integration is impossible' quoted in E. J. B. Rose et al (1969) *op. cit.*

11. Primary immigration . . . 'the admission and settlement of heads of households on their own account—as opposed to the gaining of the right to settle permanently by people (mainly wives and children) . . . by virtue of their relationship with someone already settled here' . . . 'primary immigration . . . (NCWP) averaged less than 3.4 thousand a year from 1973–1977'. *CSO Social Trends 1979* (1979). London HMSO.

12. On employment opportunities, see for example, the PEP/PSI research in the following. Daniel, W. W. (1968) *Racial Discrimination in England*. London: Penguin. Smith, D. J. (1977) *Racial Disadvantage in Britain*. London: Penguin. Smith, D. J. (1981) *Unemployment and Racial Minorities*. London: Policy Studies Institute.

13. C.f. Archbishop Coggan 'there must be a clearly defined limit to the numbers of those allowed into this country. There are signs that our present legislation needs looking into on

this point', *Birmingham Post*, 12 July 1976, quoted in Rex, J. and Tomlinson, S. (1979) *Colonial Immigrants in a British City*. London: Routledge and Kegan Paul.

14. C.f. Downing. J. (1975) The (balanced) white view. In Husband, C. (Ed.) *White Media and Black Britain*. London: Arrow Books.

15. C.f. Manchester Law Centre (1981) *The Thin End of the White Wedge*. On problems of access to health services, e.g. refusal of treatment without production of passport, c.f. Brent Community Health Council (1981) *Black People and the Health Service*. On changes in social security c.f. the White Paper, Reform of the Supplementary Benefits Scheme (1979), HMSO Cmnd 7773, para. 21: 'Where someone is admitted for settlement on the declaration of a relative already living here that he will maintain him or her, the relative will be statutorily liable for maintenance'; and its implementation in the Social Security Act 1980, paras. 17 and 25.

16. Dummett, M. (1978) *Immigration: Where the Debate Goes Wrong*. London: Action Group on Immigration and Nationality (AGIN).

17. Moore, R. (1975) *op. cit.*

18. *Ibid.*

19. A recent academic example of the equation of 'numbers' and 'problem' occurs in M. Pratt's *Mugging as a Social Problem*. (1980, Routledge and Kegan Paul). Referring in the text to 'genuine concern about immigration and its future development', he comments in a footnote: 'It must be said that this concern is not wholly without foundation. In the 1977 publication of Social Trends it was estimated by the Central Statistical Office that the coloured population is likely to rise to about 2 600 000 by the mid 1980s. Although the "official" interpretation of this figure was that fears of cities being "overrun" by coloured immigrants by the end of the century "may be exaggerated", the total is, in itself, a substantial one'.

20. Ryan, W. (1973) *Blaming the Victim,* London: Orbach and Chambers.

21. Downing, J. (1975) *op. cit.*

22. Foot, P. (1965) *op. cit.* The Conservative sticker 'Vote Labour for a nigger neighbour' should also be mentioned here.

23. OPCS *Population Trends*, 1981, No. 24.

24. CSO (1974) *Social Trends 1974*. London: HMSO.

25. Eversley, D. and Sukdeo, F. (1969) *The Dependants of the Coloured Population of England and Wales*. Oxford: Oxford University Press.

26. OPCS Migration Analysis Unit 'International Migration: Recent Trends' *Population Trends,* 1979, No. 18.

27. OPCS *Monitor PP1 81/1* (1981).

28. OPCS Immigrant Statistics Unit 'Population of New Commonwealth and Pakistani Ethnic Origin: New Projections', *Population Trends*, 1979, No. 16.

29. OPCS *Monitor PP1 79/9* (1979).

30. OPCS Immigrant Statistics Unit *Population Trends,* 1979, No. 16 *op. cit.*

31. CSO (1974) *op. cit.*

32. OPCS *Monitor PP2 79/1* (1979)—40 per cent of NCWP population born here, rising to nearly 60 per cent by the end of the century.

33. Halsey, A. H. (Ed.) (1972) *Trends in British Society Since 1900.* London: Macmillan.

34. *Ibid.*

35. *Ibid.*

36. C.f. Foot, P. (1965) *op. cit.*

37. CSO (1980) *Annual Abstract of Statistics 1980.* London: HMSO.

38. OPCS *Population Trends 1981,* No. 24.

39. C.f., for example, on implications of low population growth, Central Policy Review Staff (1977) *Population & the Social Services.* London: HMSO.

40. CSO (1980) *op. cit.*

41. Britton, H. (1980) Recent trends in births. *Population Trends 1980*, No. 20.

42. OPCS (1975) *Regional Population Projections: mid 1973-based.* London: HMSO.

43. Most recent estimates—mid 1979-based population projections (OPCS *Monitor PP3 81/1,* 1981) based on lower levels of net migration out of London—give a higher projected figure, but one which still indicates a fall over the period, the greatest fall being in Inner London:

| | Population—thousands | | |
	1979 (base)	1991	% change
England	46 396	47 485	+ 2.3
Greater London	6 877	6 539	− 4.9
Inner London	2 672	2 488	− 6.9

44. Hall, P (1977) The inner cities dilemma. *New Society,* 3 February.

45. Nabarro, R. and Watts, C. (1977) Looking for work in Liverpool. *New Society,* 20 January. This was at a time when national unemployment was under half the current (1981) level.

46. C.f. Lawless, P. (1979) *Urban Deprivation and Government Initiative.* London: Faber. Community Development Project (1977) *Gilding the Ghetto.* London: CDP.

47. Hall, P. (1977) *op. cit.* Referring to the Asian community of Small Heath identified in the Birmingham Inner Area Study (Llewelyn-Davies et al, 1977 *Unequal City: Final Report of the Birmingham Inner Area Study.* London: HMSO), he comments: 'they are steadily moving into the area, buying up the oldest and often the most dilapidated housing. Unlike the native-born English, they regard Small Heath not as an area running down, but as a place of opportunity. On present trends, by the year 2000 they would make up one-third of the population of Small Heath—and in the process a large part of the area would be upgraded.'

48. C.f. accounts in Foot, P. (1965) and Rose, E. J. B. et al (1969) *op. cit.*

49. *Manchester Guardian* 10 October 1958, quoted in Foot, P. (1969) *The Rise of Enoch Powell.* London: Penguin.

50. 5 December 1958, quoted in Foot, P. (1965) *op. cit.*

51. Moore, R. (1975) *op. cit.*

52. Patterson, S. (1969) *op. cit.*

53. Rose, E. J. B. et al (1969) *op. cit.*

54. Peach, C. (1968) and (1978/79) *op. cit.*

55. *Ibid.*

56. Robinson, V. (1980) *op. cit.*

57. Jackson, J. A. (1963) *The Irish in Britain.* Routledge and Kegan Paul.

58. Rose, E. J. B. et al (1969) *op. cit.*

59. Desai, R. (1963) *Indian Immigrants in Britain.* Oxford: Oxford University Press.

60. Rose, E. J. B. et al (1969), *op. cit.*

61. Deakin, N. (1970) *Colour, Citizenship and British Society.* London: Panther.

62. CSO (1979) *op. cit.*

63. Eversley, D. and Sukdeo, F. (1969) *op. cit.*

64. CSO (1979) *op. cit.*

65. OPCS Immigrant Statisitcs Unit (1978) Marriage and birth patterns among the New Commonwealth and Pakistani population. *Population Trends 1978,* No. 11.

66. OPCS *Monitor FM1 81/1* (1981).

67. OPCS Immigrant Statistics Unit (1978) *op. cit.*

68. *Ibid.*

69. Illiffe, L. (1978) Immigrant birth rates. *New Society,* 6 April.

70. C.f. Foot, P. (1965) *op. cit.*

71. C.f. Foot, P. (1969) *op. cit.*: Powell's 'quarter of a million' contrasts with the Kenyan Statistical Digest's 1967 estimate of Asian population as 192 000 of whom approximately 70 000 had chosen Kenyan citizenship and others had become citizens of India and Pakistan. S. Wallis (1976) The Asians' arrival, *New Society,* 27 May gives the *total* number of Asians in East and Central Africa (Kenya, Tanzania, Uganda, Malawi and Zambia) who chose British citizenship after independence in the early 1960s as 205 000.

72. Wallis, S. (1976) *op. cit.*: quota vouchers, introduced in 1969, totalled 1500 p.a.; 1971 increased to 3000; 1974, 3500; 1975, 5000.

73. Moore, R. and Wallace, T. (1975) *op. cit.*

74. Quoted in The *Guardian*, 8 February 1978.

75. On racial discrimination and the EEC, c.f. Immigration Rules ' "EEC national" means a national of one of the other member countries . . . except that a passenger who is,
a) a national of the Netherlands solely by birth in or other connection with Surinam or Antilles or,
b) a national of France solely by birth in or other connection with one of the French overseas dependent territories, is not on that account to be regarded as an EEC national.' Quoted in Moore, R. and Wallace, T. (1975) *op. cit.*

76. C.f. for example Moore, R. and Wallace, T. (1975) *op. cit.* and Counter Information Services (1976) *Racism: Who Profits?* London: CIS.

77. Eastbourne speech, 16 November 1968, in Smithies, B. and Fiddick, P. (1969) *op. cit.*

78. Manchester Law Centre (1981) *op. cit.*

79. Foot, P. (1969) *op. cit.*

80. *Ibid.*

81. C.f. Andre Gorz (1970): the import of ready-made workers amounts to a saving, for the country of immigration, of between £8000 and £16 000 per immigrant worker, if the social cost of a man of 18 is estimated for West European countries at between five and ten years' work'. Immigrant labour. *New Left Review,* 1970, No. 61.

82. Taylor, A. J. P. (1965) *English History 1914–1945.* Oxford: Oxford University Press.

83. Rose, E. J. B. (1969) *op. cit.*

84. Smith, D. J. (1977) *op. cit.*

85. Quoted in Counter Information Services (1976) *op. cit.*

86. Jones, K. (1967) Immigrants and the Social Services. *National Institute Economic Review,* No. 41.

87. The demographic characteristics of the black population result in much less expenditure on welfare on them:

% of population aged 65 and over (1976)

UK	of NCWP ethnic origin
14.3	1.8

The black population therefore, is under-represented in the use of services that cost most.
a) Income benefits for the elderly, 1978–1979: retirement pensions £7509 million; supplementary pensions £662 million; out of a total Social Security expenditure of £15 441 million.
b) expenditure per head on health and personal social services in 1978–1979: average = £180; for people aged 65–74 £300; for those aged 75 years and over £805. (Expenditure White Paper, 1981).

88. Sivanandan A. (1976) Race, class and the state: the black experience in Britain. *Race and Class,* Vol **XVII**, 4.

89. Marx, K., Contribution to the critique of Hegel's philosophy of right. In Bottomore, T. B. (Ed.) (1963) *Karl Marx: Early Writings.* London: Watts.

4

Racism, Ways of Thinking and School

M. SYER

Education is always a moral issue. It involves values, standards and judgements. In addition, it is always intellectual, because disciplined thinking is crucial. And it is always political, since the values and ways of thinking that are used favour some sections of the population, but not all. No issues can be 'merely educational' if they affect the distribution of life chances to school-leavers.[1]

The same can be said of 'race'. Race is a moral, intellectual and political issue. It is misleading, even dangerous, to suppose that it is any less than all three.

In this chapter, I take it as given that racism is morally evil. I concentrate on the intellectual problems of understanding how and why racial distinctions are made in education—often unintentionally—and what some of the implications of this are. I argue that the actual terms used are often less important than the fact that some kinds of distinction are made at all. The ways of thinking that underlie the use of racial categories are what I shall call deterministic and atomistic. I shall explain these two terms more fully later. Briefly, though, deterministic thinking involves assuming that certain things happen inevitably. It is deterministic, for instance, to see poor academic performance as an unavoidable consequence of personality, or of poverty, or of inferior genes. Atomistic thinking is often associated with this. It involves assuming that things can be explained in fairly narrow terms. The need to understand the complex relationships that make up society as a whole is ignored. Performance at school, for instance, might be explained simply in terms of a child's individual ability. It will tend not to be explained in terms of the society-wide relationships that affect how that child was treated as an infant, what kinds of experiences it had at school, what prospects actually or apparently face it after school, and how all these vary non-randomly through the population at large. These wider relationships are the wood, as it were, where atomistic thinking sees only the trees. I shall argue that these ways of thinking are inadequate, misleading and even dangerous. Among other things, they appear to make racist explanations plausible. I shall also argue that both ways of thinking are fostered, at least in part, by the way our education system works. I do not, however, wish to convey a message of pessimism, or an excuse for escapism. What is indicated is the essentially political nature of education, and of the fight against racism.

CONSCIOUS AND UNCONSCIOUS RACISM IN SCHOOLS

Racism is the belief that racial categories provide valid explanations and necessary predictions of social differences. It is supposed that people's life-styles, their attainment at school, and their position in society are all a result of racial origin. This is obnoxious because it is degrading. It is also fundamentally untrue.[2] And it is crucially political. Racism is not just bad, or false—though it is both of these. Its effects are politically momentous. This has implications for what must be done to combat it.

In our society, the intellectual aspect of education is the most obvious. Consequently, the IQ debate has been recurrent for many years. In a backlash from liberal educational policies in America, the noted psychologist Arthur Jensen revived racist aspects of this debate in 1969. He purported to show that compensatory education programmes had failed with black children because their intellectual potential was genetically inferior. He followed this with a book, *Educability and Group Difference*.[3] In Britain, the success of Eysenck's *Race, Intelligence and Education* showed that the time here was also right[4] for such views to be accepted as scientifically respectable. In the US, Jensen's monograph was immediately quoted in litigation that challenged school desegregation. In Britain, the National Front's Martin Webster acknowledged that

> The most important factor in the build-up of self-confidence amongst 'racists', and the collapse of morale amongst multi-racists, was the publication in 1969 by Professor Arthur Jensen in the Harvard Educational Review.[5]

The intellectual and scientific debate can be followed in the pages of *New Humanist* (1973–1974), *Philosophy* (1974), *New Community* (1973) and elsewhere. Competent refutations have been made by Davey, Simon and the Roses.[6] It needs to be stressed, though, that however competently refuted, the very existence of this debate tends to make it seem sensible to take racism seriously. The 'numbers game' over immigration—wherein opposing sides challenge each other's statistics—makes it much more plausible that the sheer number of black people constitutes a problem. Similarly, scientific and intellectual squabbles about the genetic (and racial) component of intelligence allow it to pass unnoticed that a particular definition of intelligence and the significance of racial or genetic differences, both come to be taken for granted.[7] Racists, in short, have dictated the terms of the debate.[8] It matters little if they are challenged here, or obliged to concede points there, if the fight is always couched in terms that allow their basic assumptions to be unquestioned.

This is considerably aggravated in schools, for there are many practices which, though not explicitly motivated by racism, are racialist in their effects.[9] Groups which *others* define in racial terms may be treated differently by *non*-racists. Some teachers in British schools are, of course, racists. But there are many more who would not recognize, and might well deny, that they, too, are unwitting racists. And there are many more again who would actually see themselves as anti-racist, yet who are party to practices which are effectively racialist. The aim of this chapter is to show how this can be, so that action can be taken to counter it.

Unconscious racism often arises where religious or sub-cultural sensitivities are overruled (or simply unrecognized) on such matters as dress, school meals or religious observance. Teachers may claim that shalwars are unsafe in PE. Or they may see dispensations for black schoolchildren over school uniform as unfair on whites. Three incidents from 1971 illustrate this. In Blackburn, a headteacher had to be ordered by the local education committee to allow daughters of Pakistani parents to wear trousers to school. Warwickshire County Council, on the other hand, ruled that Sikh children could not wear 'national dress' instead of school uniform. In Harmondsworth, a headteacher reprimanded some girls for their Afro hairstyles—an incident that led to protests from what the *Daily Express* called 'black power militants', and to counter accusations by Birmingham NUT about interference by a 'racially motivated minority' in the 'school's attempts to educate and discipline children on an equal basis.'[10] It is tempting to dismiss the last comment as an excuse for what was really racism. But in fact there *are* real difficulties for teachers, given firstly the nature of our education system (including a need to maintain particular kinds of discipline and to justify actions in terms of 'fairness') and secondly the existence of racial categories, in terms of which any such behaviour is likely to be interpreted.

Schools face many dilemmas which originate elsewhere. Because of the patterns of migration and of internal colonialism, black people tend to be concentrated in under-privileged areas.[11] Various kinds of low real income[12] may be associated with such areas, including less favourable access to adequate leisure, shopping, welfare and employment opportunities. They commonly include inadequately resourced schools—whether that be a matter of the age of buildings, the supply of teaching materials, the experience of staff, or the accepted expectations of how pupils will fare later in life.

For similar reasons, black teachers are grossly under-represented on school staffs. (In the mid 1970s about 0.15 per cent of teachers, compared with 1.5 per cent of pupils, in England and Wales, were of West Indian origin.)[13] Even when qualified black teachers were allowed relatively easy entry to the UK, many found it impossible to find teaching posts. The Centre for Information on Language Teaching estimated in 1971 that there were between two and three thousand qualified Asian teachers in the UK, but only a few actually teaching. The reasons for this given to the Select Committee on Race Relations and Immigration are revealing. We should not, however, simply dismiss them as a cover for racism. The Select Committee reported that a large proportion of those who had managed to find employment as teachers 'had proved satisfactory, but others had not, because of inadequate command of English and inability to adapt to British teaching objectives and disciplinary methods.'[14] In 1971, the Coventry branch of the NAS asked the national conference to pass a resolution condemning the employment of teachers with substandard English.[15] A Kenyan Asian, Mrs Shamshad Khan, was refused a post in Walsall because of her accent.[16] Even though, in this case, the Race

Relations Board ruled that unlawful discrimination had occurred, such cases are not all a matter of irrational prejudice. The discriminators will undoubtedly deny racist motives. They will appeal to reasons which are not only widely accepted, but which are fairly realistic, given current definitions of education. Those definitions cannot be blamed on the schools, teachers and politicians immediately concerned. But these people's actions are inevitably interpreted in terms of racial categories, given the prior existence of these categories. And they may well perpetuate a vicious circle.

In the hope of breaking into the vicious circle, the Plowden Committee recommended a policy of positive discrimination.[17] Above-average provision should be made in areas of above-average disadvantage. (One of the criteria of disadvantage, it was recommended, might be the proportion of children unable to speak English.) The Educational Priority Area policy has been criticized on a number of lines.[18] The level of extra provision was actually quite low (0.2 per cent of the total educational budget in 1973). And it is questionable how distinct and identifiable underprivileged areas are.[19] I wish to emphasize two points, however. First, wherever local strategies are aimed at solving national (and possibly international) problems, there is a tendency to overlook the real reasons for inequality and disadvantage. Second, the very identification of 'problems' can set up new and dangerous pressures. This is not to dismiss positive discrimination out of hand. But a failure to recognize real difficulties can make them that much more insidious.

Consider the case of special language provision for immigrant children, for instance, or that of dispersal ('busing') to achieve a social and ethnic mix. Both policies can be defended, in educational terms, given current definitions of schools' objectives. Whether or not it is intended, however, both have the effect of singling out one section of the population—one which is also identifiable in terms of dominant racial categories—as different. They are marked as having problems which are of their own making, and as creating problems for others. The following passage has similar implications.[20]

> The three main problems which face those who are concerned with the education of 'immigrant' children are . . .
>   (1) language education;
>   (2) problems of assessing present and potential ability levels;
>   (3) problems of social and cultural deprivation.
> The greatest advances have probably been made in the field of language education. This is undoubtedly the first necessity since without adequate language the child cannot learn in the schools, realize his potential, or interact meaningfully with those from the host community.[21]

There is no racist intent in this passage. Yet the effect of such thinking is twofold. It brands some children (almost invariably black) as *having* problems—problems which would have been avoided had they not had the impertinence to come here in the first place. And it brands them as *being* problems—for clearly special policies must be devised for them. One of the main problems is taken to hinge on the 'inadequacy' of their language. It is *their* deficiencies which are blamed, not the emphasis placed on language—*one* language, namely English—in *our* education system.[22]

The dangers of specialized provision are only more obvious than other dangers inherent in the British education system. They are not different in kind. Tapper reported a decade and a half ago on the preponderance of black pupils in the lower streams of London secondary schools.[23] In the 1960s a mass of evidence was collected by Alan Little and his colleagues[24] to suggest that black children did persistently less well at school—even those who were born and bred in this country.[25] The Committee of Inquiry into the Education of Children from Ethnic Minority Groups has found little change.[26] All this leads to differential treatment. And it results from it. A black youth interviewed by *Race Today* blamed teachers:

> The ones who have only been in this country for three or four years are in the low streams and everyone treats them as dunces. The teachers treat them as dunces. When we are doing maths, they are doing PE. When we are doing English, they are doing PE. When we are doing French, they are doing PE. And even some of our own black ones who were doing well in school would mock them because they didn't know better. And it was all through the teachers. They spoke in a different way to those kids—different to how they talked to ones in the higher streams. And nearly all the blacks were in the lower streams. (*Race Today,* April, 1975)

This youth's teachers may, of course, have been racists. But not necessarily, as the Committee of Enquiry has recently pointed out. Differentiation is central to the way our education system works. It has inherently dangerous tendencies. One of these is that *racial* differentiation comes to seem more reasonable, more natural and more likely.

Far too many black children are found in schools for the educationally subnormal. An internal report, initially suppressed by the ILEA, revealed that, in 1967, 28 per cent of the children in that Authority's ESN schools were of immigrant origin. Three-quarters of these were West Indian. Yet only 16.5 per cent of the ILEA's pupils were 'immigrant'.[27] The Select Committee heard that, in January 1971, two per cent of all 'immigrant' pupils in England and Wales, compared with 0.7 per cent of the overall school population, were in special schools, most of these for the educationally subnormal.[28] The reasons for these disproportions are, of course, complex. The DES attributed them to the sheer number of ESN school places in London—just as one used to get more eleven-plus passes in areas which had more grammar-school places.[29] Brent Community Relations Council and Brent Teachers' Association blamed teachers who misread behavioural differences as mental deficiency.[30] But one must examine carefully the view expressed by the head of an ESN school in Wandsworth. In her view, West Indian children are not unjustifiably placed in such schools. These are in any case good schools, offering 'almost a tutorial system'. And after 20 years of experience she believes that IQ tests have proved an accurate measure of the subsequent development of 95 per cent of her children. Similar views have been expressed by a special-school headteacher in Hackney.[31] What is important here is the faith in heavily institutionalized methods of assessment, and in the criteria by which such assessment is made. It is quite unnecessary to have racist motives, in order to operate a racialist system. And the criteria used for assigning children to ESN schools *are* racialist.[32]

A final way in which schools can covertly make racism seem reasonable is through their curricular and teaching materials. A great deal has been written about racist textbooks.[33] The main problems dealt with in such accounts are stereotyping, misinformation and ethnocentrism. As an example of the first, consider this extract from Longman's *Mining in South Africa* (1962):

> European labour is necessary for the more skilled jobs. Thousands of African labourers do the heavy industrial work.[34]

On ethnocentrism,[35] the following is relevant:

> Incidents such as the Black Hole of Calcutta and the Cawnpore massacre become the proverbial expressions of Indian mutiny and cunning . . . In contrast, few people know of the 'Black Wagons', the airless railway vans which conveyed 200 Moplah prisoners in hot weather without water, whereby 70 were asphyxiated. A distorted picture was presented not only by suppressing certain facts, but also by contrasting the best aspects of Western culture and contributions with the worst features of Eastern societies.[36]

Singhal has pointed out the emphasis that is put on suttee and caste, while no comparison is made with the burning of witches and heretics, or with slavery and serfdom, in the West. Many history and geography textbooks, especially, are full of distortion and bias. Even infant-school and remedial reading schemes may be less innocent than one might suppose, as the late Blair Peach pointed out.[37]

I wish, however, to make three points. First, an enormous problem for all teachers is that of resources. Books are a major form of resource, and as the Select Committee acknowledged (though it played it down as a problem),

> It has always been a weakness of some schools, for financial reasons, to use books which are out of date and/or badly written.[38]

The price of books has increased astronomically, while pressure to cut back on educational expenditure has grown.[39] Second, there is another major resource which is often even more limited. It is teachers' time and energy. Most teachers just do not have the time to check, revise, criticize, analyse and read around all the materials they use in school. Third, the very use of textbooks indicates an approach to education in which knowledge is bundled up, simplified and distorted for the sake of one-way transmission and one-way assessment. It would, of course, be desirable to remove all racist textbooks from schools. But this is more because of the way they are used—often as revered gospel—than because of their actual content. There are lots of bad books—not just racist ones. Like racist teachers, schools would no doubt be healthier without them. But the problem is much deeper than that. For it concerns the way in which education in general is organized, and the ways in which that organization leads us to think about knowledge and people.[40] Racialist distinctions are made plausible by the atomistic and deterministic thinking that pervades our education system.

ATOMISTIC AND DETERMINISTIC THINKING AND RACISM

Racial terminology is notoriously complex. As long ago as 1837, Cleave's *London Satirist* suggested that

> The niggers are rapidly progressing in respectability; they were first styled after their emancipation 'the black population', and then they became 'the sable peasantry' and now Lord Brougham designates them as his 'coloured fellow-subjects'.[41]

At different times, some terms are thought to be particularly offensive. Indeed, they are used or avoided for that reason. Other terms are often sought, ostensibly to avoid such offence. But they fool no one. The *London Satirist* knew Lord Brougham was talking about 'niggers'. Similarly, when politicians talked about 'aliens' and 'foreigners' before the 1905 Aliens Act, everyone knew they meant Jews.[42] And when the word 'immigrant' is used today, for most people that means 'black'. ('Immigrant' can, however, have other important connotations. It can imply 'stranger', and even 'unwanted' and 'repatriable'.[43]) The use of intentionally racist terms is not, of course, irrelevant, any more than the employment of racist teachers and racist textbooks is irrelevant. But even where these are avoided, there remain tendencies for people to think and see things in ways which are not fundamentally different.

It is my argument that racist beliefs are *one* kind of deterministic belief about people. Determinism is a belief in the inevitability of causal processes. If one thing is such-and-such, then another is supposed inevitably to follow. If the temperature rises, ice inevitably melts. If one's parents are black, the racist will assume, one's character, intelligence, food preferences and aptitudes for particular kinds of work are inevitably pre-determined.[44] There can be other kinds of deterministic belief about people. It may be assumed, for instance, that the son of a criminal is inevitably 'at risk'—just because of his parentage. It may be assumed that girls are inevitably tender and caring—just because of their sex. Or that young children are inevitably incompetent in various respects—just because of their age. Such beliefs can exist independently of racism. Yet their determinism arises in similar kinds of social and historical context. And they make racist beliefs, and the use of racial categories, more plausible and more likely to occur.

The British education system still has a tendency to promote deterministic thinking. It is therefore compatible with racism, however unconscious this may be, and however dressed up in overtly non-racist language. I say 'still', because deterministic thinking was most clearly seen in the widespread use of intelligence tests. These were based overwhelmingly on what Pidgeon has called a 'potential ability' theory of intelligence.[45] It was assumed that people's general ability, and therefore their educational potential, was more or less fixed at an early age—possibly even at conception. Educational psychologists and sociologists in the 1950s and 1960s paid a great deal of attention to selection (especially at eleven-plus) and to the effects of reforms associated with the 1944 Education Act. A number of official reports[46] decried the wastage or inefficiency, as well as the inequity, that this research revealed. Orthodox views of intelligence became less deterministic. Indeed, the Newsam Committee declared that

> Intellectual talent is not a fixed quantity with which we have to work, but a variable that can be modified by social policy and educational approaches.[47]

As the notion of fixed intelligence became less respectable, however, other deterministic beliefs took its place. There was the 'need for achievement', investigated by David McClelland.[48] If not our intelligence, then our motivation was supposed to be fixed in early childhood. Then there were 'language codes'.[49] Whether Basil Bernstein intended it or not,[50] this concept served a similar function. As Harold Rosen put it,

> It was just when (the prevailing theory of intelligence and the concept of the Intelligence Quotient) was looking sadly tattered . . . that the theories of Bernstein began to be available . . . Whereas in the fifties children had their IQs branded on their foreheads, in the sixties more and more of them had the brand changed to 'restricted' or 'elaborated'. The ideology vacuum had been filled.[51]

More recently, poor performance at school has commonly been blamed on 'cultural deprivation'—the supposed deficiencies of a 'bad home'.[52] Ethnic as well as class cultures are condemned as inadequate. (As we have seen, 'inadequate language' can mean a language other than English.) The myth of cultural deprivation, as Keddie has called it,[53] depends upon deterministic thinking. It depends upon an assumption that a child's intellectual potential and basic orientations to the world are more or less fixed at an early age, and will determine subsequent performance at school. It depends also on certain assumptions about the nature of knowledge, and about who 'naturally' has the right and responsibility to decide what is valid and valuable, and to decide how it should be arranged into subjects, taught and examined in schools.[54] Deterministic thinking is firmly established in British educational institutions. It is therefore hardly surprising that even those who reject racism can be a party to racialist practices.

The dominant way of thinking is also atomistic.[55] That is, there is a tendency to see the trees, but not the wood. There is a tendency to understand the growth of each tree, or each type of tree, in terms of its own characteristics, but not in terms of the terrain, or the climate, or the relative position of other trees in the wood. Not the wider education system, nor indeed the society in which that education system is situated, but the characteristics of each individual child are seen as the real causes of his or her educational success or failure. Sometimes the focus is widened a little, to take in the family, or the neighbourhood, or the ethnic group. But atomistic thinking is still narrow. For it takes the broader structures of society and of formal education as steadfastly given. They are assumed to be either neutral or even vainly progressive forces, working against unfavourable odds set by 'the home'.

It is quite understandable that people come to think in this way. What conscientious teacher would welcome the suggestion that his/her own practices may contribute to the failures and difficulties that he/she is trying so hard to eradicate? Or, if they can think less atomistically and see those practices in terms of the education system as a whole—beyond the culpability of individual teachers, just as they are beyond the fault of individual pupils—the conclusion might be that schools in general are responsible for educational failure. That is hardly more likely to boost teachers' confidence or pride in their work. When the famous Jencks *Report on Inequality* came out in America[56] suggesting the almost complete powerlessness of schools to contribute to egalitarian policies, gloom was indeed a typical reaction. Many, however, prefer to remain determinedly optimistic. (As Eric Midwinter has put it, they are like the rebellious Britons who, buried by Roman legionaries up to the necks in sand, accompanied the incoming tide with a determinedly optimistic chorus of 'Oh, we do like to be beside the seaside'!) Many more, of course, are just not confronted with such research evidence. And they have little reason to belittle their own efforts by analysing educational failure in non-atomistic terms.

Just as a climate of deterministic thinking is one in which covert and overt racism can flourish, so also with atomistic thinking. In both cases an intellectual effort is involved in trying to think, and to see things, in ways that counter dominant tendencies in our society and in our schools. The task is to look for, and to seek to understand, broad social and historical structures. These are the wood in which the trees grow. For the anti-racist, the search must be for those structures which promote deterministic and atomistic thinking. For it is on these that racism is dependent. The American sociologist, Howard Becker, once wrote:

> If we locate the responsibility for everything that happens in the individuals we work with, by making everything that happens a function of *their* attributes— *their* abilities or interests or motives—we hide our own contributions to the shaping of what we do. That contribution usually results from well-established patterns of institutional organization, in which people acquire vested interests.[57]

Anti-atomistic and anti-deterministic thinking involves a conscious examination of those well-established patterns, and of vested interests which may well include our own. A good example of this is found in William Labov's research on non-standard English, in America.[58] He suggests that when black children score badly on tests of intelligence and linguistic ability, this is not because of any inadequacy in their language. Being governed by the same deeper rules of language, their non-standard English can handle abstract ideas just as well as standard English. The differences arise, not atomistically from the linguistic capacities of individual children, but from the social contexts in which the tests are administered. Employing black investigators instead of whites can significantly improve scores.[59] Appearing non-hostile in other respects—appearing not to represent 'white' or politically and economically dominant institutions—can have further startling effects on language use. The message for anti-racists here, is not that one should try to *appear* to represent friendly instead of hostile forces; such a merely moral stance would be unrealistic and unconvincing, while deeper pressures towards racism persisted. Like it or not, teachers represent such forces, at least as much as they represent more benign ones. The intellectual task for anti-racists is to understand those pressures, which often have contradictory tendencies, in non-atomistic and non-deterministic terms.

In this and the previous section, I have stressed that to dismiss racism as mere prejudice is not enough. Indeed, it is actually dangerous to sit back smugly and claim that racism is something of which only other people are guilty. We are all involved in racism, because the very institutions of which we are parts tend to promote those ways of thinking that make racism plausible. The intellectual fight against racism entails a conscious effort to question determinism and to understand deeper social, economic and political structures. Yet still such intellectual understanding is not enough. It is itself made more difficult by those structures that promote atomism and determinism. Through understanding these, one's aims must be to transform them, by exploiting whatever *anti*-deterministic and *anti*-atomistic tendencies also exist. Opposition to racism must be more than intellectual, just as it must be more than moral. It must be political, like education itself. Before I elaborate on this, however, I shall look in the next section at some of the consequences of racial categorization in schools.

SELF-FULFILLING PROPHECIES AND SELF-CONCEPTS

The notion of 'self-fulfilling prophecies' was made famous by the American sociologist, Robert Merton.[60] Something one expects to happen may happen only *because* it is expected to do so. Merton gave the example of a bank which was rumoured to be on the verge of bankruptcy. That this rumour (i.e. prophecy) was initially unfounded made no difference. Depositors rushed to the bank to withdraw their savings in case a collapse occurred. And the prophecy was fulfilled.

Merton also suggested that the generally poor school performance of American blacks might result (at least in part) from an assumption (i.e. a prophecy) that they were unlikely to do well. Because of that assumption, he suggested, fewer resources were allocated to schools that catered for black children. Those children would in turn have an inferior education. And the prophecy might thereby be fulfilled. Evidence does indeed suggest that the level of resources available in schools is related to levels of achievement.[61] But the evidence does not all point so clearly in that direction,[62] and we should be surprised if it did. For it is unlikely that a simple and mechanical relationship inevitably exists between financial input and academic output. We should temper such deterministic expectations by noting that people's perceptions and understandings play a crucial part in the process.

Educational researchers have mostly used the self-fulfilling prophecy idea in connection with classroom interaction and the internal organization of schools. The most famous study is undoubtedly *Pygmalion in the Classroom,* by Robert Rosenthal and Lenore Jacobson.[63] As a psychologist, Rosenthal had for a long time been interested in experimental design. He was fascinated by the way experimenters themselves could unwittingly affect the results of their experiments. In one experiment, for instance, he asked two groups of research students to test some rats for their ability to solve mazes. One group was told that its rats had been specially bred for their superior ability in this respect. The other was told that its rats had been bred for their inferiority. There was in reality no difference between the two groups of rats. Yet the students' observations significantly distinguished between them. The students observing 'bright' rats may have been more on the look-out for 'bright' behaviour, or they may somehow even have communicated their expectations to the rats and thereby encouraged them. Either way, the results appeared to 'prove' that one group of rats was brighter than the other, while there had actually been no grounds for prophesying that this should be so.

Rosenthal and Jacobson saw the possible implications of this for education. After all, teachers continually form judgements about their pupils' behaviour, and they are likely to have expectations about how they will subsequently behave. The two researchers devised an ingenious experiment, which they conducted in a down-town American elementary school. All children in the first five grades were given what was in fact an intelligence test (Flanagan's Test of General Ability). But the teachers at the school were told that it was the 'Harvard Test of Inflected Acquisition', specially designed to identify those children who were likely to show marked academic improvement in the near future. After the tests had been completed, the teachers were told that about 20 per cent had shown very high 'spurt' potential. Each class teacher was given the names of the 'spurters' in his/her class. These names had actually been chosen at random, and bore no relationship to the test scores. The researchers returned to the school three times over the next two years, to retest the children. After eight months, 47 per cent of the 'spurters', compared with only 19 per cent of the rest of the children, had gained no less than 20 IQ points, as measured by the tests. The suggestion was, of course, that the teachers had shown a greater interest in these children, interpreting their behaviour in terms of the 'spurt' prophecies, and behaved in such a way that these expectations were covertly communicated to the children themselves. Those children, it was said, had then fulfilled the prophecies.

Unfortunately, this ingenious experiment had serious flaws. The most damning criticism is that the Test of General Ability was quite inadequate. (It had to be relatively unknown, of course, so that the teachers would not recognize it.) Thorndike[64] even calculated from Rosenthal and Jacobson's figures that the children in one of the school classes must have had an average IQ of 30, according to the tests. Since the national average should have been 100, and since it is unlikely that so many children were technically imbeciles, this does not say much for the validity of the Pygmalion findings.

Nonetheless, as Thorndike himself admitted, the theory was, and still is, generally plausible. I have recalled the experiment because it has been immensely influential. There is now an enormous literature on the subject.[65] Many other researchers have now examined aspects of the self-fulfilling teacher-expectancy effect. Many, but by no means all, have produced results that are compatible with Rosenthal's theory. Some, for instance, Rist,[66] have observed classrooms in action, to see what processes might be involved. They have wanted to know how teachers may unwittingly communicate their expectations of how their pupils will do. In the school which Rist observed, such prophecies were apparently formed very early in the children's school life, often on the basis of stereotypes.

The teacher expectancy effect is not, of course, only relevant to children from 'racial' minorities. But where racial categories exist, and especially where these are associated with assumptions about the innate potential, or the 'parental encouragement', or the cultural background of minority group children, many teachers may unwittingly have low expectations of these children's potential. It is reasonable to suggest that those expectations can be transmitted, subtly and not so subtly to the pupils themselves.

We should not expect such prophecies to be fulfilled automatically. That would be to assume an inevitable causal chain, looking something like that illustrated in Figure 1. Each of the links is plausible, all are relevant, but none is inevitable. First, teachers may disguise their expectations. (The suggestion is, however, that this is harder to achieve than one might suppose. It might, moreover, be seen as professionally incompetent to behave 'inappropriately', by giving children what one judges to be the wrong standard of work, for instance.) Pupils, in their turn, may 'misread' the signals, or at least interpret them in a way that rejects their teachers' judgements. Moreover, both teachers and pupils are unlikely to respond passively to external signals. People do not just receive messages. Developing an understanding of things is a creative process. It

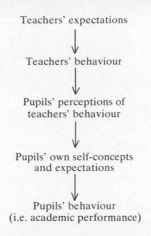

Teachers' expectations

↓

Teachers' behaviour

↓

Pupils' perceptions of
teachers' behaviour

↓

Pupils' own self-concepts
and expectations

↓

Pupils' behaviour
(i.e. academic performance)   **Figure 1**

can often happen in original and quite unpredictable ways. To expect the teacher expectancy effect to be inevitable would, in short, be deterministic.

Second, other factors also enter at various points. Each link in the chain is only one of a number of possible determinants of the next. Pupils' self-concepts are not just affected by their perceptions of teachers' behaviour, for instance. Their parents, their school friends (and enemies) and others will also behave towards them in ways likely to affect the way they come to see themselves. And their experience of the wider society— through the mass media, for instance—may be of even greater importance. Racial categories here become important. Teachers' expectations may initially have been derived from a number of sources, including racial stereotypes in popular usage and the patterns of differentiation that generate these. Pupils' own self-expectations are likely to be influenced by similar sources, quite apart from their teachers' behaviour. The very idea of a 'self-concept' is atomistic, if it is not understood to be formed and constituted in relation to wider social structures.

In short, the teacher expectancy chain is not inevitable. Nor is it the whole story. Yet it is likely to be a powerful force, firstly to the extent that other sources of self-concept are in accord with those teacher expectations, and secondly to the extent that deterministic thinking prevails. For that makes it difficult to reject the stereotypes and expectations suggested by external sources. Teachers should resist determinism, and seek conditions in which children, too, can resist it.

The most accessible British book dealing with race and children's self-concepts is David Milner's *Children and Race*.[67] He outlines a great deal of relevant research, both British and American, and reports on some of his own. He used a technique first made famous in the US by Kenneth and Mamie Clark, over 30 years ago. They asked three- to seven-year-olds to 'Give me a doll that looks like you.' The found[68] that some 33 per cent of black children chose a white doll in response to this question, often showing signs of distress. Two-thirds of them thought the white doll was 'nicer' and had a 'nicer colour'. Fifty-nine per cent thought the black doll 'looked bad'. Many studies have confirmed and refined these results. Milner's own study was conducted in two large British cities. Forty-eight per cent of the West Indian and 24 per cent of the Asian children in his sample maintained that the white doll looked more like them than the black one. Milner summarizes as follows:

Black British schoolchildren are showing essentially the same reaction to racism as their American counterparts, namely a strong preference for the dominant white majority-group and a tendency to devalue their own group.

This study, and others like it, confirm the suggestion made by Bernard Coard that

The black child is prepared both by his general life experiences and by his classroom for a life of self-contempt. He learns to hate his colour, his race, his culture and to wish he were white. He learns to consider black things and black people as ugly and white things and people as beautiful. (*Race Today*, June, 1971)

Such negative self-concepts are obviously likely to have a detrimental effect on school performance. This is one of Coard's main arguments in his *How the West Indian Child is made Educationally Subnormal in the British School System.*[69] It reaffirms much American research[70] in a British context.

It must be repeated, though, that such effects are not inevitable. They are only made more likely, not certain, by the context of British racism and the nature of British education. To be fulfilled, negative expectations of black children's performance must key in with the children's *own* determinism and atomism. Only if they themselves accept (or are unable to question) deterministic predictions of their own failure and atomistic explanations that blame their own attributes (including those of their ethnic or 'racial' groups), will they believe themselves unable to behave differently. We have here another causal chain which, like the teacher expectancy chain, is neither self-contained nor inevitable (see Figure 2).

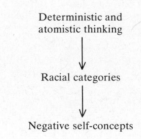

Figure 2

This is not self-contained. For racism is not caused, but only strengthened, by ways of thinking. And such ways of thinking are not historical flukes. They are generated by particular kinds of societal structure, including, not least, the education system. Nor is the process inevitable, for other kinds of self-concept are possible. Other responses to overt and covert racism can be sought. One might be a pride in blackness, or in ethnic distinctiveness. Though Davey et al seem to confirm Milner's earlier findings, London indicates a new pride of this kind.[71] Another response might be to try to create new kinds of social institutions—ones which discouraged, instead of promoted, deterministic and atomistic thinking. Anti-racist teachers should themselves be striving for this. It goes beyond a moral condemnation of racism, and beyond even an intellectual understanding of how it works.

THE BASIS OF DETERMINISTIC AND ATOMISTIC THINKING IN SCHOOL

This is not the place to document the fact or the extent of overt racism in Britain.[72] I wish here to stress three things. Firstly, racialist institutions and processes can exist without overt racism. Secondly, racism is only one kind of deterministic and atomistic thinking. It is aggravated and made harder to combat because such thinking is so deeply rooted in our society. Thirdly, our education system is itself heavily implicated in this. In theory, education, as opposed to schooling or training, should be critical and creative.[73] It should be anti-deterministic and anti-atomistic, and therefore anti-racist. But in practice education is a matter of social policy. As such, it has had two major emphases in Britain. Both have tended to bolster, rather than counter, those ways of thinking which are compatible with racism. First, mass schooling was originally a policy aimed largely at social control. Second, there has been a long-established emphasis on liberal welfare.

Let us take the emphasis on social control first. Of course, there were many, often conflicting, motives behind early educational policy. But the dominant one in the 19th century was to civilize and to discipline an otherwise unruly workforce.[74] From this aim of control, there followed—in education as elsewhere[75]—a tendency towards bureaucratization. One feature of bureaucracy is a hierarchical ranking of command. Another is an emphasis on clearly defined categories of knowledge and of people. Both aspects were clearly illustrated by the Payment by Results system in the late 19th century.

It can, of course, be argued that such origins are no longer relevant in the late 20th century. There has now been an emphasis for over two decades on efficiency and economic needs in educational policy. And there have been many strident demands for accountability and the preservation of standards in the Great Debate of the 1970s. Yet many teachers would be most reluctant to see their primary role as promoters of social control. Many, too, would set great store by their own, and their colleagues', professional judgement. They would see this as opposed to the outside interference of crudely utilitarian demands. They may be mistaken.

At least two features of professionalism are quite compatible with the social control function of schooling, even where no one advocates this as its primary purpose. The first is a tendency towards specialization. Particularly in large schools, staffs often become very specialized. Each person has his/her own area of responsibility for a given age group, or a given subject, etc. A classic study of this was carried out in an American high school by Aaron Cicourel and John Kitsuse.[76] They concentrated on the specialized vocabulary that accompanied the specialization of staff. Where there were full-time counsellors, for instance, a language developed for classifying 'conduct problems'. This justified the status and employment of specialist staff—who alone could recognize the niceties of such problems. And it categorized pupils (not least through the use of school records) in ways which deterministically predicted their subsequent behaviour. Similarly,

> A psychiatrist or social worker . . . may interpret the reported behaviour and the preliminary interview with the student as indicative of 'deep-seated problems', with the implication that he is 'sick' and in need of 'professional help'. On the other hand, a part-time teacher-counsellor may interpret the 'same facts' as a 'situation problem', or as no problem at all.[77]

Such specialization need not be far advanced. Any emphasis on the professional judgement of teachers can have similar effects. One's professional competence may be judged by one's ability to recognize and deal with particular kinds of problem in an appropriate manner. It can be in the teacher's interest, therefore, to prove that competence by refining his/her perceptions of pupil characteristics. That tendency both depends on and reinforces deterministic and atomistic thinking. A large amount of teachers' time is spent on petty administration and petty discipline, like ensuring that work is completed and that books are returned.[78] Professional competence is judged not least by the efficiency with which such day-to-day routines are handled. Professionalism is thus inseparable from some form of social control, given prevailing approaches to formal education.

The second feature of professionalism that is compatible with a social control function links closely with the first. To justify one's own professional competence, one has at least implicitly to devalue that of others. Those who are not 'properly qualified' can be a threat. Parents, for instance, tend to be welcomed (if at all) only on terms that are set by teachers' professional judgement. Sharp and Green write of the powerlessness of parents that is revealed in

> a recognition that their geographical and economic position gave the parents no choice of school; a realization that the parent had no sanctions he could bring to bear whereas the teachers had, which might result in the child being 'done down'; a lack of institutionalized authority behind the parents to give legitimacy to their complaints; a feeling of being deprived of access to information which might assist them in their case against the school; a realization that if the parents and teachers are going to get on well, then it must be on the teachers' terms.[79]

The school about which these two were writing had a widespread reputation for progressive child-centredness. Distrust of parental interference is not a feature only of 'old-fashioned' schools. It is inherent in the way formal education is organized in Britain. And the tendency is for it to exist despite overt—and sincere—expressions of a desire for parental involvement. It is revealing, perhaps, that the teachers at William Tyndale Junior School[80] rejected the interference of the school managers on the grounds that these represented only a minority of parents. Yet their own actions were justified in terms of professional judgement, not of the declared wishes of the parental majority. Teachers' professionalism has no necessary tendency to combat the social control function in schooling—on the contrary. And as the Sharp and Green study showed, the most 'progressive' resisters of utilitarian demands may covertly bolster forms of stratification and control. This is precisely because of their refusal to see that education is intrinsically political.

The second major emphasis in British educational policy has been on liberal welfare. Lately, of course, this has been more apparent than that of social control. But for similar reasons, it, too, has been quite compatible with tendencies to think deterministically and atomistically, and therefore with racism. An obvious example of liberal welfare policies in education is that of positive discrimination, which I discussed earlier. The intentions involved are generally benevolent. (It would be simplistic to dismiss them as motivated purely by a fear of civil unrest, even if they did receive a boost from Enoch Powell's 'rivers of blood' speech[81] and the spectre of urban riots comparable to those in the US.) But the benevolent deceive themselves if they see no dangers in such policies. They always run the risk of reinforcing assumptions that certain sections of the population are inherently different and inferior. They can imply that those for whom the help is intended are 'naturally' problems—to themselves and to others. To follow liberal welfare policies, one must identify problems, so that the right kind of treatment can be provided. This is so basic to the way education in Britain is organized that it seems obvious. After all, there seems no point in providing this or that kind of educational facility unless it is appropriate to the needs of the children in question. And the more clearly one can define the problems, the more effectively can one help. Unfortunately, this view of education automatically distinguishes between the helpers and the helped. Some people, as John Holt has put it, become full-time good Samaritans.[82] Others become the 'problems'—potentially in their own eyes, as well as in those of the helpers. If the helpers' efforts fail, then it is only that much more to their credit that they tried. And it is that much more to the discredit of the failures, that the opportunity was missed. 'Blaming the victim', as William Ryan has called it,[83] is not exclusively racist. But once again racism is made to seem more plausible and reasonable when liberal policies fail.

CONCLUSION: SOME POLITICAL IMPLICATIONS

We must, of course, make distinctions and use categories. Without fairly clear concepts of food, pets and furniture, for instance, we might eat the cat and put the armchair out at bedtime. But *which* distinctions we make, and how 'natural' and inevitable we take them to be, are not absolute. They vary from culture to culture, and they can be momentous in their effects. Different cultural definitions of 'family' or 'mother' crucially affect the sexual division of labour. Different definitions of 'intelligence' and 'knowledge' and 'competence' crucially affect how schools are organized, who judges the performance of whom, and how those concerned come to see their postion in society.

The distinctions we use, however, are not historical flukes. They do not just happen. Particular social and material circumstances make some kinds of distinctions—some ways of seeing the world —more pressingly likely than others. There is a history, and an ongoing social structuring, to the ways in which we classify people. John Tierney's chapter in this book looked at the broad context of racism. I have suggested that the school system itself is heavily implicated in fostering ways of thinking that make racism possible. This can be so even where those involved feel morally outraged at the consequences. Indeed, merely taking a moral stance may even exacerbate the problem. It is vital to seek an intellectual understanding of what is involved.

One must not be trapped, however, into seeing the results of social and historical circumstances as inevitable. It is possible, though difficult, to resist the inflexibilities of determinism and the myopia of atomism. No necessary causal chain exists, only a number of contradictory tendencies which on balance, at the moment, favour racism. Only through seeking to understand those tendencies can one guard against the unconscious racism that is undoubtedly widespread in British schools. It is this unconscious racism which, as Husband puts it, made it possible for ESN schools to have a disproportionate number of black pupils drafted to them. To white educationalists, it did not seem unreasonable that there should be an excessive number of black children in ESN schools, for there was a lower expectation of their intellectual ability. (This is) a view almost parodied by a headmaster who told me with a degree of pride how good relationships were in his multi-racial school, and then proceeded to comment upon how the natural athleticism of his West Indian pupils compensated for their lesser academic abilities.[84]

Nevertheless, an intellectual understanding is still not enough to defeat racism. Racism is not just irrational prejudice, as many have implied,[85] any more than it is just moral turpitude. There are strong—though not inevitable—reasons for it in our experience of how our education system works.[86] Insofar as answers can be found in that education system itself, there is one clear objective. If racism is to be eradicated, the features of school which tend to suppress critical and creative education, and to promote instead deterministic and atomistic thinking, must be challenged. That is a political objective, and one which seriously threatens many vested interests—including those of teachers. Yet, if they are to reject the roles of professional custodian or professional helper—both of which can encourage the ways of thinking I have described—teachers must realize that the fight against racism requires a democratization of education. That may be a daunting prospect. But to ignore it is to condone the tendencies that promote determinism and atomism. Once we grasp this intellectually, we must do something about it. For inaction would be escapist. It would be a political blow not against, but in support of, racism.

At the start of this chapter, I claimed that an intellectual understanding of racial distinctions in education should not lead to escapism, not to pessimism. The anti-deterministic message is an optimistic one. For it suggests that whatever the weight of dominant tendencies, these are not irresistable. There are other tendencies which we should attempt to harness. For instance, the very fact that some teachers are concerned about racism—concerned enough to read this book—is grounds for optimism. I have said that some features of professionalism tacitly condone or promote those ways of thinking which make racism plausible. But there are other features, too. A pride in one's work and a faith in the creative aspects of education are also, thankfully, common. It is not eccentric to query the features of schooling that I have criticized in this chapter. It is not misguided to seek greater, and genuine, involvement with parents and others in the community. It is not unprofessional to question the narrow and inflexible thinking that is often found in our schools. It is *more* professional to do these things. Elsewhere in this book, some things are suggested which teachers can realistically attempt to do. This chapter has attempted to show why such action is necessary in the fight against racism, why a merely moral stance is not enough, and why non-teachers—both adults and children—must also be politically involved in education.

NOTES AND REFERENCES

1. For some reasons why education is always political, see Benton, T. (1974) Education and Politics. In Holly, D. (Ed.) *Education or Domination.* London: Arrow Books.

2. Articles by scientists from various disciplines are included in Kuper, L. (1975) (Ed.) *Race, Science and Society.* New York: UNESCO.

3. Jensen, A. R. (1969) How much can we boost IQ and scholastic achievement? *Harvard Educational Review*, **39**, 1. Jensen, A. R. (1973) *Educability and Group Differences.* New York: Harper and Row.

4. Eysenck, H. J. (1971) *Race, Intelligence and Education.* London: Maurice Temple Smith. A summary of the changing acceptability of racist jokes and arguments is given by Rex, J. (1970) The concept of race in sociological theory. In Zubaida, S. (Ed.) *Race and Racialism.* London: Tavistock.

5. Walker, M. (1977) *The National Front.* London: Fontana.

6. Davey, A. G. (1973) Teachers, race and intelligence. *Race*, **3**.
   Simon, B. (1970) Intelligence, race, class and education.
   Reprinted in Simon, B. (1971) *Intelligence, Psychology and Education.* London: Lawrence and Wishart.
   Rose, H. and S. (1978) The IQ myth. *Race and Class*, **20**, 1.

7. This is argued in the American context by Marks, R. (1975) Race and immigration: the politics of intelligence testing. In Karier, C. J. (Ed.) *Shaping the American Educational State.* New York: Free Press.

8. See Parekh, B. (1978) Asians in Britain: problem or opportunity? In Commission for Racial Equality (Eds.) *Five Views of Multi-Racial Britain.* London: CRE.

9. The distinction between racism and racialism is discussed in Chapter 1. The first is a matter of beliefs. The second is one of practices.

10. *Race Today,* November, April and August, 1971.

11. See Dummett, A. (1973) *A Portrait of English Racism.* London: Penguin. Chapter 1 and pp. 132–133.

12. Pahl, R. (1971) Poverty and the urban system. In *Whose City?* London: Penguin.

13. Select Committee on Race Relations and Immigration (1977) *Report on Education*, Vol. I, para 69.

14. *Ibid.* Vol. I, para 118.

15. *Race Today,* May, 1971.

16. *Race Today,* March and June, 1971.

17. Plowden Report (1967) *Children and Their Primary Schools.* London: HMSO.

18. For a summary, see Chapters 3 and 4 of Robinson, P. (1976) *Education and Poverty,* London: Methuen.

19. See Ackland, H. (1971) What is a bad school? *New Society,* 9.9.71. Pahl, R. (1978) Will the inner city problem ever go away? *New Society,* 28.9.78.

20. Taylor, F. (1974) *Race, School and Community.* Windsor: NFER. This book summarizes and reviews a great deal of the relevant literature, and as such is very valuable, despite such passages as that quoted here.

21. *Ibid.*

22. This emphasis is nicely criticised by Rai, V. (1978) British Diary. *Times Education Supplement,* 17.11.78.

23. Tapper, O. (1963) Educating the immigrants: day school. *East London Papers* (6).

24. For a summary and commentary see the following. Little, A. (1975) Performance of children from ethnic minority backgrounds in primary schools. Reprinted in Raynor, J. and Harris, E. (1977) (Eds.) *Schooling in the City.* London: Ward Lock Educational.
    Little, A. (1978) Schools and Race. In Commission for Racial Equality (Eds.) *Five Views of Multi-Racial Britain.* London: CRE.

25. This low rate of achievement is played down, however, by Phillips, who suggests that it is a consequence of family size, etc. Phillips, C. J. (1979) Educational underachievement in different ethnic groups. *Educational Research,* **21,** 2.

26. Committee of Inquiry into the Education of Children from Ethnic Minority Groups (1981) *Interim Report,* Cmnd. 8273. London: HMSO.

27. *Race Today,* January 1971. The DES at that time used a definition of 'immigrant' which included children born in this country to parents who had themselves migrated to Britain in the previous 10 years.

28. Select Committee (1973) *op. cit.* (note 13) Vol. II, para. 32.

29. *Ibid.* Vol. II, para. 32–33.

30. *Ibid.,* Vol. I, para. 149.

31. *Race Today,* September and May, 1971.

32. For a detailed evaluation of ESN assessment and its consequences, see Coard, B. (1971) *How the West Indian Child is Made Educationally Sub-normal in the British School System.* London: New Beacon Books.

33. For instance see the following:
    Stewart, I. (1970) Readers as a source of prejudice. *Race Today,* **2,** 1.
    Glendenning, F. (1971) Racial stereotypes in history textbooks. *Race Today,* **3,** 2.
    Proctor, C. (1975) *Racist Textbooks.* London: National Union of Students.

34. Quoted by Proctor, C. (1975) *op. cit.*

35. Ethnocentrism is the tendency to see one's own people, their own culture and their way of life as superior. It may or may not be explicitly racist.

36. Singhal, D. P. (1963) Writing Asian history. *Commonwealth*, December.

37. For infant reading schemes, see Stewart, I. (1970) *op. cit.* (note 33) and Worpole, K. (1971) Ladybird life. *New Society*, 23.12.71.
    Blair Peach, who was killed following an Anti-Nazi League demonstration on 23 April, 1979, had campaigned against racism in remedial reading schemes *The Guardian*, 25.4.79.

38. Selection Committee (1973) *op. cit.* (note 13) Vol. I, para. 96.

39. Makins, V. and Rodgers, L. (1977) The emptying shelves. *Times Educational Supplement*, 18.11.77 and 25.11.77.

40. 'Textbooks assume that all students are more or less alike; that students learn in the same way; and that students are interested in the same things. For these reasons, the textbook is responsible, perhaps more than any other single factor, for the rigidity of school curricula. If we can rid ourselves of textbooks, we will open the way to some really creative changes in the curriculum.' Postman, N. and Weingartner, C. (1971) *The Soft Revolution*. New York: Delacorte Press.

41. Quoted by Shepherd, M. A. (1974) Black Slave Labour: Review of J. Walvin's 'Black and White'. *Bulletin of the Society for the Study of Labour History (29)*.

42. Foot, P. (1965) *Immigration and Race in British Politics*. London: Penguin.

43. Parekh, B. (1978) *op. cit.* (note 8). Note the similar significance of talking about the 'host' society.

44. For a slightly different argument about deterministic beliefs and racism, see Rex, J. (1970) *op. cit.* (note 4).

45. Pidgeon, D. (1970) *Expectation and Pupil Performance*. Windsor: NFER.

46. Notably The Crowther Report (1959) *Fifteen to Eighteen*. London: HMSO.

47. Newsam Report (1963) *Half Our Future*. London: HMSO.

48. McClelland, D. C. (1953) *The Achievement Motive*. New York: Appleton-Century-Crofts.

49. Bernstein's work on language and socialization is collected in Bernstein, B. (1971) *Class, Codes and Control*. Vol. I. London: RKP.

50. See his critique of the concept of compensatory education in Bernstein (1971) *op. cit.* (note 49). Another version can be found in Cosin, B. R., Esland, G. and Swift, D. E. (Eds.) *School and Society*. London: R.K.P.

51. Rosen, H. (1972) Language and class: a critical look at the theories of Basil Bernstein. In Holly, D. (1974) (Ed.) *Education or Domination?* London: Arrow Books.

52. For an overview of the cultural deprivation idea, see Freidman, N. (1967) Cultural deprivation. In Raynor, J. and Harden, J. (1973) (Eds.) *Cities, Communities and the Young*. London: R.K.P.

53. Keddie, N. (1973) *Tinker, Tailor . . . The Myth of Cultural Deprivation*. London: Penguin.

54. See Bernstein's article on the classification and framing of educational knowledge in Bernstein, B. (1975) *Class, Codes and Control*, Vol. III. London: R.K.P.

55. Bourdieu criticizes atomistic thinking and advocates a 'relational mode of thought' instead, in Bourdieu, P. (1973) Cultural reproduction and social reproduction. In Brown, R. K. (Ed.) *Knowledge, Education and Cultural Change*. London: Tavistock.

56. Jencks, C. (1972) *Inequality*. London: Penguin.

57. Becker, H. S. et al (1965) *Making the Grade*. London: Wiley.

58. Labov, W. (1969) The logic of non-standard English. In Keddie, N. (1973) (Ed.) *op. cit.* (note 53).

59. C.f. Katz, I. (1964) Review of evidence relating to effects of desegregation on the intellectual performance of Negroes. In Passow, A. H., Goldberg, M. and Tannenbaum, A. J. (Eds.) *Education of the Disadvantaged*. New York: Holt, Rinehart and Winston.

60. Merton, R. K. (1949) The self-fulfilling prophecy. In *Social Theory and Social Structure*. New York: Free Press.

61. Byrne, D., Williamson, W. and Fletcher, B. (1975) *Poverty of Education*. London: Martin Robertson.

62. Coleman, J. S., Campbell, E. Q., Hobson, C. J., McPortland, J., Mood, A. M., Weinfeld, F. D. and York, R. L. (1966) *Equality of Educational Opportunity*. Washington: US Office of Education.

63. Rosenthal, R. and Jacobson, L. (1968) *Pygmalion in the Classroom*. New York: Holt, Rinehart and Winston.

64. Thorndike, R. L. (1968) Review of Rosenthal and Jacobson's Pygmalion in the Classroom. *American Educational Research Journal* (5).

65. For a competent review, see Finn, J. D. (1972) Expectations and the educational environment. *Review of Educational Research* (42).

66. Rist, R. C. (1970) Student social class and teacher expectation: the self-fulfilling prophecy in ghetto education. *Harvard Educational Review*, **40**, 3.

67. Milner, D. (1975) *Children and Race*. London: Penguin. (2nd Edition, 1980.)

68. Clark, K. B. and Clark, M. P. (1947) Racial identification in Negro children. In Newcomb, T. M. and Hartley, E. L. (Eds.) *Readings in Social Psychology*. New York: Holt, Rinehart and Winston.

69. Coard, B. (1971) *op. cit.* (note 32).

70. C.f. Katz, I. (1964) *op. cit.* (note 59).

71. Davey, A. G., Pushkin, I., Norburn, M. V. and Mullin, P. N. (1980) Who would you most like to be? *New Society*, 25.9.80.
    London, B. and Hearn, J. (1977) The ethnic community theory of black social and political participation: additional support. *Social Science Quarterly*, **57**, 4.

72. A good overview is provided by Dummett, A. (1973) *A Portrait of English Racism*. London: Penguin. More specialized studies, for instance of 'race' in the media and of race relations in the police can be found, respectively, in Husband, C. (1975) (Ed.) *White Media, Black*

Britain. London: Arrow Books. Also in Lambert, J. R. (1970) *Crime, Police and Race Relations: A Study in Birmingham*. Oxford: OUP. A historical perspective is given in Bolt, C. (1971) *Victorian Attitudes to Race*. London: R.K.P. The connections with past colonialism and modern internal colonialism are explored by J. Tierney in Chapter 1, J. Gundara in Chapter 2 of this book.

73. See Arlblaster, A. (1974) *Academic Freedom*. London: Penguin. Chapter 1. He advocates a democratization of tertiary education to make such 'real' education possible.

74. See, for instance:
Hurt, J. (1971) *Education in Evolution*. London: Paladin.
Johnson, R. (1976) Notes on the schooling of the English working class, 1780–1850. In Dale, R., Esland, G. and McDonald, M. (Eds.) *Schooling and Capitalism*. London: R.K.P.

75. Marglin, S. A. (1976) What do bosses do? In Gorz, A. (Ed.) *The Division of Labour*. London: Harvester Press.
Gouldner, A. W. (1954) *Patterns of Industrial Bureaucracy*. New York: Free Press.

76. Cicourel, A. V. and Kitsuse, J. (1963) *The Educational Decision-Makers*. Indianapolis: Bobbs-Merrill.

77. Cicourel, A. V. and Kitsuse, J. (1968) The social organization of the high school and deviant adolescent careers. In Cosin, B. R., Esland, G. and Swift, D. E. (1971) (Eds.) *op. cit.* (note 50).

78. Hilsum, S. (1974) *The Teacher's Day*. Windsor: NFER.

79. Sharp, R. and Green, A. (1975) *Education and Social Control*. London: R.K.P.

80. Gretton, J. and Jackson, M. (1976) *William Tyndale—Collapse of a School—or a System?* London: Allen and Unwin.

81. Foot, P. (1969) *The Rise of Enoch Powell*. London: Penguin.

82. Holt, J. (1974) *Escape from Childhood*. London: Penguin.

83. Ryan, W. (1971) *Blaming the Victim*. London: Pantheon Books.

84. Husband, C. (1974) Education, Race and Society. In Holly, D. (Ed.) *op. cit.* (note 1).

85. e.g. Bibby, C. (1969) *Race, Prejudice and Education*. London: Heinemann.

86. Of course, there are also strong reasons why our education system works in this way. It has not been the purpose of this chapter to explore these.

5

Approaches to Multicultural Education

J. GUNDARA

The title of this chapter suggests that it is a relatively new field. There is, as such, no generally accepted theoretical framework for the subject matter. Terms like 'multi-cultural education', 'multiracial education' and 'multi-ethnic education' are used inter-changeably[1] by educationalists and have yet to be defined. This comparative review of the literature on the subject highlights some problem areas in the field of *multicultural* education.

DIVERSITY AND INEQUALITY IN SOCIETIES

One point on which the critics of Anglo-centric education agree is that a bias in favour of the dominant community is detrimental to minorities. Comparative educationalists interested in multicultural education have isolated five criteria of diversity in societies: language, religion, social class, territoriality and race. Hence, at the lowest possible level one can attempt to theorize about multicultural education on the basis of the above five criteria of diversity in societies without losing sight of the crucial variables of social class and race as analytical categories.[2] Given the changing attitudes about sex discrimination in the last two decades, a sixth category based on gender differences can be added to illustrate the issues and sharpen the focus on racism in individual and institutional terms.

However, within this wider framework, this chapter will emphasize diversity on the basis of race. While some educationalists maintain that the criterion of race tends to be blurred by the term multiculturalism, others hold that it is not a relevant category. This chapter assumes that race is an important variable in many societies, there being no firm evidence to the contrary. The 1976 Race Relations Act (however weak) and the Commission for Racial Equality (however ineffectual), both of which are intended to eliminate racism, are in themselves indicators of the existence of racism at both individual and institutional levels in British society.[3] Looking at the other side of the coin, the colonial and imperial past of British society, its involvement in the black slave trade and the existence of current racist immigration legislation on the statute books are also indicators of the past and present existence of race as a category which is important as an aspect of diversity in British society and societies generally.

In America, as a response to the assumptions implicit in assimilationism that some cultures were superior to others, a study of majority–minority groups relations was undertaken. Acceptance of diversity was based on three propositions:[4]

1. That since individuals have no choice as to their ancestry it was undemocratic to penalize them for an aspect of their permanent identity over which they had no control.
2. Each minority group culture has within itself valuable and positive attributes and the denial of these aspects lessens the value of the dominant culture.
3. The proposition that all men are created equal does not mean that there are no differences between people but that all merit equal respect and treatment.

These assertions were made by Kallen and other liberal philosophers early in the twentieth century after European immigrants were expected to reject totally their national backgrounds and assimilate into an Anglo-centric American society.

Pluralism

In the 1960s an American scholar, Gordon, postulated that the United States was a plural society. He stated that there exists (a) structural pluralism and (b) cultural pluralism in American society.[5] Structural pluralism can be demonstrated by the existence of diversity among minority groups which are separate on linguistic, religious and racial lines. At the minority group level, structural pluralism exists in the form of institutions which were relevant to specific communities. The existence of the media (minority group press), religious organizations (temples, synagogues) and educational institutions (Jewish schools) is an indicator of this.

At the dominant level, cultural pluralism exists and focuses on the ideologies and institutions of society with the 'structurally assimilated' schools in the public institutional framework. In the British context this is exemplified by the comprehensive state school system.

At the wider social level, cultural pluralism is complicated by:

1. Autonomy of groups which either demand a high degree of equality or already possess a high degree of equality; or
2. Segmentation and dominance.

A society which illustrates segmentation and dominance is South Africa, where the politically dominant white minority segments and autocratically governs the majority black Azanian population. In other countries like the United States and Britain, the trend is from segmentation and dominance towards a situation of group autonomy within a context of equality. In other words, distinct cultural groups within this institutional setting maintain their distinction over time. If, for instance, the minority groups are not allowed their autonomy, they could then make demands for separate institutions, be they on linguistic or religious grounds.

A major theory of cultural pluralism has been integration as racial assimilation, i.e. the socialization of black children with children from the dominant white community. If and when some elements of minority communities accept this postulation, they might do so on the grounds that if their culture resembles that of dominant group they may become more acceptable. Conversely such groups may fear that failure to accept the dominant value system would leave them open to oppression and persecution in the future. Those of the minority group who experience self-hatred might also adopt the dominant norm and reject others of their own culture. The school curriculum under these circumstances retains a traditional white Anglo-Saxon Protestant orientation. Because of this, integration as racial assimilation is merely 'token desegregation'.[6] It involves no changes in the social structure and the content of education, nor does it reflect the presence of diverse cultural groupings. A major proportion of minority communities consequently rejects this form of assimilation or integration.

British models of the 1960s and 1970s, including Roy Jenkins' ideas of cultural pluralism, were basically integrationist. Translated into educational terms the policy of 'dispersal' of immigrant students was based on assumptions of integration. In the London Borough of Ealing these policies were continued until 1973.

While the dominant group might support racial assimilation, those from racial minority communities might favour the cause of racial diversity. This perspective on the part of the latter, would allow for the affirmation of values which are other than Anglo-conformist or Anglo-centric. One justification for this perspective might be that the minority communities are often bicultural and bilingual and possess traits of the dominant group as well as a culture distinctive to themselves. A school which accepts diversity in racial terms presupposes that pupils, parents and teachers have equal status based on equal power. However, this is not always the case in schools, because in institutional and structural terms the dominant group does not allow power to slip from its hands. In the American context particularly there has been a tendency to ask for community control, while in Britain demands for separate schools based on religious (Pentecostal, Muslim, Sikh) grounds are increasing. In terms of schools there are certain factors, such as social class and diverse languages, which make the pedagogic issues complicated, particularly if the schools are controlled by local communities or religious groups, yet face national examinations to legitimize their knowledge. Furthermore, as minority groups, they do not control the economic resources or political power to become independent of the dominant group.[7]

Deprivation and Disadvantage Models

The existence of social classes raises the concept of assimilation on a class basis and the issue of those who are poor or 'disadvantaged'. In the British context this means that those from social classes 4 and 5, using the classification of the Registrar General, are considered to be 'culturally deprived' or 'culturally disadvantaged'. The conservatives in this debate tend to postulate an inferiority based on genetic factors. The liberals in the debate tend to stress that the disadvantage is really a result of the past discrimination based on sex, race, class and ethnic or territorial grounds which has resulted in the existence of a disadvantaged section of the community. A combination of these forms of discrimination may contribute to family breakdown, which may have led to the inadequate socialization of individuals, accumulated intellectual deficit and a resistance to schooling. Educational researchers and teacher-training courses have used such theories to explain poor performances in schools: such explanations form the basis of various remedial or compensatory programmes. In the United States, such thinking determined the initiation of programmes like Head Start. In other words, what children from poor classes needed was an initial dose of socialization to acquaint them with the values, behaviour and ideas of the middle-class white population.[8]

Since this model is firmly entrenched in class assimilation, it tended to ignore any racial differences which were considered irrelevant to education. In societies like the United States, Canada and Australia,[9] which are fragments of Europe, the capitalist elite uses this model to stress the possibility of mobility. In the class-based capitalist society like Britain, the poor can be blamed for remaining poor.

Psychological Deficit

However, these liberal reforms of the 1960s failed in most cases and evoked a more conservative bias or backlash in education. In the United States, Jensen[10] wrote an article from the University of California in 1969. He argued that intelligence was largely (about eighty per cent) determined by genetics and that differences in IQ represented genetic differences. In this argument he reversed the postwar psychological theory and addressed the problem of compensatory education. He asserted that since intelligence was largely determined by genetics, the efforts to raise the intelligence of people with low IQ scores by compensatory education programmes were bound to fail. Intelligence, as such, was not defined except in as much as the intelligence tests could measure this undefined phenomena.

Jensen focused on the racial differences in IQ scores and gave a genetic explanation: that blacks on average do not possess the same innate intellectual qualities as the whites. Such American research was swiftly supported by Eysenck, a member of the Institute of Psychiatry in London.[11] The arguments found favour with right-wing politicians and those who favoured cuts in educational budgets. This can be illustrated by the Black Papers episode, which brought together practising teachers like Rhodes Boyson under the same umbrella. Their conservative stance under the guise of demanding higher standards resulted in a negative appraisal of the liberal curriculum content and urged the withdrawal of financial support.

The whole position is, however, suspect, because any psychological analysis which deals with individual differences and ignores ideology as a problem does not provide a fair analysis but compounds issues of disadvantage.[12] Criticisms of Jensen and Eysenck were also made because of the data on which they based their hypothesis. It was suggested that the data of Sir Cyril Burt, on which both Jensen and Eysenck relied had actually been fabricated.[13] Sir Peter Medawar, a biologist and Nobel Prize winner has suggested that 'intelligence' cannot be summarized by a single IQ score. He stated that human capabilities and potentialities are far too diverse for this type of simplification.[14]

The important issue to remember is that Jensen's and Eysenck's work has been picked up without using the details of their arguments. Fascist groups saw these two psychologists as vindicating their racist ideologies. Eysenck's books are on the reading list of fascist groups like the National Front.

In fact, the hypothesis of IQ test scores needs to be rejected, as does the so-called rigorous testing and measurements which support this thesis. The groups who are labelled because of the genetic inferiority thesis face disaster in educational as well as social terms. As Kamin has argued, the research involving IQ testing is inherently political:

> With respect to IQ testing, psychology long ago surrendered its political virginity.
> The interpretation of IQ data has always taken place, as it must, in a social and
> political context, and the validity of the data cannot be fully assessed without
> reference to the context.[15]

Academics have to play a positive role in rejecting these theories, particularly since they revive race-science in a milieu which is susceptible to the acceptance of fascist ideology. Psychologists in these terms are neither detached nor can they claim to seek dispassionate truth because psychologists in the Eysenck/Jensen mould are involved in creating cultural racism.[16]

The Social Deficit

The social dimensions of the deficit debate have even wider implications than the individual-oriented psychological theories. It can be postulated that both the liberal and conservative positions in this issue are incorrect and that people are disadvantaged because of *present* forms of racism, *present* forms of structural inequalities and *present* barriers to choice.[17] While older forms of inequality might be removed, new forms of inequality are continually being instituted. Until institutional forms of inequality are removed, the education of those who are considered disadvantaged will not improve.

The anthropological and sociological models of 'cultural deprivation' and the 'poverty of culture' have taken as their evidence the low-level social organization of minority communities, and an intellectual and cultural resistance to the norms of the dominant group. This emphasis on client behaviour and the need for its modification for entry to middle-class culture is similarly not valid, because basic or causal issues such as elimination of poverty itself are not tackled.

The environmental deficit model stated that lower-class children failed in schools because of lack of literacy and social skills, where the family provided no intellectual or social stimulation. The theory of restricted language codes, lack of books at home, and non-intellectual life-styles had supposedly contributed to stimulus deprivation. It was alleged that in terms of performance at school this led to an inability to delay gratification and sustain attention, resulting in a lack of perceptual discrimination skills.

There is considerable research to support the thesis of the functional inferiority of black and white working-class children. Aspects of special education (including units for 'disruptive children') and remedial education serve to replicate existing racial and class differences and ensure that the above groups have unequal schooling with no paper qualifications to improve their economic status.

Psychology as a profession also contributed to this debate by formulating the issue as one of inadequate socialization. Disruptive family patterns, single-parent families and the lack of adequate adult models are held responsible for the supposedly interrupted social growth. This environmental version of a determinist model of social behaviour was propounded by Patrick Moynihan in his 1965 Report to the US Department of Labor on the black family.

He held that the matriarchal black family had been enhanced by the emasculation of the male by slavery and was inconsistent with the patriarchal norms of American society. In the British context, the matriarchal argument has been used to assert higher achievement among the girls from matriarchal single-parent families.[18]

This pathological condition of the black family as analysed by Moynihan also gained currency in Britain in another form. In 1974 Keith Joseph stressed issues of eugenically 'transmitted deprivation' which attempted to concentrate on the poor family as an agency of perpetuating poverty. He also stated that the poor families 'threatened the balance of our human stock'.[19] The Department of Health and Social Security has jointly funded an extensive research programme on 'transmitted deprivation' with the Social Science Research Council. These projects are carried out at various academic institutions in Britain and there have been some recommendations about compensating for the debilitation of the personal family life of the child. The structural and institutional reasons which allow the schools as part of the state system to replicate the parental occupational inheritance and socio-economic backgrounds do not receive the scrutiny they merit.

DIFFERENT APPROACHES

The personality-oriented model of analysis continues the long process of deflecting attention away from the larger social system as a determinant of social inequality. In other words, the concentration is on individuals in powerless positions and not on powerlessness itself, and issues of cause and effect are not clearly demarcated. 'It can be argued that in the pursuit of "equal" opportunities for education through compensatory and remedial programmes, the more we do, the worse the students get!'[20] This only compounds and further entrenches the powerlessness of subordinate groups.

For instance, one could argue that the various deficit theorists, on whose work policy has been based, have deflected their analysis from the real issues and, as a result, resources have been misdirected. Rather than schooling a population to accept a lower status in social terms, the real issue is how to educate a society that no longer requires a disadvantaged class of people. The curriculum could be used to analyse the reasons for disadvantage and offer proposals to redress the present forms of inequality. A prevailing assumption is that the schools have some measure of autonomy which would allow educators who recognize diversity to alter the curriculum. On the critical issue of race in education, it is important to look at racism in terms of dynamics between dominant and subordinate groups, and racism as such would then be seen to be a problem for the dominant group. Obviously educators and teachers in a diverse society have to expect conflict in these heterogeneous contexts. Teachers have to expect that racist feelings are derived out of direct experiences; for example, the limited opportunities for employment result in stress in areas which are already under pressure. Similarly, housing problems and cultural or racial conflict as a result of geographical proximity in the inner city worsen opportunities and prospects of education. This in fact means the acknowledgement of class diversity in a society without a unified value system and the affirmation of the values of the working class and its culture. Various features of the British colonial connection, the presence of racial minorities in urban areas and the educational implications of this black presence need to be taken into account in discussions on multicultural education.[21]

British Typologies

In the British context very little conceptual work has been done in this field. One writer states: 'In spite of many isolated innovations and a few LEA initiatives there is much less agreement on either the theory of multicultural curriculum or its practice among teachers.'[22] Mary Worrall maintains further that the gap between the practitioners and experts is a wide one. She quotes Roger Watkin (1978), who referred to multicultural education as a comprehensive term for a variety of educational objectives and strategies of a diverse kind, and makes the point that this valuable initiative has failed 'because the terms have not been sufficiently clarified'. A simplified typology, as done by Jenny Williams, has three main categories.

The first category—the technicist category—is based on positive discrimination and is basically part of the compensatory education tradition which has been referred to in some detail in this chapter. In this model the low achievement of non-English-speaking children and children of Caribbean origin is seen to be the main problem to be remedied, as exemplified by Alan Little's studies in 1975 and 1978. The Community Relations Commission also stressed this dimension in its evidence to the Bullock Committee (1975). Curriculum changes suggested in this direction by organizations like the National Association for Multiracial Education (NAME) also stress the improvement of basic skills and issues of images. NAME and the Redbridge Report (1978), which focuses on the self-concept of West Indian children, both view the emphasis on the use of negative pictures and images as the main cause of education under-achievement by black children. As early as 1971 Bernard Coard had stressed that the compensatory model would lead to stereotyping of black children as educational and behavioural problems. The Plowden Report and its implementation, however, epitomizes LEAs' dilemmas on the compensatory approach.

The second model is the moral education approach, and the Lawrence Stenhouse work in 1975 and 1978 argues for open discussion on issues of race using well-prepared sets of materials. In other words, the emphasis is on individual feelings and not instruction in the history of nations. The initiatives at various schools in the country to unite morally against the use of racist remarks fall into this category but are rarely followed through with changes in educational practice. Even though the staff might have received some in-service training, the institutional structures of the school have not changed to correct the biases.

Robert Jeffcoate (Open University)[23] attempts to concentrate in his work (1975, 1977, 1979) on how respect for self and respect for others underpin a non-prejudiced society, but only from the point of view of the dominant community. His work is criticized by various writers for its 'neutral' stance.[24] Alan James from Derby Lonsdale College extends the debate in several ways. He argues that the concern with roots as stressed by some educators is regressive and that educated people do not need roots but take their ideas from any culture. He also argues that stereotyped thinking is functionally related to control in schools and that there is a link between intolerance and obsessive conformity.

One might perhaps fit Jeffcoate and James into Williams' category of moral persuasion, as well as into a separate category outlined by Clara Mulhern for (ALTARF)[25] that racism is a result of ignorance. In fact there is some overlap between the two.

While ALTARF's third category is based on anti-rascist teaching, that of Williams stresses a socio-political perspective. This perspective acknowledges that what passes for knowledge is in fact the dominant ideology of that society, reflecting the needs of, and control by, the ruling groups. Hence, Williams argues that the change to a multicultural curriculum would involve a move away from value consensus in British society, leaving open the possibility of a diverse society of relatively separate but equal groups.

The dangers of this approach are the stereotyping of cultures and the identification of cultures with religions.[26] For instance, the Punjabi culture of the North Indian region may be inclusive of Hindu, Muslim and Sikh religious groups. In the British context there is stress on religious groups without any emphasis on the similarities and differences among cultural and linguistic groups from various regions of the sub-continent. A second alternative within this socio-political framework is to focus upon the history and literature of a particular country, illustrating the effects of colonialism on the country and the political and literary responses to these historical experiences (some years ago referred to as Black Studies). While the earlier Black Studies dimension has subsided, the 'resistance to domination' theme is still central. This wider emphasis on multicultural education through all subjects means that all teachers need a wider knowledge of their subjects. According to Williams, teaching about race relations in Britain should focus on the reasons for migration, government legislation and other controversial issues. This would entail studies similar to those undertaken for Sociology O Level examinations, with emphasis on both objective facts and subjective impressions of what it is like to suffer discrimination. The World Development Education's project on the history of mankind, the School of Oriental and African Studies and the Ministry of Overseas Development (1978) have given some emphasis to this issue in both the development of syllabuses and the in-service training of teachers.

The link with the Third World prevents an exclusive focus on the discussion of race relations in Britain but Mary Worrall[27] discusses the problems of combining the two different foci. These problems arise because many of the images from the Third World reinforce the negative stereotypes already existing in the British context. The connection with the Third World can be made more substantive and instructive if the thesis of the development of the northern hemisphere as against the underdevelopment of the southern hemisphere, or Third World, is used. This approach becomes more viable as more black children are born in Britain and their images of the Third World coincide with those of the white British children.

The British model of multiculturalism has a large input of what is referred to as mother-tongue teaching. At the present time mother-tongue teaching is carried out by voluntary groups which to a certain extent are aided by LEAs. The Bedford Project on teaching Italian and Punjabi was funded by the European Economic Community and despite its success did not receive funding from the Bedford LEA. Unless the local education authorities take a direct initiative in the teaching and funding of mother-tongue teaching, the distance between the languages of home and school will continue to persist. However, any direct work on integrating language teaching is in its initial stages and more recent research tends to adopt[28] a different perspective on issues of linguistic diversity. This shift in emphasis involves the teaching of English to dialect and English-as-a-second-language learners by building on their knowledge of their first language and dialect.

In the Australian context, the work on community languages is more advanced and the work of Professor Smolicz at the University of Adelaide has made a contribution in this area by establishing the link between the languages of the minority communities and their culture. The predominant link between culture maintenance is seen to be the expansion of bilingual education programmes in the school curricula. He maintains that mother-tongue teachers can be systematically trained to teach community languages in the school. The school of linguistically oriented multiculturalists also has extremely strong adherents in the United States and Canada.[29]

In Britain, the initial responses to multicultural education were also articulated by English-as-a-second-language teachers, as Eric Boulton pointed out as a DES Inspector on Multicultural Education in 1979.[30] The SCOPE project financed by the Schools Council is a case in point. While Boulton as an HMI would like to see a multicultural curriculum lest the 'divisions in our society' widen, the radical members of the black community are critical of precisely this type of perspective. Their position states that conflict between school and authorities is an important development. The peer group which rejects adults, whether parents or teachers, is more able to foster a positive identity rather than the academic identity as postulated in schools.

These critics of the multicultural concept argue that it is used to control the rebellious second generation. Dhondy states that black youth reject such policies because schools are seen as processing agencies for the labour market. Their main critique is that schools act as social reproductive agencies which perpetuate rather than diminish social class differences. The more respectable and acceptable multiculturalism becomes within the state, the more suspect it becomes as an instrument of social control.[31]

GENERAL CRITIQUE OF MULTICULTURALISM

A more detailed critique of multicultural education has been carried out in a comparative study by Bullivant. His main contention is the need to refine the concept in terms of various societies, given different types and levels of heterogeneity and pluralism.[32]

At a wider political level, the concept of multiculturalism has been criticized in Canada. For instance, a radical critique referring to that country says 'Canada is a prison of nationalities'.[33] The concept of 'one Canada, one Nation', as outlined by the 'Prairee Lion' Diefenbaker, has been written off as chauvinism on the part of the dominant English community, in which the minorities cannot take pride in themselves or feel a sense of belonging because of the inequalities and indignities they suffer. Similarly, in Britain, Gus John calls any integration with the majority which is racist, 'madness'.

This historical inequality is expressed by the American melting-pot theory as being oppressive of American minorities, and this theory is similar to the Canadian one-nation concept. Trudeau's 'two-founding race' theory which led to the formulation of a policy of bilingualism and biculturalism, also masks the real inequalities between English and French Canadians and other minorities. This formulation also entrenches ideas based on a false equality and stifles the struggles of French Canadian minorities inside and outside Quebec.

The concept of 'unity in diversity' is further criticized for actually hiding the differences between historically oppressed minorities in Canada and institutionalizing racism against visible immigrant minorities. The criticism of the concept of multiculturalism in Canada has as much validity in the British context. This is so because issues of diversity on linguistic, religious, class, racial and territorial bases are applicable in both countries. Any new conceptualization therefore needs to re-examine these issues and attempt a more realistic and workable framework.

CONCLUSION

Any theoretical framework needs to take into account many of the above critiques. Much recent literature, despite its opposition to 'cosmetic educational planning',[34] continues to make the mistake of only tackling teacher attitudes and issues of ethnic diversity.[35]

A conceptual framework for multicultural education can only become clearer if the issues of institutionalized racism and the problems between dominant and subordinate groups are identified. It is unfortunate that some of the recent critiques of multicultural education tend not to come to grips with the substantive issues raised by this concept.[36] They also tend to develop those perspectives which only deal mechanistically with issues of racism while ignoring institutionalized inequalities and the contradictory strands within multicultural education which can be used to address issues of diversity in society.

NOTES AND REFERENCES

1. As an example see: ILEA (1977) *Multi-Ethnic Education* (mimeo).

2. Rist, R. (1978) *The Invisible Children: School Integration in American Society.* Cambridge, Mass.: Harvard University Press.

3. It might be useful to study the effectiveness or otherwise of the Commission for Racial Equality and the Equal Opportunities Commission in dismantling institutionalized racism and sexism in British society.

4. This arises out of early work by Kallen, H. M. (1924, reprinted 1970) *Culture and Democracy in the United States*. New York: Arno Press.

5. Gordon, M. (1964) *Assimilation in American Life*. New York: OUP.

6. Rist, R. (1978) *op. cit.*

7. Carby, H. (1980) Multiculture. *Screen Education*, **34**, 64–65.

8. *Ibid.,* pp. 18–19.

9. Hartz, L. (1964) *Founding of New Societies*. New York: Harcourt, Brace & Jovanovich. This provides an analysis of these fragment societies of Europe.

10. Jensen, F. N. (1969) *Harvard Education Review*, **39**, I, 1–123.

11. Eysenck, H. J. (1971) *Race, Intelligence and Education*. London: Temple Smith.

12. Hogan, R. and Emler N. (1978) The biases in contemporary social psychology. *Social Research*, **45**, 3, 748–534.

13. Kamin, L. J. (1977) *The Science and Politics of IQ*. London: Penguin.

14. Billig, M. (1979) *Psychology, Racism and Fascism*, pp. 8–9. Birmingham: Searchlight Press.

15. Kamin, L. J. (1977) *op. cit.* p. 16.

16. See Billig, M. (1979) *op. cit.* pp. 11–30, for links between Eysenck, Jensen and fascist publications.

17. Claydon, L., Knight, T. and Rado, M. (1978) *Curriculum and Culture*. London: Allen & Unwin.

18. Driver, G. (1980) *Beyond Underachievement. Case Studies of English, West Indian and Asian School-leavers at Sixteen Plus*. Commission for Racial Equality.

19. The *Sunday Times*, 1.6.81.

20. Claydon, L., Knight, T. and Rado, M. (1978) *op. cit*, p. 57.

21. Street-Porter, R. (1978) *Race, Children and Cities*. Milton Keynes: Open University Press. An Open University Handbook.

22. Williams, J. (1979) *The Social Science Teacher*, **8**, 4.

23. Jeffcoate, R. (1979) *Positive Image: Towards a Multicultural Curriculum*. London: Writers and Readers Co-operative/Chameleon Books.

24. Dodgson, P. and Stewart, D. (1981) Multiculturalism or anti-racist teaching: a question of alternatives. *Multiracial education*, **9**, 3, 41–44.

25. ALTARF (1978, 1979) *Teaching Against Racism.* London.

26. Hoggart, R. (1969) *The Uses of Literacy.* London: Penguin.
Williams, R. (1971) *Culture and Society.* London: Penguin.
Thompson, E. P. (1970) *The Making of the English Working Class.* London: Penguin.
Earlier work by these authors is reviewed by Johnson, R. (1980) Cultural studies and educational practice. *Screen Education, op. cit.,* pp. 5–16.

27. Worrall, M. (1978) Multicultural education and development education. *Approaches to Multi-racial Education.*

28. Rosen, H. and Burgess, T. (1980) *Languages and Dialects of London School Children.* London: Ward Lock Educational.

29. Cazden, C. B. and Dickenson, D. (n.d.) *Language in Education: Standardization vs Cultural Pluralism.* (mimeo) Cambridge, Mass.: Harvard University.
Smolicz, J. S. (1976) Ethnic cultures in Australian society: a question of cultural interaction. *Studies in Education.* Melbourne; Melbourne University Press.
Khan, V. S. (1980) The 'mother tongue' of linguistic minorities in multicultural England. *Journal of Multilingual and Multicultural Development*, **I,** I.

30. Boulton, E. (1979) Multicultural education. *Trends in Education,* **4.**

31. Dhondy, F. (May/June 1978) Teaching young blacks. *Race Today,* 80–86.

32. Bullivant, B. (1979) *Pluralism, Teacher Education and Ideology.* (mimeo) Faculty of Education and Centre for Migrant Studies, Monash University, Melbourne.

33. *October* (Autumn, 1979) **7,** 88.

34. Cross, D., Baker, G. and Stiles, L. (1977) *Teaching in a Multicultural Society.* New York: Free Press.

35. Banks, J. (1981) *Multiethnic Education: Theory and Practice.* Boston: Allyn & Bacon.
Banks, J. (1979) *Teaching Strategies for Ethnic Studies.* Boston: Allyn & Bacon.

36. Stone, M. (1981) *The Education of the Black Child in Britain.* London: Fontana.

6

Multiracial Education in Britain: From Assimilation to Cultural Puralism *

C. MULLARD

Since the early 1960s when the Commonwealth Immigrant Advisory Council recommended to the Home Secretary that special provision should be made for the education of 'immigrant' pupils, the multiracial education movement in Britain has tended to view black pupils as a *problem*.[1] They were a problem because they were black; they were a problem because many, especially those from India and Pakistan, could neither speak nor write English well enough to take an effective part in, or benefit from, school education. Numerically, they allegedly posed an administrative problem for already overcrowded inner-city schools, and a political problem which was expressed in terms of the fear that 'the whole character and ethos of the school' would be radically altered.[2] In short, their numbers, which were recently estimated to be in the order of 750 000 or roughly eight per cent of the total school roll, represented on one level a threat and on another a challenge to our educational system, its professional organizers and political protectors.[3]

While exploratory in nature, the purpose of this chapter is to trace the educational response to the so-called 'problem' and to evaluate critically the social meanings and educational practices of multiracial education. The argument that will be unfolded here, however, will be concerned more with the social and assumptive base of multicultural education than directly with the multiracial classroom or situational conflicts arising from teaching in a multiracial school. It will be suggested that the various multiracial

---

* In a slightly different form this chapter was originally published as a paper, Black Kids in White Schools: Multiracial Education in Britain, in *Plural Societies*, Summer, 1981.

education models developed and employed since the early sixties have attempted to foster the cultural subordination and political neutralization of blacks; they have started to achieve the very thing many of their advocates attempted to prevent—the social isolation and alienation of blacks in our society.

To begin with, however, the meaning and aims of multiracial education can be best understood if seen as the outcome of a continual process of development from intention to action, from reformulated intention to reformulated action, all stemming from a common social imperative—to maintain as far as possible the dominant structure of institutions, values, and beliefs. Although the three phases of development and meaning through which concern has travelled are to some extent interconnected and interdependent, for the purposes of our analysis here we will view them separately. They can be broadly designated the assimilationist phase, and its incumbent worldviews and model of social action which characterized thinking on race and education from the early 1950s to the *1965 White Paper*; the integrationist phase and model from 1965 to the early 1970s; and finally the present cultural pluralist phase and model which, as will be shown, is essentially a revised version of the integrationist model.

THE ASSIMILATIONIST MODEL

At the base of this model, which was dominant in the early to mid sixties and which today still influences the thinking of many educationalists, rests the belief that a nation is a unitary whole, politically and culturally indivisible. Immigrant groups, black or white, should thus be absorbed into the indigenous homogeneous culture so that they can take an informed and equal part in the creation and maintenance of our society. While a certain respect should be encouraged for other cultures and social traditions, this should be only a secondary concern. In no way should it be encouraged to the point where it could possibly undermine the social and ideological bases of the dominant white culture, or threaten the stability of what was seen as the 'host' society.[4]

For education generally the policy of cultural assimilation meant an almost obsessive attachment to the view forthrightly expressed in CIAC's Second Report; namely that:

> A national system of education must aim at producing citizens who can take their place in society properly equipped to exercise rights and perform duties the same as those of other citizens. If their parents were brought up in another culture and another tradition, children should be encouraged to respect it, but a national system cannot be expected to perpetuate the different values of immigrant groups.[5]

For teachers, as Williams describes in her study of schools in Sparkbrook, such a policy meant in practice that teachers continued to see 'their role as putting over a certain set of values (Christian), a code of behaviour (middle-class), and a set of academic and job aspirations in which white-collar jobs have higher prestige than manual, clean jobs than dirty . . .'[6] Taking the point a little further, Townsend and Brittan in 1973 reported three comments on assimilation by heads of humanities departments.

The first raised the question:

> Should immigrants—from wherever they come—be encouraged to maintain the
> traditions and cultures of their own societies, or through an educational process,
> be *weaned* gradually away from this towards the adoption of the standards of the
> country in which about 90 per cent of them will spend the rest of their lives. The
> aim of the twentieth century educationalists should be to deliver mankind from
> the 'ghetto' mentality, be it religious or cultural . . .[7]

The second assumed that segregation was the only possible alternative to assimilation:

> It is assumed that immigrants wish to be absorbed into the community into which
> they enter; this has been indicated through experience in teaching immigrants.
> Features relevant to life in the British Isles are taught through the media of
> History, Geography and Social Studies. There are no courses in Asian History or
> Geography, for example, since the whole aim of the school is towards social
> integration. We cannot account for practices in the home which may be towards
> segregation.[8]

While the second teacher was quite unaware of the significant contradiction between
his first and last sentences—one that perhaps helped him to justify his stance through
alluding to inter-generational conflict—the third possessed few doubts over the integrity
and logic of his position:

> We are after all trying to create an integrated society—and a great many of our
> pupils while retaining their racial and religious 'peculiarities' think of themselves
> as British. I think that we (the teachers) need to be made fully aware of the
> differences but I think in teaching we must be careful not to create divisions.
> Following this my History syllabus and the Humanities syllabus developing is and
> will remain basically British and possibly Euro-centred.[9]

Although their research is in many ways inconclusive, Townsend and Brittan show
that many teachers by and large 'formed their own definition of our society and worked
towards it'; definitions which ranged 'from complete assimilation through various
degrees of integration (assimilation) to separate development'.[10] And from a later study
conducted by Brittan it is also clear that a significant proportion of teachers perceived
blacks in hostile and stereotyped terms, a threat, unless assimilated, to the smooth
running of formerly all-white schools and society at large.[11] That such attitudes and
indeed assimilationist conceptions of educational and societal aims often resulted in a
disturbing lack of sensitivity, 'forcing' Hindu and Muslim children to eat pork and beef
by adopting an English-food only school menu, coercing Muslim girls to change into PE
kit and have showers through the process of social ostracism described by Brittan and
Townsend, is evidently clear from the descriptive studies that proliferate in the field.[12]
But what is so often overlooked and under-analysed, as Street-Porter rightly points out,
is what exactly constitutes this British society and way of life cherished by assimilationists?[13] Or to put it another way, what, apart from the unitary notion of the nation, are the
other assumptions on which the assimilationists' model is based?

From the teachers' statements quoted above, it is clear that the second assumption,
which, of course, is intrinsically related to the first, is that there exist an almost definable

shared value, belief system and code of behaviour into which *all* should be assimilated. This is not only, as Williams noted, interpreted to be predominantly middle class in all respects, but it is also seen to include quite centrally a stratified view of society in which pupils or adults-to-be will be placed hierarchically and ranked according to how well they have internalized middle-class values and norms.[14] That is to say, a basic tenet of assimiliationist ideology appears to reflect and dovetail with the way in which many teachers perceive the social aspects of their educational roles, such as the assessment of social as well as intellectual ability, the preparation of pupils to take up their already designated and presumed positions in the adult world of work and the social structure in general. Whether or not this, as a visible aspect of institutionalized racism, partly accounts for Smith's 1976 finding that only 31 per cent of black graduates in his sample compared with 79 per cent of white graduates managed to gain professional or man-agement positions is debatable.[15] But, according to Smith, what is not is their command and standard of English. He concludes:

> It might be suggested that inadequate English is the explanation of the low job levels of Asian men, even after their qualification level has been taken into account but this is not so. We have seen that there is a very strong relationship between fluency in English and academic qualifications—so strong, in fact, that nearly all Asian men with degree equivalent qualifications speak English fluently. Nevertheless a substantial proportion of them (21 per cent compared with 0 per cent of white graduates) are doing manual jobs.[16]

To invert this finding slightly, a third assumption embedded in the assimilationist's model embraces the theory and rationale behind the massive 'English for Immigrants' campaign launched by the DES in 1963, taken up by the 45 or so community relations councils, and implemented almost without question by literally hundreds of primary and secondary schools designated 'multiracial'.[17] If black children could be taught English quickly and to an acceptable level then just as quickly they could be assimilated into the British educational system, and ultimately into society as a whole. Although there was then and possibly still is now a need for special and extra tuition in English, the point we are making is not one about standards or even extra-curricula activity. Hinted at by James, it is a point about social stability as expressed in the view:

> That a dose of systematic language teaching, preferably carried out in the monas-tic security of a special class or centre, using the seemingly efficient sub-behaviourist 'direct method' of the 1950s, would act as a lubricant; the children could be fed into the educational machine on completion of this treatment without causing it to seize up.[18]

In other words the assimilationist perspective was seen by many educationalists, politicians, and race professionals alike as one that embodied a set of beliefs about stability. The teaching of English along with a programme of cultural indoctrination and subordination, as we shall see below, would help in short to neutralize sub-cultural affinities and influences within the school. A command of the dominant group's lan-guage would not only mean blacks could 'benefit' from the 'education' provided in school, but, more significantly, it would help counter the threat an alien group appar-ently poses to the stability of the school system and, on leaving, to society at large.

Closely related to this viewpoint, as both a political and educational strategy for implementation and as a further base assumption of the assimilationist model, rested a notion of coercion and control. Visibly detectable in the recent much criticized government and LEA policy of dispersal, which was not officially abandoned by the former body until 1973/4, its genesis stemmed from the prevalent belief in the early 1960s that:

> The presence of a high proportion of immigrant children in one class slows down the general routine of working and hampers the progress of the whole class, especially where the immigrants do not speak or write English fluently. This is clearly in itself undesirable and unfair to all the children in the class . . .[19]

Taking up the CIAC Report's main conclusion that the dispersal of black children would be preferable, as a last resort, to *de facto* segregation, the then Minister of Education, Sir Edward Boyle, informed the House of Commons in November 1963 that:

> If possible, it is desirable on education grounds that no one school should have more than about 30 per cent of immigrants . . . It is both politically and legally more or less impossible to compel native parents to send their children to school in an immigrant area if there are places for them in other schools.[20]

Eighteen months later the idea that white pupils would be protected educationally against the needs of black children, that they would be neither 'bussed' nor forced to change schools, was endorsed in Circular 7/65 which, in effect, officially introduced the policy of dispersal. Under a section headed 'Spreading the Children', it stated:

> It will be helpful if the parents of non-immigrant children can see that practical measures have been taken to deal with the problems in the schools, and that the progress of their own children is not being restricted by the undue preoccupation of the teaching staff with the linguistic and other difficulties of immigrant children.[21]

Thus in order to maintain standards of education in schools attended by 'large numbers of immigrant children with language difficulties' special arrangements must be made to teach them English:

> Such arrangements can more easily be made, and the integration of immigrants more easily achieved, if the proportion of immigrant children in a school is not allowed to rise too high. The Circular 7/65 suggests that about one-third of immigrant children is the maximum that is normally acceptable in a school if social strains are to be avoided and educational standards maintained. Local Education Authorities are advised to arrange for the dispersal of immigrant children over a greater number of schools in order to avoid undue concentration in any particular school.[22]

Embedded then in this racially discriminatory policy and indeed in the philosophy on which it was based lurked not only the dubious contentions that the education of white pupils would suffer in schools which possessed a large number of black pupils, that large numbers of blacks in a particular school by virtue of their being black, culturally different, would be disruptive; and that social strain allegedly caused by *them*, as blacks, would somehow inevitably lead to a general lowering of educational standards. But less difficult to fathom was the idea that assimilation could be achieved through the controlled dispersal of black pupils; that, furthermore, a measure of coercive control, national and local state direction was socially necessary to both stimulate the process of assimilation and, ultimately, to guarantee the absorption of black immigrants into white society.

All these four assumptions rely, as does the whole assimilationist model, on a fifth and in many ways a crucial belief in the cultural and racial superiority of the 'host', metropolitan society—on racism. Hidden in the recesses of rationalized thought, and built into the very structure of policies ostensibly concerned with English tuition, dispersal, and educational testing is, as convincingly demonstrated by Coard, the imputation that black culture is inferior, that black values and beliefs are of secondary importance, even whimsical, when considered against those held by dominant white groups.[23] To assimilate, for blacks, is to discard voluntarily or to be forced to discard all that culturally defines their existence, their identity as West Indians, Asians, or Africans. To assimilate, for whites, means to stay the same. That such a model's social anchorage and, moreover, political thrust depends upon an ethnocentric conception of our society, an almost rigid belief in the superior value of western culture and institutions, is also evident in headteachers' statements on the subject of multiracial education. Simply:

> Continuous discussion of racial differences in culture and tradition serves only to perpetuate them. I do not consider it the responsibility of an English state school to cater for the development of cultures and customs of a foreign nature. I believe our duty is to prepare children for citizenship in a free, Christian, democratic society according to British standards and customs . . .[24]

THE INTEGRATIONIST MODEL

Compared with the model out of which it evolved, the integrationist perspective is less crude. Many politicians, including the former Home Secretary, Roy Jenkins, and possibly even more teachers by the mid 1960s, had already started to reject the inherently racist nature of the assumptions underpinning the assimilationist model. The former, for instance, urged that what was required was 'not a flattening process of assimilation but equal opportunity, accompanied by cultural diversity, in an atmosphere of mutual tolerance'.[25] In other words, and on the surface at least, the idea of cultural superiority, which had sustained the early and continuing influence of those who advocated assimilation, should be replaced by the intrinsically more liberal and humanitarian concept of cultural tolerance. Further, and an important departure from earlier views, this definition of integration accepted that equal opportunities did not exist, that racist views and practices, institutionalized or otherwise, had in fact inhibited the development of equal opportunity structures and the creation of a racially harmonious and equal society. It also attempted to shift the emphasis of thought and policy away from social and cultural imperatives, and towards political integration. From a position

of expected equality which in turn would be achieved through providing equal educational, social, and economic opportunities, black groups, or so it seemed, would be able
to renegotiate their position in society with the various dominant power groups.
Although this seemed eminently preferable to the assimilationists' overt injunction 'to
integrate on our terms', (or else), the gap, as Street-Porter stresses, between the
idealism expressed by Jenkins and the practical implementation of integrationist
policies was acute and clearly demonstrated in educational practice.[26]
   She opens:

> The late sixties saw the start of several small policies which reflected partly the
> views of the Jenkins statement and also the assimilationist hangover . . . There was
> a mushrooming of courses and conferences to inform teachers about the home-
> land of such British-born children and there was an increasing number of advisory
> posts created to deal with the 'problems' of 'immigrant' education . . . Dispersal
> was officially abandoned, concern expressed about West Indian children in ESN
> schools, and an increasing amount of money was being spent on the special needs
> of such children.[27]

By way of an overall explanation, she concludes:

> Cultural integration seems to have been accepted merely as a modest tokenism, an
> acceptance of that which is quaint in a minority culture but a worried rejection of
> those cultural aspects that seem not just alien but threateningly so. In other words
> minority groups in practice are allowed complete freedom to define their own
> cultural identity only in so far as this does not conflict with that of the white
> indigenous community.[28]

   While this might appear to represent a plausible analysis of why integrationist
educational policies have not worked in practice, it fails, unfortunately, to come to grips
with the actual assumptions on which the integrationist model is based. Together with
Jenkins' original definition in the wider context in which it was forged (namely as a
policy goal for government-sponsored community relations groups), and the response
of the Select Committee to demands for black studies in the school curriculum, it is
possible to strip off the liberal-white gloss work and uncover an ideological undercoat
that looks very similar indeed to the one already exposed.
   But first the Select Committee had this to say in response to the Committee on Black
Studies memorandum:

> The demand for black studies has arisen because the content of education in
> Britain is seen as Anglo-centric and biased against black people. We can under-
> stand this. But we doubt whether black studies in the narrow sense would make a
> contribution to wider education and better race relations, and we are not attracted
> by the idea of black teachers teaching black pupils in separate classes or estab-
> lishments . . . We come down firmly on the side of unity through diversity.[29]

Although the phrase 'unity through (cultural) diversity' appears to be a paraphrasing of
the explicit social ends of Jenkins' original conception of an integrationst policy, it
differs little from the assimilationist's belief in a politically and culturally indivisible
society. Where it differs is only in a matter of degree. Within this perspective, political
diversity is discouraged in favour of political integration; cultural diversity is tolerable

so long as it neither impedes progress to political integration nor explicitly challenges the cultural assumptions of our Anglo-centric society. That is to say the political imperative of assimilation in this model is no longer, as construed in the early sixties, dependent upon complete cultural subjugation: the means to the ends have slightly changed, but the ends remain the same. But even on this level of analysis it is still questionable whether or not cultural diversity is openly promoted. From the Select Committee's statement above, which was greeted with the full approval of the government, it is, of course, clear that blacks should 'not be expected to get rid of all their own customs, history and culture'; but by the same token it is also clear that 'those who come here to settle must, to some extent, accept the ways of the country'.[30] In other words, there exists an expectation that they will in fact 'get rid' of most of their customs, history, and culture. Indeed this covert end will be assisted by 'the educational process (which) influences and helps to shape (society)'.[31] Thus it would seem from this standpoint that toleration should be considered as a short-term social objective; an awareness and appreciation that the integration-assimilation goal can only be achieved harmoniously if blacks are conditionally allowed to maintain aspects of their culture in order to provide the sense of social security, independence, and possible confidence to integrate or assimilate at a later stage, after contact with and involvement in 'the educational process'.

The assumptions, then, of cultural superiority, social stability, and shared values and beliefs still figure prominently in this second model. Though reformulated in terms of conditional cultural diversity, the first manifests itself often in the emphasis placed on integration into *our* society, *our* way of life, which in turn undervalues, even negatively values, other cultural traditions and ways. In the school, as described to some extent by Jeffcoate and to a greater extent by Searle, it takes on an added dimension.[32] *Our* society and *our* way of life are firstly juxtaposed and secondly subtly inculcated through the adoption of a liberal ideology which promotes and stimulates classroom discussion on multiracial issues within the framework of dominant white British norms, values and beliefs. Or, to put it another way: other cultures, other ways of life whether introduced as part of the formal or informal curriculum are seen and often openly evaluated against not their own value and belief patterns but, instead, those of the school and the wider British society. Through such a process a deceptive pressure to conform is inevitably exerted; one that is channelled obliquely through the posture of liberal, multiracial education.

In fact, ultimate conformity and eventual cultural absorption become, as the assimilationist model demonstrates, preconditions of a stable and racially harmonious society. Stability as both an assumed continuing aim and present social condition likewise is based on the further assumption that there exist values and beliefs to which we *all* subscribe. All the integrationist model affords, as possibly distinct from its predecessor, is that, while immutable, these dominant values and beliefs can in effect be reinforced through following a policy of mutual tolerance and reserved respect for other cultural values and beliefs. For what matters is not total but selective value orientation and acceptance. In short, political and economic values and beliefs, those on which our society and its major institutions are based, need to be separated from the rest—religious beliefs, cultural customs, and so on. And, as the most important values and beliefs in the sense of their determining the substructural base of our society, they become the ones that must be protected at all costs and to which black pupils and adults must be persuaded to subscribe. By allowing limited diversity in respect of religious beliefs, customs, dress and even language, it is assumed within the framework of the model that blacks will be more likely to accept than reject outright those which actually shape our society.

Seen from this position, the notion of equal opportunity which occupied a central place in Jenkins' definition in essence means social control. Firstly, on a theoretical level equal opportunity for all can only exist in a society where there prevails, among other things, a general acceptance of the dominant values and beliefs. Where this does not exist, equal opportunity is dependent upon the degree of mutual tolerance to be found. But given the necessity in the first place of relying on mutual tolerance—that racism exists—it is highly likely that the degree of equal opportunity to be attained at any one time by any one group will correlate quite closely with that group's orientation towards a society's dominant value and belief system. If it rejects this system, equal opportunities of access to key positions in the power structure where social or political change can be effected will be denied; if it accepts, equal opportunity of access will possibly be granted with the understanding that the existing system of beliefs will be upheld. In other words, given the racial dimension of the structural inequality that exists in our society, equal opportunity in practice means equal opportunity only for persons whose ideas and values conform to those of the dominant white middle-class culture.

On an educational and more practical level, the provision of equal opportunities is already defined in terms of the objectives of education in British schools. For black pupils, as in many cases for white working-class children, this means the rapid development of conceptual tools, language and arithmetical skills, white middle-class values, and so on, in order to achieve academically—pass GCE examinations with the view to entering higher education. Equal opportunity tends to be interpreted in the school setting as the provision of services, facilities, resources and so on to all in order for all to have an 'equal' chance of achieving the explicitly middle-class social and educational objectives revered by the school. Those who desire social and academic achievement need foremost to conform, to accept, if only passively, the school ethos before they can usefully gain from the supposed equal opportunities provided. To integrate in this sense is to suppress the cultural symbols of one's social existence; to submit to a form of control that denies that very existence. Or, as Gus John has put it:

> To wish to integrate with that which alienates and destroys you, rendering you less than a person, is madness. To accept the challenge to join it and change it from within, when it refuses to accept that you are there in your fullness and refuses to acknowledge the results of interaction between you and it, is double madness.[33]

CULTURAL PLURALISM

If the integrationist model is in fact a more sophisticated and liberal variant of the assimilationist model, then that which is constructed around the concept of cultural pluralism is in effect a more refined version of both. In many ways it is not a separate model at all; it really expands the idea of cultural diversity and establishes the existence of this idea as a central observable feature of the social structure. Certainly, in contrast to the assimilationist's view of our society as being politically and culturally homogeneous, its advocates maintain that our society consists of different groups which are culturally distinctive and separate. Therefore within a plural society there exists a positive commitment to difference and to the preservation of group culture, traditions and history. The only thing that is acknowledged as binding on all groups is the political authority of the state. Whether or not Britain is a plural society in this somewhat simplistic sense or indeed whether it exhibits any of the defining characteristics outlined by Van den Berghe is not as important a question to resolve in the context of our argument here as is the question of its relevance *vis à vis* multiracial education.[34]

On this count it appears to take the liberal idealism of the mid sixties and remould it into an operational philosophy for educational innovation and policy action. For a start cultural pluralism can mean all things to all people. For some it can mean the pursuing of a policy of total cultural segregation which in turn could lead to demands for political segregation; for another group it could mean a policy of revised integration based upon a more equitable distribution of power; and yet again for others it could be used to justify and encompass more educational development, curricular expansion and educational sensitivity.[35] Given this problem with the concept and the way it is beginning to be employed in Britain—as a revised policy of integration—it is perhaps more useful at the moment to see it not as a distinct model but as a more liberal and possibly progressive version of the integrationist model.

Although some might argue that this is a neat way of dismissing it altogether, it does, however, provide us with the opportunity, firstly, to address briefly a common underlying assumption of the two main models; and, secondly, tentatively to bring our thoughts together on the meaning of multiracial education. With respect to the first issue, one of the main problems associated with the pluralist perspective in general and that of cultural pluralism, as a multiracial education model, in particular, arises from the way in which it views the distribution of power in our society. In theory at least, it sees power as a residual commodity possessed by the culturally different groups that constitute a plural society. That is, simply, all groups possess power; all groups possess roughly equal amounts of power; or, if not exactly equal amounts, all groups acquire enough power to ensure the maintenance of a high degree of cultural sovereignty and distinctiveness; and all groups are able equally to assert pressure on the political state and negotiate with its agencies to see that a certain amount of cultural equilibrium is maintained. Leaving aside the crucially problematic question of the actual socio-cultural composition of the state and the even more difficult question of the nature of state power *vis à vis* that held by constituent cultural groups, the problems implicity in this perspective are still fairly obvious. Equal distribution of power will not theoretically only depend upon group size, the economic base of each group, history, the organizing ability of each group, and a host of other variables, but more significantly in a dualistic international and interlocked economy based on two competing political and economic ideologies, it will depend upon at least three other factors:

1. The precise relationship that the plural state maintains with the international economy.

2. The relationship the plural state builds with class- and ethnic-based constituent groups.
3. The relationships that exist between the constituent groups themselves.

In the context of Britain it is empirically difficult to establish that we live in a plural society in most senses of the concept. Neither West Indians, Pakistanis, Indians, nor Africans, nor blacks as a whole, possess anything like the same amounts of power as the white dominant 'British' group. So even if we were to take cultural pluralism seriously as a multiracial education model separate from that of integration, it is patently clear that black groups in a white society, black pupils in white schools, could not develop their cultural traditions without the unconditional permission, approval and encouragement of white society as a whole and of white dominant power groups in particular. What this then suggests is that the power assumption located at the base of the cultural pluralism model as interpreted by its mainly white British advocates—as a culturally defined form of integration—and at the base of the other two models of assimilation and integration is to all intents and purposes identical.

One headteacher got very close to the point when she asked rhetorically:

> Is (Britain) a society into which immigrants are gradually absorbed into English culture? Is it a society in which the best is taken from, say, West Indian, Asian and English culture to form a basis for a new culture? Is it a society in which the English culture must adapt itself to new and increasingly powerful voices of the different cultures? Are immigrant cultural forces sufficiently powerful to encourage the indigenous population to change its cultural heritage? Will a 'ghetto' situation contain immigrant cultures and cause the indigenous population to ignore and disregard immigrants, causing a multiracial society to remain really a racial one (with the same power structure)?[36]

The point is, of course, that all the models assume various degrees of cultural change on the part of black groups in school and society without any corresponding change on the part of white groups in school and society. Power is held by white groups in society; white groups and schools can insist that black groups and pupils assimilate or integrate. Real power in a capitalist and, as shown in earlier chapters by John Tierney and Mike Syer, a racist society is indivisible. Although disguised and dressed up with platitudes or good intentions, the three multiracial education models are in fact power models. They are power models constructed by dominant white groups for the protection of the power of white groups, for the continuation of our society as it is basically perceived by those groups.

CONCLUSION

Multiracial education in Britain, then, has above all meant the assimilating or integrating of alien black groups, without disruption, into a society dedicated to the preservation of social inequality and a seemingly unchanging and cherished stock of central values, beliefs and institutions. As interpreted and practised by many, multiracial education has appeared to become an instrument of control and stability rather than one of change, of the subordination rather than the freedom of blacks in schools and or society as a whole. In the context of schools and against a wider societal background of institutionalized racism, multiracial education programmes, from the assimilationist's view on English teaching to the integrationist's stance on multicultural and black studies, have in fact integrally contributed to the increased alienation of black youth. To be told, however politely and cleverly, that your culture and history count for nothing is to invoke responses ranging from low self-esteem and lack of confidence, as Verma and Bagley et al have convincingly shown, to political oppostion and resistance.[37] To be told that your culture and history count for something only within the pedagogic boundaries of the school curriculum and not outside the school gates in the white dominated world of work and politics is to foster the response of a 'blacks only for the black studies class'.[38] To be goaded to integrate politically and then in practice to take up your place at the bottom of society with as much of your culture intact as is permitted is, to extend Gus John's conclusion, a madness that not even a mad and subordinated black can any longer contemplate.[39] Simply, what multiracial education, as viewed in British schools, is teaching black pupils is that they will always remain second-class citizens; and, ironically, that in order to survive or exist as blacks it is necessary to resist racist authority within and outside school.

Without a radical reappraisal of multiracial education theory and practice, our society's materialist and racist culture will continue to be transmitted by all schools: without a radical reconstruction of our society as a whole and of the meaning and practice of multiracial education in particular, we shall for some time to come continue to talk about black kids in white schools, rather than merely children in schools.[40]

NOTES AND REFERENCES

1. See *Second Report by the Commonwealth Immigrants Advisory Council.* (Cmnd 2266) (1964) London: HMSO.

2. *Ibid.*, para. 25.

3. Although from 1966 to 1973 the DES made some attempt to collect statistics through the instrument of Form 7 (1), these proved to be inaccurate as children of mixed (black) immigrant and black/white non-immigrant parentage were excluded; a ten-year rule also excluded those black children who had resided in Britain longer than this arbitrary period; and finally it also excluded the children of blacks who were themselves born in Britain. For an official discussion on the reliability of DES statistics consult Chapter 9 of the Select Committee on Race Relations and Immigration's *Report on Education*, Vol. 1 (1964) London: HMSO. For a more up-to-date evaluation, see Street-Porter, R. (1978) *Race, Children and Cities,* pp. 63–69. Milton Keynes: The Open University Press.

4. The concept of the 'host' society as part of the 'stranger' hypothesis in race relations illustrates not only the kind of attitude that prevailed during the early 1960s but also the kind of approach developed in the study of race relations at that time.

5. *Second Report by the Commonwealth Immigrants Advisory Council* (1964) *op. cit.,* para. 10.

6. See Jennifer Williams, Chapter 10 in Rex, J. and Moore, R. (1967) *Race, Community and Conflict: A Study of Sparkbrook.* Oxford: Oxford University Press.

7. Quoted in Townsend, H. E. R. and Brittan, E. M. (1973) *Multiracial Education: Need and Innovation,* p. 31. Schools Council Working Paper 50. London: Evans/Methuen Educational.

8. *Ibid.*

9. *Ibid.*

10. *Ibid.,* p. 83.

11. Brittan, E. M. (1976) Multiracial education 11: Teacher opinion on aspects of school life. *Educational Research,* **18** pp. 82–191.

12. Townsend, H. E. R. and Brittan, E. M. (1973) *op. cit.*

13. Street-Porter, R. (1978) *op. cit.,* p. 77.

14. Williams, J. (1967) *op. cit.*

15. Smith, D. J. (1977) *Racial Disadvantage in Britain.* London: Penguin.

16. *Ibid.,* pp. 76–77.

17. See *English for Immigrants.* Ministry of Education pamphlet, No. 43. (1963). London: HMSO.

18. See James, A. (1977) Why language matters. *Multiracial School,* Summer.

19. Second Report by the Commonwealth Immigrants Advisory Council, (1964) *op. cit.,* para. 25.

20. See Hansard, Vol. 685, cols 433–444, 27th November, 1963.

21. *The Education of Immigrants,* Department of Education and Science Circular 7/65, London (June, 1965). This circular was sent to local education authorities and certain other bodies concerned with race relations and education.

22. *Immigration from the Commonwealth.* (Cmnd 2739) (1965). London: HMSO. Para. 41–42.

23. Coard, B. (1971) *How the West Indian Child is made Educationally Sub-normal in the British School System: The Scandal of the Black Child in Schools in Britain.* London: New Beacon Books.

24. Townsend, H. E. R. and Brittan, E. M. (1973) *op. cit.,* p. 13.

25. Rt. Hon. Roy Jenkins (1966) *Address given by the Home Secretary to a meeting of Voluntary Liaison Committees.* London: NCCI.

26. Street-Porter, R. (1978) *op. cit.,* pp. 80–81.

27. *Ibid.*

28. *Ibid.*

29. Select Committee *Report on Education* (1973) *op. cit.*, paras 102, 103 and 104.

30. For governmental approval see in particular, *Educational Disadvantage and the Educational Needs of Immigrants: Observations on the Report on Education of the Select Committee on Race Relations and Immigration.* (Cmnd 5720) (1974) London: HMSO.

31. Select Committee *Report on Education* (1973) *op. cit.*, para. 104.

32. See Searle, C. (1978) *The World in a Classroom* and Jeffcoate, R. (1979) *Positive Image: Towards a Multiracial Curriculum.* Both are published by Writers and Readers Publishing Co-operative/Chameleon Books, London.

33. Quoted in British Council of Churches (1976) *The New Black Presence in Britain: A Christian Security.* London: BBC Publications.

34. For a full list of the defining features of a plural society see Van den Berghe, P. (1967) *Race and Racism: A Comparative Perspective*, p. 35. London: John Wiley and Sons.

35. As Street-Porter, R. (1978) *op. cit.* notes, the concept, certainly in America, has become a catch-all for a whole number of policies, ranging from compensatory education to affirmative action and women's educational equality; it has become overworked and empty.

36. Townsend, H. E. R. and Brittan, E. M. (1973) *op. cit.*, pp. 16–17.

37. For a number of interesting papers on the subject written mainly within a social psychological tradition and a comprehensive account of the literature see Verma, G. K. and Bagley, C. (1979) *Race, Education, and Identity.* London: Macmillan. Although somewhat out of date, two further books are worth consulting in this respect: Milner, D. (1975) *Children and Race.* London: Penguin; and McNeal, J. and Rogers, M. (Eds) (1971) *The Multiracial School.* London: Penguin. Read the latter more for the assumptions made than its actual content.

38. A discussion of this phenomenon is to be found in Jeffcoate, R. (1979) *op. cit.* in Chapter 6 on 'Schools and Racism'. Unfortunately, though, Jeffcoate's peculiar brand of educational liberalism, which permits and indeed even urges that the National Front should be allowed to put its case across in the classroom, tends to prevent him from seeing the real political point black pupils are making.

39. Gus John in the British Council of Churches, 1976, *op. cit.*

40. I have attempted this task in the following publications:
    Racism in Society and Schools: History, Policy, and Practice (1980) Centre for Multicultural Education, University of London Institute of Education; The social context and meaning of multicultural education, *Educational Analysis* Vol. **3**, No. 1 (1981); and, forthcoming, The racial code: its features, rules, and change, in Len Barton (Ed.) *Race, Class, and Gender in Education*, (1982) London: Croom Helm.

7

Educational Responses to Racism
C. JONES AND K. KIMBERLEY

The analysis in earlier chapters has already indicated ways in which those concerned with making and carrying out educational policy appear to have made little more than minimal changes to their central values, beliefs and practices in the face of the facts of institutional racism and increasingly visible racialist activity in society and schools. This has been accounted for in terms of the preservation of the material advantages of the dominant group and by explanation of the ways in which the racism deriving from Britain's imperial past, and neo-colonial present, functions to sustain inequality. Schooling has been seen as providing the means of reproducing the dominant ideology and of controlling resistance which might otherwise force changes in the existing structures and value systems of society.[1]

Considered in the context of arguments such as these which push towards,

> . . . ways of understanding how this society actually works and how it has arrived where it is,[2]

it will be seen that racism brings into sharp focus many difficult issues for those in education and that this in turn helps to explain both the attempts that are made in schools to deny the connection between educational issues and those of the larger, social, economic, and political background[3] and the coexistence, even within individual schools or colleges, of dramatically differing views on how to analyse and respond to racism.

Little and Willey (1981) bear witness to the extreme reluctance of some LEAs and schools across the country to respond even to mild DES exhortations that the curriculum for all students should reflect the multi-ethnic nature of society at large. While their survey revealed that there is now wide agreement within LEAs in multiracial areas that the presence of minority ethnic groups in Britain has implications for the curriculum in all schools, they were also forced to conclude that,

... where there are few or no such pupils the general view is that the wider multi-ethnic society has little relevance for their schools.

Some replies suggested that this was 'not an issue that concerned them' and that 'to take any sort of positive action would only be divisive and generate hostility.'[4] That these teachers and administrators are either unable or unwilling to identify the implications for all students in all schools of the facts of society's diversity suggests a poor prospect for their ability to analyse, and act upon, a phenomenon as difficult to analyse and as deeply embedded as racism.

It may help if at this point we restate the main ways in which racism manifests itself in education in the hope that these distinctions may help to highlight some of the ever-present confusions which arise in discussions about racism.

Firstly, and centrally, decisions about the curriculum are taken within a largely taken-for-granted framework of assumptions which draw on Britain's history and present social structures. Insofar as there is racism embedded in those assumptions, it is possible for those making seemingly straightforward choices about what to include or exclude to slip into unintentional racism. What is chosen for transmission to students can only with some difficulty and by means of careful presentation be freed from the taint of racism. Debates about racism in the curriculum are often fundamental arguments about the nature of society. This means that suggestions for change in what is taught are often bitterly contested though, put more optimistically, the curriculum provides important spaces where teachers can assist students to analyse racism and uncover its origins and realities.

Secondly, schooling is itself an integral part of the operation of institutionalized racism in society. Schools have a bad record for devising forms of organization and setting levels of expectation which match the aspirations of black students and their parents.[5] A survey commissioned by the Rampton Committee based on DES figures gives, for example, evidence of a dramatic shortfall for West Indian students at O and A Levels in comparison with the national average.[6] This will not have come as a surprise to those black parents and community leaders who have, for a decade, criticized the placing of disproportionate numbers of children of West Indian origin in low streams, special schools, and disruptive units.[7] As with the curriculum, change is not necessarily easy to achieve in the face of a defensive stance by those who organize schools and who argue good intentions in the face of contrary statistical evidence. However, it is arguable that there exists sufficient autonomy for LEAs, schools and teachers to work individually, or collectively, to remake such structures and redefine those expectations which work to the disadvantage of certain groups of students.

Thirdly, schools and colleges are arenas where racism surfaces. In schools where there are few black students, racialist attitudes and activities have made their ugly appearance in the classroom and playground and in so doing pose a clear challenge to teachers, LEAs and the government. In schools with large minority groups, some teachers and white students have been forced to face up to the black students' daily experience of racist attacks and of the subtler forms of discrimination which operate in and around the school. When students are overtly racist in such schools they are kept firmly in their place by black students and anti-racist white students. This surface racism has, by its sheer nastiness, sometimes provided a sufficient stimulus for action to be taken at various levels. It provides blatant evidence of the need for policies which tackle racism simultaneously at the levels of institution, ideology, attitudes and actions.

RESPONSES BY THE DES AND THE LEAS

It will be clear by now that we are arguing for the need to understand the complexity of what has to be done in responding to racism and for a recognition of the divisions of opinion that has arisen in education at various levels. As in many other educationally controversial areas, it is often the classroom teacher who both takes the blame for the failure of the whole schooling system and what it is expected to do for society and, in addition, has to struggle to make some sense of it for the pupils that s/he is in contact with. In this chapter we look at the interworking of the parts of the education system, from the Department of Education and Science (DES) to the classroom. We have done this because we maintain that if so little seems to be being done in classrooms it is at least in part because so little is being done at those levels in the educational system which, in theory, should support and sustain classroom practice.

Looking separately at the various levels of the educational system does not suggest that each level can be looked at as if divorced from the others. Obviously that would be nonsense. It does not imply either that there is some form of chain of command. The whole education system interacts and reacts both within itself and with other institutions in society.

For example, many people would argue that the tension between the DES and the Local Education Authorities (LEAs) is a creative one, preventing the system from becoming monolithic and by implication inefficient and lacking in humanity. This belief may be true over some issues but it has proved a major obstacle to progress in the area of race relations and education. One example of this is an EEC educational directive on the teaching of EEC nationals' children and other migrant workers' children. Under the directive, their children have the right to a certain amount of mother-tongue maintenance wherever they are being educated in the EEC.[8] This directive has reluctantly, been accepted by the DES on behalf of the British Government. However, as the DES does not control the school curriculum, they have no way of enforcing the directive.[9] The LEAs, who do, are unwilling to take on this new task, either for reasons of expense or because of a lack of commitment to the concept. Some of our EEC partners regard this use of the DES/LEA division of power as casuistry to avoid compliance with the directive.

The relationships between the formal organizations of schooling (DES/LEAs/ schools) are affected by their relationships with the rich variety of educational interest groups. Foremost among these are the teacher unions, although in the area of race relations organizations such as the National Association for Multiracial Education (NAME) and the Anti-Nazi League (ANL) can be important, particularly at a local level. Some local community organizations, notably those within black groups have also had significant impact especially on issues like suspension. Some teacher groups, like the All London Teachers Against Racism and Fascism (ALTARF) and Teachers Against the Nazis (TAN) have not only been active pressure groups but have also produced curriculum materials, a point taken up later in this chapter.

To disentangle educational responses from this mix of interest groups is clearly a difficult task for so short a chapter. By looking in more detail at the DES, a single LEA and some examples of school and classroom practice some idea of this variety can be gained. In addition, some of the confusion subsequent to this diversity is made a little easier to understand.

In looking at the DES, the first question to be established is, has the DES responded at all to the issue of race in education? The answer is that it has, but not necessarily to good purpose. Its response is most interesting in so far as it reveals the way in which the state has tried to avoid action in this area.

Its initial stance, which dates back to Arnold, was an extension of the long-standing concern with gentling the masses, or in its slightly more sophisticated form, educating our masters. Stuart Hall[10] has shown how the urban school system responded to this task and how the urban working class responded in their turn. The arrival of large numbers of black immigrants in the postwar period was seen by the DES and government in general as posing similar problems for education. How were such numbers to be assimilated peacefully into the 'British way of life'? This worry is quite clearly shown in the DES Circular 7/65 on the dispersal of immigrants. It stated boldly that 'serious strains' could arise in schools if the proportion of black children in any one school rose above one-third. An implication behind this statement is that white parents would protest at what they perceived as the 'taking over' of 'their' school. In other words, the DES was tacitly supporting a racist response to the presence of black children. This position was earlier put even more clearly by Sir Edward Boyle, the then Minister of Education, who, after visiting schools in Southall in 1963 reported to Parliament:

> I must regretfully tell the House that one school must be regarded now as irretrievably an immigrant school. The important thing to do is prevent this happening elsewhere.[11]

The consequence of this circular was to legitimate dispersal policies in many LEAs, policies which continued right through the seventies in some local authorities. The DES itself, in 1971, recognized that these dispersal policies were inherently racist, a recognition aided by the objections to the practice made by black and other organizations concerned with race relations.

This policy of reacting to events rather than anticipating them typifies much of the DES's policy on race and education through the seventies. The late seventies saw a slightly more positive commitment to these issues, with a small group in Her Majesty's Inspectorate (HMI) taking a real interest in these issues. Courses were organized for teachers on a more intensive scale, and a small unit, the Educational Disadvantage Unit (EDU) was set up within the DES. In addition, the DES helped to set up the, now defunct, Centre for Educational Disadvantage (CED) in Manchester.[12] Despite the efforts of a small group of committed HMIs within the DES, it has not in any way taken the lead in this area, even when some form of national policy was urgently needed. Two examples of this might be helpful. The first is the use and abuse of monies disbursed through Section II of the 1966 Local Government Act. This section of the Act allowed local authorities to claim back 50 per cent (later 75 per cent) of the salaries of people employed to deal with the special needs of immigrants. At quite an early stage the DES had statistics of the unequal and inequitable take-up of the money and knew of the allegation of widespread misuse of the money. Because the money was distributed by the Home Office and spent by the local authorities, the DES was, and is, reluctant to enter into this debate.[13,14]

A second example is the way in which the DES chose to respond to the complaints in the 1977 report of the Parliamentary Select Committee on Race Relations and Immigration. This report[15] indicated discontent within the West Indian community about a wide range of issues, including education. The DES's response was to set up the Rampton Committee to enquire into the educational needs of children from ethnic minority groups.

Similarly, it is true to say that certain individuals within the DES are trying very hard to implement change. By the 1980s the DES has publicly adopted a policy of cultural pluralism.[16] The plethora of documents on the curriculum emphasize the importance of multicultural education, but in such general terms that a variety of policies, from assimilationist to plural, could follow from it. Racism is scarcely mentioned. The implication is that this is still seen as something like smallpox; susceptible to an educationally effective innoculation.

Partly because the DES has not given a decisive lead in these matters, LEAs reactions have varied enormously, from apathy to a sincere attempt to grapple with some of the issues. Many of these latter LEAs are those controlling schools in the large conurbations where the effects of racism are often clearly visible. As an example of one such authority's response[17] that of the Inner London Education Authority deserves closer examination. Even today, it is one of the few authorities to have made a public policy statement on multi-ethnic education and a commitment to positive teaching against racism.

A significant factor in the establishing of this public commitment in 1977 was pressure from both within the authority and outside. Individual teachers, schools, and certain teacher organizations, such as London NAME and the teacher unions were all seeking a more public stance on these issues. Black parents and black students in the schools were also a very important factor, both in influencing the group within education just mentioned and exerting pressure on the authority through organizations like the local community relations councils.

For the various interested parties, the public policy document ILEA 269—the 1977 paper on multi-ethnic education—was a significant step forward.[18] There had been recent, overt racialist events within London and involving schools which had alerted the elected members. A new education officer, Peter Newsam, was deeply committed to issues of cultural diversity in education, views which had been reinforced by a visit to New York with a group of ILEA teachers and officials the previous year. The document that emerged from all the consultations was meant to be a guideline for policy and also an official statement of support for the initiatives, many of them individual, that were already underway. The document is an interesting one. Its underlying assumptions were thought to be pluralist but a close reading of the document reveals a restatement of the Roy Jenkins' integrationist statement of the mid sixties, a viewpoint discussed by Chris Mullard in an earlier chapter.[19]

The ILEA stated that the authority wished

to sustain a policy which will ensure that, within a society that is cohesive though not uniform, cultures are respected, differences recognized and group and individual identities are secure.[20]

What is also interesting about this statement is that it in many respects parallels current mainstream thinking on this subject in the USA. There, the rejection of an assimilationist ideology has been coupled with a rejection of cultural pluralism.[21]

Within this multi-ethnic framework, the ILEA documented four key area that needed to be carefully examined and developed. The first was to obtain accurate information and statistics on the basis of which policies could be framed. The second was to encourage work that was already being done. The third was to find ways of relating more effectively with the ethnic minorities within the ILEA, and the fourth was to examine how the authority could respond positively to the 1976 Race Relations Act, particularly the sections supporting positive discrimination. Although there was initially no specific reference to racialism, a commitment to positive teaching against racism was added to the document—on the initiative of a Conservative member.

The document was generally welcomed within the authority, though this may have had something to do with the vague wording of certain key passages. Even so, there was opposition to it, usually covert, at all levels of the authority. The most specific and potentially divisive element of the document—the commitment to prepare material on how to teach against racism—has taken over four years to be fulfilled and the work, at the time of writing (mid 1981), has not yet been published.[22]

In the four areas there were developments. On the collection of statistics, an annual survey of schools has been instituted by the Research and Statistics branch. This has revealed not only the large number of bilingual children in the schools, slightly over 10 per cent but also the need for an expansion of the English as a Second Language service within the authority. Monitoring the 'disruptive' units to ensure that certain groups of children are not over-represented has also been undertaken.

In terms of encouraging and developing existing practice perhaps the most significant action was a rapid expansion of the inspectorate and other advisory staff in the area. In addition, certain specific curriculum development projects were either set up or assisted with funds. Some of these initiatives are worth mentioning briefly. Following the success of the 'whole school' curriculum development project run in an ILEA primary school by the Schools Council/NFER Education for a Multiracial Society Project, two larger projects, to be run on similar lines, were set up: The Lambeth Whole School Project based in Brixton and the East London Whole School Project based in Tower Hamlets and Hackney. The major aim of these projects was to work with schools in an attempt to ensure that

the cultural base of a successful school is compatible with the cultural base of the community it serves. The entire school (becomes) involved in exploring changes in curriculum and organization designed to foster a growth in self and mutual identity amongst all the pupils.[23]

A second example links with the third objective of the document, namely, closer liaison between the ethnic minorities and the local authority. Many ethnic minorities have expressed their disenchantment with the school system by setting up and running a whole range of supplementary schools. These fall into three main groups, namely, those concerned with mother-tongue maintenance, those with religion and those with basic education. The latter group in particular are a direct criticism of the failure of the school system to meet the educational needs of ethnic minority children. In an attempt to open the channels of communication between the supplementary schools and the ILEA, the latter have helped to fund ten such language-based supplementary schools and ten dealing with basic educational skills.[24]

The question of liaison has generally proved a difficult one for the ILEA, for a variety of reasons. Knowing whom to consult is one problem. In addition, there is the feeling among some people that established channels are adequate and any extension would give ethnic minority groups special privileges. It is as a consequence of this that the fourth major objective, relating to support of the 1976 Race Relations Act, has also met with some difficulties.

To give the full list of initiatives that were undertaken as a result of this policy commitment would be beyond the scope of this present chapter. A fuller analysis is needed and would be a most useful document, particularly if it chronicled both the successes and the failures. It is to be hoped that the ILEA will encourage such an analysis.

The general conclusion that can be drawn from the ILEA example is that although a public commitment to multi-ethnic education is an essential first step, it is only the beginning. The problems of racism do not go away as a result of making a public statement opposing it. What this document has done is to bring the issue into the open, so that the public debate on the issues is widened and publicized. It has consequently become more difficult for people opposed to any idea other than that of crude assimilation to go quietly on their way as they have done in the past.[25]

NATIONAL RESPONSES: THE SCHOOLS COUNCIL AND THE TEACHER UNIONS

Having discussed how the DES and a particular LEA have responded to the challenges of racism and education, it may be useful to examine other national initiatives before moving to the level of the individual school and classroom.

The last 15 years have seen a series of initiatives at national level to deal with the issue of race. The most important of these have been the curriculum projects emanating from the Schools Council, the efforts of the teacher unions, and the influence of a major national pressure group, NAME. The influence of NAME has been more general than specific, acting as a pressure group or body of informed opinion which other agencies have consulted. The teacher unions have acted in a similar manner. The response of the various unions has, however, differed greatly, ranging from apathy to a reasonable degree of commitment, though even this latter stand has varied within the same union. The NUT has attempted to follow a coherent and systematic line in recent years partly in response to pressure from local branches, especially those located in multiracial areas.

The result of this pressure, particularly in the middle and late 70s, was a series of documents on multiracial education from the various unions, notably the NUT and the National Association of Teachers in Further and Higher Education (NATFHE).

'All our Children', produced for the 1978 NUT Conference, gives an account of the NUT's contributions to multiracial education. It is the voice of those who have been

... pressing for action in the area of multiracial education for many years.[26]

Successive Conference resolutions on racialism have reaffirmed a positive view of teachers helping to develop 'a harmonious multiracial society', called for positive discrimination in the form of increased resources and for a strengthening of the Race Relations Act. This continues a history dating back to 1968 in which the NUT has shown an unwillingness to consider, in any depth, factors in schooling, the curriculum and the attitudes of teachers, which might contribute to black students' educational difficulties. Blame is laid firmly at the door of the government, in not providing sufficient resources for well-intentioned teachers, and on the growth of racist activity in society at large.

Of the documents prepared in this period perhaps the most controversial was that on race and intelligence produced for the NUT by Stephen Rose of the Open University.[27] It had the dubious honour of being criticized in a *Daily Telegraph* leader, but it provided in a clear manner the research evidence regarding the various claims about the links between race and intelligence. It was distributed free to members of the union and was an influential document in many staffroom debates.

The major initiatives in this area were undertaken by the Schools Council, with the support of teacher unions, the DES and NAME. Three projects in particular deserve closer attention: the Humanities Curriculum Project (HCP); the Education for a Multiracial Society Project (EMS); and the Studies in the Multi-ethnic Curriculum Project (SMC). These three display quite clearly the ambiguity that has often been shown by those in control of the educational system towards the area of race and education.

The Humanities Curriculum Project, led by Lawrence Stenhouse, ran from 1972 to 1976. Its emphasis on the teacher as a neutral chairperson was considered controversial, as were the major themes that the project introduced into the classroom. It was the last theme, race, that finally united the opposition; complaints, including those from the NUT, ensured that that particular pack was never adopted. In the mid seventies Stenhouse went on to do further research on teaching about race relations but interest was never very strong, perhaps because of all the initial adverse publicity.[28] However, the later work did show that using the pack, with either a neutral chairperson or with directive teaching did actually influence favourably the racial attitudes of a significant number of the children involved. A national association of teachers and other people interested in this work was set up, called NARTAR, and the dissemination and development work continues, albeit on a minor scale.

There was criticism of the Schools Council and the NUT for their rejection of the Stenhouse material. Partly in response to this criticism and pressure, the NUT helped to sponsor a second project organized by the NFER called, Education for a Multiracial

Society, which ran from 1972 to 1976. Problems over the direction of the project were finally brought to a head when the draft report of the project team was rejected by the Schools Council. Again the major opposition came from the teacher union representatives, including the NUT, who said the report was too critical of teachers and too polemical in its style. Leaked extracts were published in both the *Times Educational Supplement*[29] and *New Society*[30] and a reading of them was a revealing insight into what was considered 'too critical of teachers' in the area of race. They merely stated in a clear fashion what many teachers in multiracial schools perceived as being the reality.

Neither the report, nor its equally important evaluation report have as yet been published, despite efforts to produce an acceptable final draft. It is likely that 'acceptable' means a considerable watering down and even distortion of the findings of the original report. To many teachers and members of minority communities, this reluctance to publish was a confirmation of the belief that the issues of race were difficult, if not impossible, to investigate and report on unless areas like racism *within* school were ignored.

The unions, particularly the NUT, were placed in a difficult position by this public fight over the report. They were concerned about this issue, or claimed that they were, but had been seen to be acting in a reactionary and obstructive manner in two major Schools Council projects. Their solution was to set up another project, but this time ensuring that it investigated only the non-controversial areas. Consequently, the Studies in the Multi-ethnic Curriculum project was set up in 1978. The project, under Professor Alan Little, was basically an updating of the earlier pioneering work of Townsend and Brittan[31]. The message that emerges seems only too obvious: head-counting and similar exercises are acceptable, but investigation into the realities of racism within education is not.[32]

TEACHERS AND RACISM

Turning now to the schools and those who teach in them we find that 'multicultural' and/or 'anti-racist' initiatives are framed and put into practice in the context of a teaching profession which is predominantly conservative.[33] As at other levels in the education system, there are many who are unwilling often because they see no need to undertake any re-examination of the curriculum and schooling in the light of either those factors which Alan James identifies as forming 'multicultural' philosophy and practice:

> . . . that diversity of lifestyle, beliefs and cultural traditions which post-war immigration has brought to our country;[34]

> . . . the need to prepare all children for life in a society where such diversity is functional, a source of social energy and a richer life;[35]

or in the face of overt and covert racism.

Such conservatism is most crucially found at policy-making levels in many inner-city schools influencing the content of the curriculum shaping the school's structures making 'public' pronouncements to assemblies and to parents, and informing decisions on how to deal with students who pose difficulties for the smooth running of the school. It manifests itself in the provision of courses which cut off the students who participate in them from the mainstream expectations of the school and society and in the evolution of strategies for keeping 'problem' students out of the classroom. The widespread use of exclusion and suspension and disruptive units, which have recently been brought into play as methods of control,[36] have by no means supplanted the subtler methods: 'guided' option choice, long-term exclusion from lessons, teacher-condoned truancy, referral to educational psychologists and transference to special schools.[37] The drift of this thinking and its accompanying practices has been reinforced by mainstream Tory policies on law and order, immigration and nationality on the one hand, and by the fears generated by cuts and falling rolls on the other.

There are, however, large numbers of broadly liberal/progressive teachers who have modified their practice in response to their experience of linguistic and cultural diversity in the classroom and who have regarded the school as having an important contribution to make to harmonious race relations. They have accepted the need for changes both in the curriculum and in aspects of school organization which work to the disadvantage of black students.

Although such teachers sometimes act from different assumptions in different situations, most of this large group can be said to have progressed from regarding immigrants as a 'problem' needing particular measures to enable them to fit into English schools and society to a view which sees the recognition of diversity as of positive benefit and relevance to *all* students in our schools. At their most energetic they have worked assiduously through their stockrooms checking existing materials for negative images and stances, sought more positive textbooks, designed new courses and rewritten sections of existing ones. Their thinking has both contributed to, and been influenced by, LEAs and the DES. They have thus been engaged in curriculum change in a period remarkable for a general flight away from any kind of innovation. They have, generally, been against the cruder forms of streaming and some have seen mixed ability and a response to diversity as being essentially interlinked.

However, most have stopped far short of an analysis which takes a critical look at the system in which schooling is located, and it has been argued forcefully by Hazel Carby that, by espousing multiculturalism *uncritically*, teachers have acquiesced to an emerging educational strategy for the 1980s which,

> . . . is apparently to win consent in the classroom and if and when that fails, to bring coercion into play: and increasingly it is black students who are subjected to coercive strategies.[38]

As Carby points out, the weakness in the current versions of 'multiculturalism' lies in the location of what might otherwise be positive practices in a context of discipline and control.

> The purpose of educational policies is thus to promote tolerance between social groups and so produce a society displaying an equilibrium among ethnic groupings and between classes. The school is made a site for containing the effects of racism.[39]

From this viewpoint, even the most well-intentioned multicultural initiatives can be seen then as functioning as a means of defusing difficult inner-city school situations[40] and as an attempt to pacify a black community beginning to be more vocal in criticizing the educational provision made for its children.

> The paradigm of multiculturalism actually excludes the concept of dominant and subordinate cultures—either indigenous or migrant—and fails to recognize that the existence of racism relates to the possession and exercise of politico-economic control and authority and also to forms of resistance to the power of dominant social groups.[41]

The Organization of Women of Asian and African Descent, similarly, sees racism, institutionalized in schooling, as at the heart of the maintenance of existing power relations in Britain,

> Through the whole process of school, the system is designed to make Black people uncritical, passive, insecure and unable to challenge the system that wants us to take the worst jobs.[42]

It may have been the reluctance of teachers to recognize the role of the school in the perpetuation of racism which ensured that until about 1977/78[43] there was hardly any use by teachers of the word racism and that it is still used, somewhat uncomfortably, usually with reference to incidents on the street or things said by students or politicians. Even now, only a few teachers use the term both to refer to these surface manifestations of racism, and as a means of defining the ways in which the exploitation of people on the basis of their country of origin and/or colour is woven into Britain's past and present,[44] shaping its values[45] and institutions.[46] Preferring to think of themselves as tolerant and liberal and able to inspire these qualities in their students, teachers find the idea that racism, institutionalized in schools as elsewhere in society, is necessary for the maintenance of existing power relations sits uneasily with their image of themselves and their role in society. Such territory is considered dangerously 'political' so that even some of those who care about social justice draw back from the consequences of getting to the root causes of white racism and the inequality it helps to maintain. In this, these teachers are at one with the wider society which, even though it may be willing to acknowledge other cultures, has not shown any intention of changing the existing power relations between the groups concerned.[47]

There remains a minority of teachers who have adopted a stance which is 'oppositional' in that it challenges the definitions and practices of mainstream society. They have regarded multiculturalism as providing a space[48] in which an analysis might be developed which was capable of tackling race, gender and class, and which does not stop short of considering the relationships of teacher and taught to each other and to society generally.[49] They recognize that education functions as part of society but do not believe that education should be expected to produce conformity to dominant values or to defuse the problems created by unequal power relations. If students are to become critically aware and autonomous, it is argued, they must know how they themselves and their schooling relate to society and the racism that underpins it,

> if one really knows one's place, one knows and understands how it comes to be, and how it might be otherwise.[50]

Racism in school and society is seen as something which can and ought to be taken on jointly by teachers, parents and students, but which, in the end, can only be eradicated through structural changes in society since,

> ... diverse cultural groups co-existing in a harmonious atmosphere of mutual tolerance cannot be a reality when the chances in life of members of cultural minorities—and of many of their neighbours in the inner-city areas—are limited by inequality in wealth and access to power.[51]

In adopting an 'oppositional' stance in school and classroom, these teachers have located themselves within the framework of a general critique of progressivism which seeks to exclude those practices which operate against the interests of working-class students while building on those which offer students both 'competence in society' and 'the skills and knowledge they will need to change it'.[52]

In the inner-city schools in which most of them teach, these teachers have been made aware that it is not black students who constitute a problem but the white racism that black students encounter. They have learned from their students how acutely they feel the racist oppression of a whole society which is taking a move to the right and delivering a clear message that, particularly in times of recession, schools, employers, the police and the laws of the country work against those who are identifiable by the colour of their skin.

They have also begun to recognize that challenges to teacher authority in the classroom (like the challenge to LEA provision through the setting up of supplementary schools) must be seen as part of an inevitable black resistance to institutionalized racism. This development of teacher consciousness has been brought about by the students and their parents as exemplified in this statement by OWAAD:

> The children themselves have resisted the attempts to be brainwashed, stereo-typed, classified, and controlled. They refuse to sit quietly and have their roles defined for them.[53]

It is, of course, difficult for teachers to come to terms with the implicit or explicit hostility of their students. Oppositional teaching offers a partial resolution of this dilemma by focusing on ways of developing a student's critical framework without diminishing his or her anger at injustice. Teachers who have adopted this stance largely agree with Farrukh Dhondy that the antagonisms in society should not be covered up but be at the centre of an honest education. They differ from him in being marginally more optimistic about the possiblity of being allowed, or appropriating, space in the classroom for starting from the facts of conflicting interests,

> that young blacks fight the police, they refuse dirty jobs; their forms of culture gathering always bring them into conflict with the rulers of this society, their very music, professed philosophies and life-styles, contain in them an antagonism to school and to society as it is.[54]

Equally important as the lessons that these teachers have learned from black resistance are those that they have learned in their dealings with their white, inner-city students. Especially in areas where fears of recession and unemployment have taken firmest hold, though by no means only there, racism, as was suggested earlier, has been visibly increasing in the classroom and playground. Its expression varies according to what is thought possible with any individual teacher but it has become quite common for teachers to be criticized and persecuted by young white racists for favouring 'the blacks'[55] or to have racially obscene written work given in by students who know that their parents will be sympathetic to their behaviour. As on buses and in train compartments, graffiti on exercise books proclaim allegiance to the slogans and emblems of the National Front alongside allegiance to Chelsea or Millwall.[56] In fact, because the racism of white working-class students is enmeshed in peer group networks and activities and in the deep-seated insecurities of individual students, it has presented radical teachers with some serious challenges to their theory and practice. This is especially true for those who have seen building on the experiences and culture that students bring to the classroom as a key factor governing the choice of lesson content and activities.

On the other hand, the same teachers have also become aware in recent years of the anti-racist potential of school students: black students who confidently and articulately unpick the conscious, and unconscious, racist statements of white students; black and white students who have come together in huge gestures of solidarity such as the anti-racist rallies to Victoria and Brockwell Parks; and white students who have learned enough from such involvements want to make some space in school for their anti-racism.[57]

TACKLING RACISM IN SCHOOLS AND CLASSROOMS

In order to find examples of what teachers have done in schools and classrooms, it is necessary to draw mainly, though not exclusively, on initiatives set in motion by the group of teachers whose stance has been described as 'oppositional'. The publication in 1977 of the National Front magazine *Bulldog* and the document 'How to spot a Red Teacher' can be seen as triggering a period of intensive activity by teachers to combat racism both within the schools themselves and on an interschool level. As a result, some alliances were made with parents and groups within the labour movement with whom teachers do not regularly come into close contact, and some of the initiatives made substantial inroads into the 'middle ground' of teachers who, in the context of the National Front at their own school gates, became willing to make a harder analysis of the role that racism plays in society. Some of the initiatives foundered within a year or so: others have had a much greater staying power.

Certain questions had to be answered: What should be done about the people distributing leaflets outside the school? What should be done about the National Front literature brought into school? Should the National Front be allowed to use the school building for meetings? What should be done to show the students—white as well as black—that the school opposed racist thinking of all kinds? What should be taught that wasn't already being taught—and how?

Because of the very specific nature of these questions, the driving force for joint local and national anti-racist teacher activity came from the schools themselves. The policies that were evolved were established first at the school level and then spread through the means of local NUT associations and publications such as *Issues* rather than being initiated from above.

A well published example, but one which has similarities with school initiatives scattered much more widely, is the policy 'Fighting racialism in school' which was adopted by Holloway School in the ILEA. In this document the school sees itself as counteracting the racist poison of the National Front. As a harmonious multiracial school they say:

Our very existence spits in the eye of the National Front and their avowed aim of forcing black people out of the country.

They then set out some of their aims,

We should undertake a campaign of education in assemblies, in lessons and during form periods. Such a campaign should seek to achieve the following:

(a) Impress upon pupils that discrimination against people because of the colour of their skin or origin is wrong.
(b) Explain why black people, Cypriots and Asians have a right to live in this country. This is particularly important because of the numerous myths that are perpetuated about immigration.
(c) Prevent any racialist abuse occurring inside the school wherever we possibly can. For example, if epithets like 'coon', 'nigger', 'wog', 'yid' or 'paki' are heard, they should not go unchallenged. We should explain why they are offensive and prevent them from becoming common currency inside the school. . . If any racialist literature appears or is circulated in school it should be confiscated. . .[58]

The head of Holloway three years later, and despite having encountered some hostility to the school's policy, makes the position the school has adopted very clear,

we have to make a choice: do we ignore the problem of racism and racialist organizations and hope they will disappear, or do we as a multiracial school take a principled stand against them? The same dilemma presented itself to the German people in the early 1930s and they took the former course with disastrous consequences. We cannot afford the same mistake.[59]

Beyond these responses to the immediate situation, many schools adopted policies which seek to affect the whole ethos of the school and take on racism within the curriculum and school organization. A model resolution drawn up for use in school NUT meetings was widely used in London.

That this Association adopt the following as guidelines for its members:

1. To discourage as strongly as possible the myths and stereotypes on which prejudice and hatred feed;
2. To adopt curricula that accurately reflect contributions which civilizations and people from outside Western Europe have made to world history, and which present in a positive light the culture and background of those minority groups which form an integral part of our society;
3. To examine critically the books and other learning materials used in schools and to guard against those which are racially biased;

4. To look closely at the systems of selection and streaming and pattern of organization in schools for evidence of discrimination (intentional or unintentional) against minority groups.[60]

In all cases, success has depended on the establishment and maintenance of long-term committees that either have power to make changes or can continue to exert pressure on all aspects of school life. Such committees are neither common nor popular and few schools can claim to have whole school policies which have permeated the thinking of the teachers to such an extent that such groups are no longer needed.

The description that follows shows how by 1981 a school in North London has evolved a complex response to racism. This is part of a dossier of racist incidents relating to schools in the process of compilation by ALTARF though here it is being used as an example of a coherent anti-racist school policy:

SCHOOL—8 Form Entry Secondary School
AREA—Residential North London
Our school has a reasonably good record for taking positive measures to construct a multicultural curriculum. There has been a school working party which has held discussions and published various documents. In the last year, however, several developments have forced the school to face the need for a clear policy on specifically racist behaviour. There has been a general increase in the activities of fascist groups in the area; one of our fifth year Asian students was knifed out of school by skinheads; NF and BM graffiti and stickers began appearing in school and there seemed to be a rise in overt racial abuse. In the wake of these events the school produced a policy document on racist behaviour which included the following points:

(a) the school should state clearly and unequivocally its anti-racist position to students, parents and the community;
(b) records of *all* incidents should be logged;
(c) teachers should make their anti-racist position clear to students at all times. This should include assemblies;
(d) students should be involved in a discussion on the implications of such incidents. Purely disciplinary measures are inadequate;
(e) distinctions should be made between hard-core racists, those on the periphery, and 'unintentional' racists;
(f) efforts should be made to engage students in the political/economic causes of racism.

The effectiveness of this policy is being monitored by the working party. Racist incidents generally inside school have decreased. However, the 'hard-core' racists now confine their activities to outside school, as was evident by their presence on the BM march in the area last November. At our school, a motion was passed deploring the decision to let the march go ahead and the school made it clear to pupils, community and parents of our anti-racist stand. The Head reaffirmed the school's anti-racist policy in all assemblies and social education lessons followed, allowing students to explore the issues raised by the march. Letters were also sent home to parents stressing the concern of the school about the march and asking them to support our policy. Local press was contacted in order to publicize the views of the school.[60]

The 1978 ALTARF rally, which brought together 2500 teachers across a broad spectrum of opinion, did a considerable amount to give those who attended a sense of commitment and mobilization in the task of countering racism. It can be seen as drawing strength from a whole interrelated pattern of anti-racist, anti-fascist campaigns of that time and by seeking the support of local NUT associations, trades councils and gaining the wholehearted support of London NAME and other professional and political groups, ALTARF can claim to have made a major impact[61] on the London education scene. This was achieved by focusing teachers on an understanding of the structures and operations of racism in society which went a long way beyond their previous assumptions and by calling on them to take action against all forms of racism, specifically with respect to achieving effective anti-racist policies in all educational establishments and within the NUT but, more generally, to work with all organizations and groups, including school students who shared their analysis and concerns.

A parallel example of the hardening of teacher thinking can be found in *Issues,* as is evidenced by this quotation from *Issues,* 15, where the concerns of ALTARF, and incidentally of *Issues* itself, are distinguished from those of NAME.

NAME is a national organization, with about 800 members, a quarter of them in London. It concentrates on ways in which the schools and other educational institutions can meet the needs of all their students—by curriculum innovation; by establishing non-racist organizational practices within the school; by changing teachers' attitudes. But *Issues* has always taken the view that work within the school or the education system is not enough—it will not eradicate the schools' failure to give minority group students an equal education, because that failure is *endemic in a racist society.* So we have also tried to highlight issues on which parents, teachers and students can take action in the wider society—our racist immigration laws: the coming nationality laws; the NF's propaganda and their use of schools during elections etc.[62]

As a result of the activities of the post-1977 period, an appreciable amount of material has become available for teachers who wish to explore with their students alternatives to the political explanations found in existing textbooks and materials. Committed teachers are modifying this new material[63] to their needs and developing their own. On the other hand, there are very few statements available in which teachers have been prepared to say what they do in the classroom.

A notable exception has emanated from the work of the ALTARF workshops since the 1978 Rally; particularly the discussion document 'Teaching and Racism'[64] the preface to the first edition of which (December 1978) is a forthright statement of how they see themselves in relation to both the wider society and the classroom,

We do not believe that an anti-racist struggle can, for teachers, be confined to areas of the curriculum. Indeed ALTARF has held a majority of its meetings during the past year on areas outside the curriculum: on subjects such as the 'Sus' laws, the NF use of schools and discrimination against black teachers, for example. Cultural struggle cannot substitute itself for the fight against injustice and material inequality. But we do believe that in a way that manifests itself more immediately in some areas of the curriculum than others, our work as teachers in the classroom compels us to take sides on social and political questions.[65]

Clara Mulhern puts the position even more strongly in relation to what kind of activity should happen in the classroom. Talking of Tankits 1 and the Thames TV series 'Our People', she argues that they inevitably bring politics into the classroom and that

> The right to have open political discussion in the classroom, on racism or any other 'sensitive' issue, will have to be fought for by teachers and students.[66]

She does not, however, mean by 'open political discussion' the 'openness' of Robert Jeffcoate in *Positive Image*.[67] Rather, she appears to be arguing for the freedom of teachers to provide 'oppositional' political explanations. Of Tankits 1 and 'Our People' she continues,

> The really dangerous element in them is that they present a challenge to orthodox political explanations. The fact is that information about the true role of the immigrant communities fits uneasily into the political consensus . . . When un-assimilable 'facts' are submerged or repressed, the mere truth can appear danger-ously explosive.[68]

The ALTARF Secondary Workshop does not concede that what constitutes 'worth-while' knowledge has been determined once and for always in terms of the mainstream culture and, interestingly, it is a non-teacher, Alan Horrox, writing about the Thames TV 'Our People' series which he and Gillian McCredie produced, who puts the case for alternative content most strongly. He argues that one way to tackle the prevalent myths of black inferiority and British tolerance and humanity which underpin 'the great deal that people *do* know about race' is with 'facts'.

> So, the 'Our People' programmes counter them [the assumptions] with factual information from historical sources, from official statistics and from people's personal experience. The programmes also examine the institutional racism of the immigration laws: discrimination in employment, housing, education, the law; the history of Europe's colonisation of other countries right up to the post-war period when Europe called for immigrant labour from its colonies and from the Mediter-ranean; and the growing wave of racism and violent racist attacks and the struggle of anti-racist groups to oppose this process.[69]

The programmes make problematic the formation and production of 'facts' from within people's sets of values and assumptions. Horrox declares that there are criticisms to be made that the programmes[70] are not hard enough in their analysis. For instance, the history of slavery and colonization should give greater place to resistance so that there is no possibility of the process being seen as 'passive or inevitable'; the programme on racist attacks failed to locate them firmly enough in the context of inner-city decay, the pattern of institutional racism in employment, housing, education and policing, the influence of politicians and the impact of a medium which condones and reproduces the element of racism in British society. He also admits to having failed to confront under-development, the process by which the European countries of the past became with independence the neo-colonies of the ever growing multi-national giants, which today dwarf even the ex-colonisers. What is needed is an explanation of how neo-colonialism maintains and reproduces precisely the conditions of poverty, unemployment and under-development which drive people to abandon their own countries and to emigrate.[71]

It is unsurprising that the series, even without these elements, has been seen as a threat to the 'due impartiality' expected of educational television.

The parallels between the producer deciding on appropriate content and a stance to it and the individual classroom teacher are obvious. Teachers in the classroom are similarly in the firing line if they

> depart from and argue against those usual perspectives in a way that could never be described as impartial.[72]

However, it would be wrong to conclude, as the critics of 'Our People' no doubt do, that what is being argued for in these papers is the teaching of a particular political theory. What the writers primarily have in common is an interest in more comprehensive explanations than the established orthodoxies.

Jan Pollock, writing on history teaching, for example, argues for something that goes beyond and is more vigorous than mere changes in content. She does, of course, note the 'absences' from the text books and suggests that topics like Ancient Roman History can and should be studied as a means of understanding imperialism and neo-imperialism, and the nature of a slave and colonial economy. But her main argument is for a 'critical reading' of history. In her words,

> An ability to read critically is part of an understanding of history. Thus to teach in an anti-racist way requires the real development of the historian's skills on the part of both the teacher and the taught.[73]

There is no watering down of the curriculum here. Not that O-Level syllabuses, and their like, place more emphasis on understanding than content, but there seems little likelihood of teachers who adopt this position selling examination candidates short. There could even be the side benefit of students being able to locate the examination system itself in terms of its functions and history.

The paper on geography teaching by Chris Kelly has good examples of how important the 'quality of explanation' is,

> ... because developing countries are primarily in tropical regions, under-development and poverty may be seen as being due to climatic and environmental factors. Thus, one series still selling thousands of copies annually, reveals that progress is made difficult because the human brain does not work at its best where the air is always hot and moist and that *even* English men find it a strain to think hard for more than a few hours a day.[74]

This highlights the need for a recognition that contrasts in development need detailed explanations and that if they are not given directly by the teacher, the students will draw their own conclusions from the way the subject matter is presented inside the classroom (and outside through the mass media).

Liz Lindsay takes up the same theme in writing about science teaching.

Science/Biology should not be regarded as a subject in which students are required to memorise what one particular textbook writer would have them believe are undisputed facts.[75]

Her case is that

Science attempts to socialise students to interpret reality in a particular way and the nominally scientific approach is likely to be accepted as the truth.[76]

Using examples from human biology, evolution, genetics and nutrition, she argues her case for fuller explanations. For example,

Two topics in most Biology syllabuses, Nutrition and Disease, are often treated by textbooks in a distorted and patronising way with respect to Third World countries. The 'scientific analysis' of nutrition and disease resulting from malnutrition is done in a reductionist [way] and/or within a particular framework excluding the major political, economic and social factors involved. Most textbooks like Nuffield Biology consider these problems can be solved by more doctors, better birth control policies, more international aid, and by increasing production and producing more crops. Susan George asks 'increasing production for whom?'. Nuffield Biology acknowledges that foreign investment has resulted in the enrichment of a small local elite, but overlooks the fact that it is the foreign investors who have been and are being most handsomely enriched by their exploitation of the Third World countries whose workers must produce for export at starvation wages, cheap minerals and cash crops, the latter often monopolising the best land where once people grew their own food.[77]

Echoing Jan Pollock, she concludes,

the ability *to read critically* is as important a skill in science as it is in history.[78]

On the teaching of English, Hilda Kean suggests it is possible to develop an anti-racist stance by pointing up particular issues. She gives an example the way in which a standard text like *Of Mice and Men* by John Steinbeck can be placed in the context of a broadly-based discussion of social relations and unemployment in 1930s California and, she, like many of the contributors, sees the development of critical thinking as a central aim.

It is [therefore] important that we foster an awareness of racist language and concepts so students can look critically at books and the media for themselves.[79]

A further contribution of English teaching by Bob Brett and Irene Payne draws on work that has been developed at Langdon Park School over a number of years and which has been more fully documented than that of most teachers, in particular, in Chris Searle's *The World in a Classroom*,[80] and in a previous article by Bob Brett 'Charcoal and Chalk' in *Teaching London Kids* 11.

In that article, Bob Brett puts forward a set of preconditions for anti-racist teaching:

1. That the orientation of multicultural education, while continuing to recognize the needs of black students, must urgently be turned towards combating racism among white students.
2. That teachers have to grasp the fact that while they can have little effect on the racism of those students whose racism is central to their sense of themselves and who are conscious and committed fascists of long standing, they can have some effect on those whose racism is full of contradictions, who have taken it in as slogans, as part of the atmosphere they breathe, but do not depend on it for their self-image.
3. That the underlying material causes of racism must be understood by the teacher. 'It's no good condemning racism as something not quite nice, a lack of taste or culture, or as some sort of sin of which some unpleasant people are guilty. If we take up a moral attitude we can never understand why kids are racist and so can never come to grips with it.'
4. That the views of anti-racist students have more effect on attitudes than their teacher's can and should be seen as an important resource in classroom activities.

In 'Charcoal and Chalk', Bob Brett raises the issue which he and Irene Payne take to be of central importance in the 'Teaching and Racism' contribution: how do teachers learn how to create the conditions in which 'a long-term process of persuasion' can take place?

New ideas can't be imposed. If you are going to change somebody's opinion then that opinion has first to be in the open.'[81]

In 'Teaching and Racism', they take this thinking a stage further and begin to question their way of handling content—one which seeks to locate exploitation of all kinds in terms of material causes and which seeks far wider ranging explanations in terms of class, race and gender than most English or Social Studies teachers have yet attempted.

We are not rejecting it completely but we feel that a context needs to be created in which the kids are more receptive and more critical in relation to the ideas we are offering.[82]

Their strong reliance on content, on presenting alternative explanations, has itself come to look too much like the confrontation of students' attitudes by teacher authority. So they argue for 'open' debate as part of the development of the student's critical thinking and autonomy, what they term a 'real exchange of views' in a 'relaxed and open relationship'.[83]

In this stance the teacher cannot be seen as neutral or 'laid back'[84] but as having a vital structuring and informative role. It is the teacher's role to work within the space created by students' contradictory attitudes, to make the space in which anti-racist kids can speak out, or, like the girl who wrote the poem 'Charcoal and Chalk' quoted in the TLK article, work out the contradiction between the fact of racism and the fact of her own friendship with black students. It is also clear that, in such open debate on content as they are advocating, the teacher will be able to express forcefully his or her own views.

> So we had to begin by throwing the whole topic open to debate; their racism and our opposition was up for discussion. The previous implict and explicit taboo on expressing racist opinions in our classrooms was now to be open to objection and investigation.[85]

It is a delicate and difficult set of decisions that is required of the teacher and success hangs by the thread of whether the students perceive the situation and their relationship with the teacher in the way the teacher hopes; that is to say, one in which the students' emotional commitment to racism becomes negotiable, one in which, to use Mulhern's terms, the tensions that exist in classroom and society are articulated rather than alleviated.[86]

Like their students, teachers occupy positions in relation to racism which contain contradictions. Those who are most actively engaged in tackling racism in their classrooms, schools and communities are the most acutely conscious of their complicity in grading and containing both black and white working-class students, and of the difficulties they have in living up to their aims of autonomy and critical thinking when they themselves encounter student resistance in the classroom.

It is argued that schools as institutions, and the teachers who work within them, have such a degree of involvement in the racism embedded in the existing framework of social relations that understanding and confronting racism has to take place elsewhere.[87] This argument is challenged by the writers of 'Teaching and Racism' who assert that it is both possible and necessary to use the limited space and resources available in schools and colleges for anti-racist teaching. They place great importance on teachers having high expectations for their students and similarly put stress on a combination of intellectual and social development as key factors in an educational response to racism. They are well aware that programmes of work which expose the inequalities in society are inevitably regarded with suspicion but are determined to enable their students to understand how political power is organized and whose interests are served. This is not, they argue, in order to get over a particular ideology but to ensure that their students receive a balanced education—one which finds explanations for the racism inherent in the present structures of society and helps *all* their students to see how things might be otherwise.

NOTES AND REFERENCES

1. See Tierney, J. Chapter 1; Syer, M. Chapter 4; and Mullard, C. Chapter 6.

2. Hall, S. (1980) Teaching race. *Multiracial Education*, **9**, 1, 13.

3. The editorial of the *TES*, 22.5.1981, commenting on the resignation of Mr Anthony Rampton as chairman of the departmental committee on the education of children of ethnic minorities shortly before the publication of the committee's interim report, notes the differing position within the committee and states its own position:

. . . all along there has been the difficulty of separating the educational issues from those of the larger, social, economic, and political background. In a real sense which everyone can recognize, it is impossible to do justice to the educational issues in isolation. And yet, this is what a committee like this must somehow succeed in doing, if it is to be any use to anybody—broad, generalized, sentiments about socio-political questions will cut no ice with the government; they may even obscure more limited and specific proposals for positive action which the committee in its wisdom may seek to pass on.

4. Little, A. and Willey, R. (1981) *Multi-ethnic Education: The Way Forward*, Schools Council Pamphlet 18.

5. This is also true of the provision made and the expectations set for other groups in schooling: girls, working-class students etc., c.f. Spender, D. and Sarah, E. (1980) *Learning to Lose.* London: Womens Press.

6. DES. (1981) *West Indian Children in Our Schools.* (The Rampton Report) London: HMSO.

7. Attention was drawn to such forms of institutionalized racism by Coard, B. (1971) *How the West Indian Child is Made Educationally Sub-normal in the British School System,* and again by Redbridge CRC (1978) *Cause for Concern.* More recently, the Organization of Women of Asian and African Descent has pointed to the widespread abuses which they see as persisting,

   If there are no sin-bins black children are frequently suspended from school. This often happens in the 5th year, just before they are due to take their final exams. Many schools will get rid of pupils on the quiet (a couple of months before they are due to leave). They thus avoid the prescribed suspension procedures and keep the official figures down. OWAAD (1980) *Black Women in Britain Speak Out,* p. 7.

8. For an analysis of the doubled-edged nature of this directive see Brook, M. (1980) The 'mother tongue' issue in Britain: Cultural Diversity or Control. *British Journal of Sociology of Education,* **1,** 3.

9. DES (1981) *The School Curriculum.* London: HMSO. This follow-up to *A Framework for the Curriculum* states clearly that the government does not intend to take statutory powers in relation to the curriculum and re-states the principle of DES–LEA partnership.

10. Hall, S. (1974) Education and the crisis of the urban school. E351 *Urban Education,* Block 1. Milton Keynes: Open University Press.

11. For further information on Boyles' visit to Southall in 1963 and the later Circular 7/65 see Power, J. (1967) *Immigrants in Schools.* Councils and Education Press. Also see Hiro, D. (1973) *Black British, White British*, pp. 68–70. London: Penguin.

12. The Centre for Educational Disadvantage was closed down in 1980 as part of the governmental quango extermination policy.

13. For example, see the findings in Community Relations Commission (1976) *Funding Multi-racial Education: A National Survey.* London: Community Relations Commission.

14. The NUT has produced two statements on Section 11: NUT (1978) *Section 11—An NUT Report;* NUT (1979) *Replacing Section 11—An NUT Commentary.*

15. Select Committee on Race Relations and Immigration (1977) *The West Indian Community,* Vol. 1, Report Session 1976–1977 London: HMSO.

16. See for example Bolton, E. (1979) in *Trends in Education*—4. London: HMSO.

17. It will be clear in this example, as in many which follow, that we have drawn on London experience. This is not because we undervalue initiatives elsewhere but because the LEAs (and teacher initiatives) with which we are familiar are located in the South East and we believed it necessary to give substance to our arguments as far as possible by means of concrete examples. We hope that, in drawing on what we know, we do not give rise to a view that all important initiatives in response to racism emanate from London. This would be false and deny the importance of work being done to fight racism in many other urban centres and individual schools.

18. ILEA (1977) *Multiethnic Education.* Joint report of the Schools Sub-Committee and the Further and Higher Education Sub-Committee presented to the Education Committee on 8 November 1977.
    ILEA (1979) *Multiethnic Education—Progress Report.* Joint report of the Schools Sub-Committee, the Further and Higher Education Sub-Committee and the Staff and General Sub-Committee presented to the Education Committee on 12 June 1979. London.

19. See Chapter 7.

20. ILEA (1977) *op. cit.,* p. 4.

21. For example, Banks, J. (1981) *Multiethnic Education: Theory and Practice*. London: Allyn & Bacon. See particularly Chapter 5.

22. Camden CCR has demanded that the ILEA:

    —issue a specifically anti-racist statement;
    —urge heads to issue anti-racist statements;
    —require heads to report all racist attacks to County Hall;
    —provide in-service training which focuses on methods of countering racism.

    See *Issues in Race and Education*, No. 26, May/June 1980; No. 31 March/April 1981.

23. ILEA (1977) *op. cit.,* p. 3.

24. To give some idea of the range of these, the approved mother tongue schemes for 1978/79 included classes in Turkish, Bengali, Punjabi, Urdu, Gujarati, Hindi, Greek and Chinese.

25. Another example of an LEA focusing attention for all teachers in all schools can be found in 1978 in the London Borough of Haringey which produced a document on racism in schools and how it should be dealt with that was given to all teachers in the borough. It dealt principally with acts of overt racism within and near school premises.

26. NUT (1978) *All Our Children*, pp. 2–3. This document gives the developing history of NUT responses by quotation from its submissions to various enquiries. It reads as if the Executive is struggling to keep up with Conference pressure; busily realigning existing policies but this is perhaps an unfair comment since the section 'Extremist Groups' includes a commitment 'to oppose racialism in all its forms, at national and local level,' p. 15. The recommendations for teacher action are, however, extremely limited; encouraging open discussion, championing the cause of social justice for all their students, education for co-operation along with competition, and working in harmony with the home and community. This was certainly a far weaker programme than many local associations had hoped for.
    A follow-up to the section 'Textbooks in schools' in NUT (1979) *In Black and White—Guidelines for Teachers on Racial Stereotyping in Textbooks and Learning Materials*, is in sterner vein:

Do not pass over or ignore a racist concept or cliché in a textbook; if you have decided to use the book, point out its inadequacies and false assumptions and use it to stimulate discussion.
Check that books do not either by text or illustration reinforce the image of a power structure in which white people have all the power and make all the decisions, with ethnic minorities functioning in subservient roles . . . (p. 9).

27. NUT (1978) *Race, Education and Intelligence: A Teachers' Guide to Facts and the Issues*. The clarity of the argument and the aggressive stance can be seen in the following quotation.

No new scientific evidence has been adduced since 1951 to challenge this conclusion. Authors of popular books designed to 'prove' racial differences and the propagandists of extremist racist groups, such as the National Front, are forced to dig back into the long-discredited 'research' of the 1920s and 1930s to support their claims. What has happened is that over the last decade of economic stagnation, inflation and rising unemployment, racist groups have attempted to play on the cultural differences between ethnic groups in Britain to foster racist thinking and attitudes, to 'blame' immigrants and the Indian subcontinent for the problems of British society. Racism dressed up in pseudo-scientific clothes, even when it attempts to look respectable by quoting apparent 'scientific authority', remains racism and should be combated today in our schools. Teachers, especially those in schools with significant numbers of ethnic minority children but also those in largely 'white' schools, have a particular role and responsibility in this context (pp. 14–15).

28. Stenhouse, L. (1975) *An Introduction to Curriculum Research*, Chapter 9, pp. 123–132. London: Heinemann.

29. *TES*, 24.2.78.

30. *New Society*, 16.2.78.

31. Townsend, H. E. R. (1971) *Immigrant Pupils in England: The LEA Response*. Windsor. NFER.
Townsend, H. E. R. and Brittan, E. M. (1972) *Organization in Multiracial Schools*, Windsor. NFER.
Townsend, H. E. R. and Brittan, E. M. (1973) *Multiracial Education: Need and Innovation*. London: Evans/Methuen Educational, Schools Council Working Paper 50.

32. Since the Schools Council Education for a Multiracial Society Project was not extended to methods and materials, to all-white schools, or to whole school policies as was at one stage envisaged, it will be noted that there is a very substantial gap at the level where research and policy might be expected to inform practice.

33. Cretton, J. (1975) Teachers in the British General Election of October 1974: A Report on a Survey carried out by NLP on behalf of the *THES*, Times Newspapers.

34. James, A. (1979) The Multicultural Curriculum. *New Approaches in Multiracial Education*, **8**, 1.

35. *Ibid*.

36. See for both monitoring of this development and a critique, *Issues in Race Education* Nos. 19 & 22, 1979; & no. 26, 1980. Suspended—A True Story. *Teaching London Kids*, 15.

37. See note 7 above.

38. Carby, H. (1980) Multiculture. *Screen Education*, 34, Society for Education in Film and Television. London. SEFT.

39. *Ibid*., p. 63.

40. Sometimes this 'defusing' is seen as of central pedagogic importance. A discussion document produced for the National Association for the Teaching of English argues that it is preferable to tackle racism through such means as the study of literature and the discussion of issues 'a little removed from ourselves' in a classroom context 'where there is a history of calm talking-things-over' rather than attacking it 'head-on'.
    The success that such tactics have in removing conflict from the classroom is achieved, as the document acknowledges, by playing down 'the suggestion that the phenomenon of racism is an aspect of working-class struggle against capitalist pressures' and thus reducing the likelihood that students will find themselves considering the conflicting interests and contradictions of the society they live in. N.A.T.E. (1979) The teaching of English in multicultural Britain; J. Goody, (1977) Classroom interaction in the multiracial school, *English in Education*.

41. Carby, H. (1980) *op. cit*., p. 64.

42. Organization of Women of Asian and African Descent (1980) *op. cit*., p. 7.

43. It is at this time that National Front activity aimed at influencing school students—leafletting, the publication of *Bulldog*—together with increased National Front use of schools for election meetings etc., obliged teachers to talk about and take action on the racism on their doorstep.

44. See Williams, E. (1964) *Capitalism and Slavery*. London: Deutsch.
    Rodney, W. 1972 *How Europe Underdeveloped Africa*. London: Bogle-L'Ouverture Publications.
    Sivanandan, A. (1980) *Imperialism in the Silicon Age*. London: Institute of Race Relations.

45. See: Rose, S., Richardson, K., Rose, S. *et al.* (1978) *Race, Education, Intelligence*. London: NUT.
    Emler, N. and Heather, N. (1980) Intelligence: and ideological bias of conventional psychology. In Salmon, P. (Ed.) *Coming to Know*, London: RKP.

46. See OWAAD (1980) *op. cit.* CIS *Racism, Who Profits?* (Anti-Report 16). London: Counter Information Services.

47. Mullard, C. (1981) Black Kids in White Schools: Multiracial Education in Britain. *Plural Societies*, Summer.

48. Mulhern, C. (1979) Multicultural education and the fight against racism in schools. *Teaching and Racism*. London: ALTARF.

49. Williams, J. (1979) Perspectives on the multicultural curriculum. *Social Science Teacher*, **8**, 4. (Section 4—The Socio/Political Perspective.)

50. James, A. (1979) *op. cit.*

51. *Ibid.*

52. *Ibid.*

53. OWAAD (1980) *op. cit.,* p. 7.

54. Dhondy, F. (1978) Teaching young blacks. *Race Today.*

55. The National Front pamphlet *How to Spot a Red Teacher* begins with these words,

    Commies (they call themselves 'Marxists' or even 'Socialists') have infiltrated our schools.
    They are trying to indoctrinate you with Commie ideas. They sneer at our British race and
    nation, and everything that has made Britain great. Don't let them get away with it! Be
    proud to be British and fight back against Commie brainwashing.
    Commie teachers use many tricks to bend your mind. Here are some of them and the way to
    answer back.

56. While it is clear that there has been very little support for the National Front and similar
    groups in local elections, it seems unwise to minimize the insidious nature of the attempts by
    the National Front and the British Movement to recruit among school students, soccer fans
    and pop group followers. Moreover, there are significant opportunities open to them to
    capitalize on the effects of increasing unemployment among young people. The independent
    research group, the Centre for Contemporary Studies, in their report. *Nazis in the Play-
    ground,* draw attention to the lack of awareness among teachers, unions, LEAs, and the
    government of the increasing infiltration of schools by racist groups. The report recom-
    mended the monitoring of the extreme right's activities in schools, the positive use of political
    and multicultural education, the confronting of classroom racism, and the strengthening of
    the law. CCS *Nazis in the Playground,* available from the Centre for Contemporary Studies,
    163/175 Shoreditch High Street, London E1.

57. Brett, R. (1977) Charcoal and chalk. Teaching London Kids, 11. On the responsibility of
    teachers to create the conditions in which anti-racist white kids can speak out.

58. See *Issues in Race and Education* 13, 1978, for an account of this policy by Shaun Doherty.

59. *Times Educational Supplement*, 22.5.81.

60. To be found in *Issues in Race and Education,* 11, 1977.

61. Since 1978, ALTARF's initiatives have been on a smaller scale: consisting of Primary and
    Secondary Workshops and occasional conferences. In 1981, monitoring racist incidents
    relating to schools began to take on considerable importance.

62. *Issues in Race and Education,* 15, 1978.

63. Some examples of the range now available.
    Tankits 1–5 produced by Teachers Against the Nazis.
    Whose World is the World? Poster Series produced by The Poster Film Collective.
    Our People, One World, Viewpoints 2, produced by Thames Television.
    Divide and Rule—Never A film produced by Newsreel Collective and booklet produced by
    Newsreel Collective with ALTARF.
    Our Lives, The English Centre, ILEA.
    Ashton, P., Simons, M., 'Reading and Race', The English Magazine 3 & 4.
    (This list is representative rather than exhaustive for details consult the Resources Guide.)

64. Mulhern, *et al* (1978) *Teaching and Racism.* London: ALTARF. This is the work of the
    Secondary Workshop which was set up at the Robert Montefiore Conference in June 1978
    following the ALTARF rally. The booklet consists of short papers by classroom teachers
    across a range of school subjects, with reference to specific material.

65. Mulhern, C. *et al* (1978) *op. cit.* p. 2.

66. *Ibid.*, p. 6.

67. Jeffcoate, R. (1979) *Positive Image,* London: Chameleon/Writers and Readers Publishing Co-operative. See, for example, p. 119 where talking of *The World in a Classroom* he makes his own ideology clear. 'Teachers have no business thrusting their cherished ideologies on young and malleable minds; it is for children to determine for themselves where they stand politically and culturally. They are not going to be helped in the realization of this inalienable right by the kind of biased version of "oppression" offered by Searle and his colleagues!!!'

68. Mulhern, C. *et al* (1978) *op. cit.*

69. *Ibid.*, p. 19.

70. The six programmes in the original *Our People* series are available on hire from Film Forum, 56 Brewer Street, London W1. The titles are: 1. Immigrant. 2. Facts. 3. Empire. 4. A long way to work. 5. Law and order. 6. Carnival. Of these, 1, 2 and 4 were chosen for screening in Thames Television 'English Programme'.

71. Mulhern, C. *et al* (1978) *op. cit.*

72. *Ibid.*, p. 21.

73. *Ibid.*, p. 14.

74. *Ibid.*, p. 23.

75. *Ibid.*, p. 27.

76. *Ibid.*, p. 27.

77. *Ibid.*, p. 28.

78. *Ibid.*, p. 29.

79. *Ibid.*, p. 8.

80. Searle, C. (1977) *The World in a Classroom.* London: Writers and Readers Publishing Co-operative.

81. Brett, R. (1977) *op. cit.*

82. Mulhern, C. *et al* (1978) *op. cit.*, p. 11.

83. *Ibid.*, p. 12.

84. Goody, J. (1977) *op. cit.*

85. Mulhern, C. *et al* (1978) *op. cit.*, p. 11.

86. Ibid., p. 3.

87. Dhondy, F. (1978) *op. cit.*

Resources Guide

We have aimed to provide a comprehensive guide to resource material for students taking courses in multiracial/multicultural education, practising teachers, and staff in universities and colleges, as well as other groups interested in race relations, minorities and migration/immigration.

Although much of the material is to do with multiracial education, we have by no means restricted ourselves to this field, rather we have tried to gather together a wide range of material, especially in the bibliography. No attempt has been made to detail specific resources for use in the classroom in the sense of, for instance, listing children's storybooks, but we have indicated where teachers will be able to locate such material. However, some of the books mentioned will be suitable for older children.

While every effort has been made to ensure that the guide is correct at the time of going to press, there will inevitably be some errors and omissions. Telephone numbers change, organizations find new premises, and important organizations may have been overlooked. Because things can change so rapidly we have avoided including the name of an individual currently associated with a particular project, group, etc., and we have made no attempt to list every publication available from an organization. Prices of books, periodicals and films have been omitted as nowadays these are likely to be out of date when this book is published. Up-to-date lists and prices can, of course, be obtained from the organizations concerned.

The Resources Guide is made up of five parts:

1. Books.
2. Organizations and groups.
3. Periodicals.
4. Bookshops.
5. Film distributors.

Please write to the editor of this book through the publisher so that any errors/omissions/recommendations may be noted.

PART 1: BOOKS

SECTION A: GENERAL

This covers a very wide range of material relating to modern Britain, though we have included some texts on issues and problems in Europe and the United States where appropriate. Books in this section deal with such themes as race relations, minority groups, immigration legislation, religious beliefs, employment and housing. Not all of the books are of equal quality, of course, but we have not made any evaluative comments.

Abbott, S. (Ed.) (1971) *The Prevention of Racial Discrimination in Britain*, Oxford University Press. A collection of readings which examine the notion of racial discrimination and the efforts made to eradicate it.

Acton, T. (1974) *Gypsy Politics and Social Change*, RKP. Subtitled: The development of ethnic ideology and pressure among British gypsies from Victorian reformism to romany nationalism.

Adams, B., Okely, J., Morgan, D. and Smith, D. (1975) *Gypsies and Government Policy in England*, Heinemann. An examination of the ways in which policies and practices of central and local government affect travelling people.

Age Concern (1974) *Elderly Ethnic Minorities*, Age Concern. This looks at the special problems experienced by this minority within a minority.

Alcock, A. E., Taylor, B. K. and Welton, J. M. (Eds.) (1979) *The Future of Cultural Minorities*, Macmillan. A collection of readings looking at possible developments.

Ali, A. (Ed.) (1979) *West Indians in Britain*, Hansib Publications. This first appeared in 1973, and is now in its fourth edition. It is a detailed compendium of West Indian achievements—from cricket to politics.

Allen, S. (1971) *New Minorities, Old Conflicts*, Random House. An exploration of racial and ethnic conflict.

Anwar, M. (1979) *The Myth of Return: A Study of Pakistanis in Britain*, Heinemann. The author concludes: 'The limited participation of Pakistanis in British institutions is due to the external constraints, such as prejudice and discrimination, to the internal cultural norms of pressures on them to conform, and also to the myth that they are in Britain to work, save, invest and subsequently return to villages back home'.

Banton, M. (1967) *Race Relations*, Tavistock. A general discussion in which the 'stranger' hypothesis and role theory approach have been criticized.

Barret, L. E. (1976) *The Sun and the Drum*, Heinemann. A study of the African influences on the customs, festivals, speech patterns, medicine and religion among Jamaicans.

Barret, L. E. (1977) *The Rastafarians: The Dreadlocks of Jamaica*, Heinemann. The author argues that the promises of redemption made by the cult are used as a way out of cultural and economic poverty.

Baxter, P. and Sansom, B. (Eds.) (1972) *Race and Social Difference*, Penguin. A book of readings dealing with race as a social rather than a biological fact. It includes sections on stereotypes in ideology, literature and folk images, and sections of race relations in a variety of social situations and societies.

Berger, J. and Mohr, J. (1975) *A Seventh Man: The Story of a Migrant Worker in Europe*, Penguin. An evocative and sobering piece of work which includes photographs.

Berry, J. (Ed.) (1978) *Bluefoot Traveller: An Anthology of West Indian Poets in Britain*, Limestone Publications.

Bethnal Green and Stepney Trades Council, *Blood on the Streets*, published by the Trades Council, 58 Watney Street, London, E1. This publication looks at attacks on immigrants in East London.

Bohning, W. R. (1972) *The Migration of Workers in the U.K. and the European Community*, Oxford University Press.

Bowers, J. and Franks, S. (1980) *Race and Affirmative Action*, Fabian Tract 471. The authors compare British and American policies for dealing with black unemployment. They argue for equality rather than equality of opportunity.

Bowker, G. and Carrier, J. (Eds.) (1976) *Race and Ethnic Relations*, Hutchinson. A collection of sociological readings.

Braham, P., Pearn, M. and Rhodes, E. (Eds.) (1981) *Discrimination and Disadvantage: The Experience of Ethnic Minorities in Employment*, Harper and Row. The authors look at the economic and political backgrounds, the nature of employment for minority workers, equal opportunities and trade unions.

Brent Community Health Council (1980) *Black People and the Health Service*. Available from 16 High Street, London NW10. This study focuses on disadvantage and health care and points to a disturbing increase in rickets among black children.

Brooks, D. (1975) *Race and Labour in London Transport*, Oxford University Press. This work illustrates some of the less obvious ways in which racial hostility can operate.

Butterworth, E. (1979) *Minority Groups*, Longman. A general discussion.

Butterworth, E. and Kinniburgh, E. (1970) *The Social Background of Immigrant Children from India, Pakistan and Cyprus*, Longman. The book provides informative material on ethnicity.

Butterworth, E. and Weir, D. (Eds.) (1972) *Social Problems of Modern Britain*, Fontana. This contains a chapter made up of six papers on the theme of 'Minorities'.

Cashmore, E. (1979) *Rastaman: The Rastafarian Movement in England*, Allen and Unwin. A description of the emergence of Rastafari.

Castles, S. and Kosack, G. (1973) *Immigrant Workers in the Class Structure in Western Europe*, Oxford University Press. An analysis of the position of migrant workers in the richer countries of Europe. They show how such labour has contributed to the postwar economic growth of Europe.

Cheetham, J., Loney, M., James, W. and Prescott, W. (Eds.) (1981) *Social and Community Work in a Multi-Racial Society*, Harper and Row. A reader dealing with social and community work in terms of issues of policy and the day-to-day work of practitioners.

The Churches Committee on Migrant Workers (1978) *Migrant Women Speak*, Search Press/World Council of Churches. A collection of essays based on interviews with women who have migrated from North Africa and the poorer areas of Southern Europe to the more affluent north. It illustrates the special problems encountered by migrant *women* workers.

Clarke, S. (1980) *Jah Music*, Heinemann. An examination of the origins and development of Jamaican music.

Clay, R. (1976) *Focus on Europe: Minorities*, Harrap. The author examines the history and experiences of European minorities.

Cottle, T. J. (1978) *Black Testimony*, Wildwood House. Life on the receiving end of racism: West Indians talking about life in Britain.

Counter Information Services (1978) *Racism: Who Profits?* A general discussion with a journal format.

Crampton-Smith, G. and Curtis, S. (1978) *It's Not Easy: A Longman's Thinkstrip*, Longman. On the theme of understanding a multicultural/multiracial society.

Crishna, S. (1975) *Girls of Asian Origin in Britain*, YWCA. A descriptive booklet on the cultural experiences of Asian girls.

Das, M. S. and Bardis, P. D. (1979) *The Family in Asia*, Allen and Unwin. Informative material on family patterns in Asia, though mainly written for the specialist.

Davies, J. (n.d.) *The New Black Presence in Britain*, Lutterworth Press. On the subject of race relations and Christianity.

Davies, J. (n.d.) *Creed and Conflict*, Lutterworth Press. A follow-up to his earlier book.

Davis, S. and Simon, P. (1979) *Reggae Bloodlines: In Search of the Music and the Culture of Jamaica*, Heinemann. A well illustrated book about West Indian music.

Deakin, N., Cohen, B. and McNeal, J. (1970) *Colour Citizenship and British Society*, Panther. A shortened, though more up-to-date version of Rose (1969), written for the general reader.

Dench, G. (1975) *Maltese in London*, RKP. A rare study of the Maltese as an ethnic group.

Ellis, J. (Ed.) (1978) *West Indian Families in Britain*, RKP. A collection of readings covering the social and economic experiences of West Indian families.

Field, F. and Haikin, P. (Eds.) (1971) *Black Britons*, Oxford University Press. A brief description of the historical background and the legislation restricting immigration, followed by extracts dealing with the living and working situations of second generation black Britons.

Fitchett, N. (1977) *Chinese Children in Derby*, Bishop Lonsdale College of Education. A brief report of a local study.

Foner, N. (1978) *Jamaica Farewell: Jamaican Migrants in London*, RKP. This book looks at how Jamaicans have adjusted and reacted to living in London.

Foot, P. (1965) *Immigration and Race in British Politics*, Penguin. A study of racism in British politics, including a historical outline and special emphasis on the Smethwick by-election and party political stances in the sixties.

Foot, P. (1969) *The Rise of Enoch Powell*, Penguin. A history of the official response to NCWP immigration, bringing out, in particular, Powell's inconsistencies: his sudden shift to an anti-immigration stance in 1964. Essentially the book is a critique of Powell's racism.

Gainer, B. (1972) *The Alien Invasion*, Heinemann. A history of right-wing responses in Britain, especially moral panics and ethnic/racial stereotyping.

Garrad, J. E. (1971) *The English and Immigration*, Oxford University Press. An analysis of postwar black immigration which discusses white attitudes and responses.

Glendenning, F. (Ed.) (1980) *The Elders in Ethnic Minorities*, Beth Johnson Foundation Publications. A report of a seminar involving the Department of Adult Education at the University of Keele, the Beth Johnson Foundation and the CRE.

Griffin, J. H. (1969) *Black Like Me*, Panther. An account of a white American reporter who (temporarily) had his skin colour chemically changed in order to experience at first hand what it meant to be black in the Southern States. Given the limita-

tions, some important issues are illustrated.

Hall, S., Critchley, C., Jefferson, A., Clarke, S. and Roberts, B. (1978) *Policing the Crisis: Mugging, the State, Law and Order*, Macmillan. Focusing on the 'mugging' panic of the early seventies, the authors provide a Marxist analysis of social control in a capitalist society, especially one that is suffering an economic recession. They examine how and why, in Britain in the seventies, arresting and convicting black muggers came to be synonymous with 'policing the crisis'.

Handsworth Law Centre (1979) *Immigration Law Handbook*, published by the Centre. An informative booklet for immigrants in Britain.

Harrison, S. W. (1978) *Hinduism in Preston*, Preston Curriculum Development Centre.

Harrison, S. W. (1979) *Sikhism in Preston*, Preston Curriculum Development Centre.

Harrison, S. W. and Shepherd, D. (1975) *Islam in Preston*, Preston Curriculum Development Centre.

Heinemann, B. W. (1972) *The Politics of the Powerless*, Oxford University Press. An examination of black responses to their subordinate position in British society.

Heinemann Education Books, *Heinemann African Studies Catalogue*, Heinemann. This lists publications concerning Africa. Also available: *Heinemann African Writers Series*.

Hepple, B. (1968) *Race, Jobs and the Law*, Penguin. The author looks at the way that immigrants are treated by the law and examines historical material in terms of restrictions, etc.

Hill, M. J. and Issacharoff, R. M. (1971) *Community Action and Race Relations*, Oxford University Press. This illustrates the limitations of such action.

Hiro, D. (1973) *Black British, White British*, Penguin. This book is divided into three sections: the first dealing with immigration from the West Indies, the second with Asian immigrants and the third with the attitudes of the native population towards black people. It is written mainly for teachers and sixth formers.

HMSO (1967) *Gypsies and Other Travellers*,

Ministry of Housing and Local Government.

HMSO (1975) *White Paper on Racial Discrimination*.

HMSO (1977) *The West Indian Community*, Select Committee on Race Relations and Immigration.

HMSO (1978) *The West Indian Community: Observations on the Report of the Select Committee on Race Relations and Immigration*.

HMSO (1981) *White Paper on Nationality Law*.

Hoch, P. (1980) *White Hero, Black Beast: Racism, Sexism and the Mask of Masculinity*, Pluto Press. This work analyses the various ways in which 'masculinity' has been conceived. It includes an examination of racism, nationalism and sexism.

Hodge, J. J., Struckmann, D. K. and Trost, L. D. (1975) *Cultural Bases of Racism and Group Oppression*, Berkeley, California: Two Riders Press. Subtitled: An examination of traditional 'Western' concepts, values and institutional structures which support racism, sexism and elitism.

Holmes, C. et al (1979) *Immigrants and Minorities in British Society*, Allen and Unwin.

Home Office (1980) *Race, Crime and Arrests*, HMSO. This publication shows that blacks are 14 times more likely to be arrested for violent theft and 15 times more likely to be arrested for 'sus' than whites. Forty per cent of those arrested for 'sus' in London in 1979 were black.

Humphrey, D. (1972) *Police Power and Black People*, Panther. A book offering many and varied proofs of the police harassment of black people in Britain.

Humphrey, D. and John, C. (1971) *Because They're Black*, Penguin. The authors use case studies to describe what it is like to be the victim of discrimination. They advocate a form of black power as a way out, rejecting white liberal versions of 'integration'.

Humphrey, D. and Ward, M. (1974) *Passports and Control*, Penguin. An examination of the politics behind the Ugandan Asian expulsion and resettlement.

Jeffrey, P. (1979) *Frogs in a Well: Indian Women in Purdah*, Zed Press. An examination of the Muslim practice of Purdah (the exclusion of women).

John, D. (1969) *Indian Workers' Association in Britain*, Oxford University Press. A historical analysis.

John, G., Taylor, I. and Zeldin, D. (1978) *Social and Community Work in Specific Settings 1*, DE206 Block 7, Units 21–23, Open University Press. This includes sections on social work with minorities, particularly West Indian youth.

Jones, C. (1977) *Immigration and Social Policy in Britain*, Tavistock. The author examines the impact of immigration on British social policy over the past 100 years.

Jones, K. and Smith, A. (1970) *The Economic Impact of Commonwealth Immigration*, Cambridge University Press.

Kalra, S. S. (1980) *Daughters of Tradition*, Diana Balbir Publications. Subtitled: Adolescent Sikh girls and their accommodation to life in British society.

Katz, J. (n.d.) *White Awareness Training Handbook*, available in the U.K. from Houseman's Bookshop, Caledonian Road, London, N1. A handbook for anti-racist training. It aims to show how racism can be present in all kinds of groups and individuals.

Katznelson, I. (1973) *Black Men, White Cities*, Oxford University Press. A book which shows how blacks entered into and were treated in urban areas in the UK. It looks at the political strategies of the major parties.

Khan, S. V. (Ed.) (1979) *Minority Families in Britain*, Macmillan. The contributors look at the 'positive aspects of minority family life and community organisations'.

Krausz, E. (1972) *Ethnic Minorities in Britain*, Paladin. The author looks at the cultural backgrounds of people migrating to Britain, the motivations for migration and the situation in housing and employment as well as the historical background.

Kuepper, W. G. (1975) *Ugandan Asians in Great Britain*, Croom Helm.

Kwee Choo, N. (1968) *The Chinese in London*, Oxford University Press. A general discussion illustrating how the Chinese have fitted into British society in specific ways.

Lawrence, D. (1974) *Black Migrants, White Natives*, Cambridge University Press. The author shows that racial stereotyping and feelings of white superiority are common in Britain. These are seen as being cultur-

ally transmitted within the context of an
imperial past.

Leech K. (n.d.) *Christians and Fascism*, available from Jubilee Group, St. Mary's
House, Eastway, London, E9. A transcript of a speech made at a public meeting
in the East End of London.

Lester, A. and Bindman, G. (1972) *Race and
the Law*, Penguin. A detailed examination
of the 1968 Race Relations Act and the
way it operates.

Longman, *'Africana' Catalogue*. Also available: lists of books on Africa for schools.

Madan, R. (Ed.) (1979) *Coloured Minorities in
Great Britain: A Comprehensive Bibliography 1976–77*, Aldwych Press. A major
reference work covering a vast amount of
research.

Mamdani, M. (1973) *From Citizen to Refugee*,
Frances Pinter. This discusses the expulsion of Asians from Uganda and their subsequent experiences in British resettlement camps.

Marland, M. and Ray, S. (1978) *The Minority
Experience: A Documentary Collection*,
Imprint Books, Longman. Produced originally for use with the Thames Television
programme 'The English Programme', it
looks at Gypsies, American Indians,
minorities in Britain, the old and the disabled.

Mason, P. (1970) *Race Relations*, Oxford University Press. The book includes a discussion of the nature of prejudice. The author
argues that it acts as a vehicle for prejudging people or situations in 'positive' or
'negative' ways.

McIntosh, N. and Smith, D. (1974) *The Extent
of Racial Discrimination*, Political and
Economic Planning. A very comprehensive piece of research which provides a
great deal of evidence of racial discrimination in Britain.

McKay, D. (1977) *Housing and Race in Industrial Society*, Croom Helm. This examines
the extent of discrimination and disadvantage in the housing markets.

Miles, R. and Phizacklea, A. (Eds.) (1979)
Racism and Political Action in Britain,
RKP. The contributors show that current
events have precedents in the past 100
years, outline the politics of white racism
and assess the impact of white and black
racism on the British political system.

Miles, R. and Phizacklea, A. (1980) *Labour*

and Racism, RKP. This attempts to put
forward a 'new framework of analysis for
studying racism'. It analyses important
considerations such as consciousness,
trade unionism and political action. The
research is based on an area in London
containing a high proportion of black
workers.

Miller, R. and Dolan, P. J. (1971) *Race
Awareness*, Oxford University Press. A
social psychological study of racial
attitudes.

Moore, R. (1975) *Racism and Black Resistance
in Britain*, Pluto Press. The author discusses the experiences of the black community *vis à vis* the courts, the police, immigration practices, etc. One of the few studies
in the early seventies to break away from
the policy-oriented investigation which
had dominated race research.

Moore, R. and Wallance, T. (1975) *Slamming
the Door: The Administration of Immigration Control*, Martin Robertson. This
analyses the way in which the 1971 Act
has been implemented.

Mullard, C. (1973) *Black Briton*, Allen and
Unwin. A former Newcastle Community
Relations Officer, in the book he analyses
his own experiences as a British-born
black.

National Youth Bureau (1979) *Young People
and the Police*, available from NYB,
17–23 Albion Street, Leicester, LE1
6GD. Written evidence of the NYB to the
Royal Commission on Criminal Procedure.

Oakley, R. (Ed.) (1968) *New Backgrounds*,
Oxford University Press. A collection of
readings on the experiences of immigrants.

Owens, J. (1979) *Dread: The Rastafarians of
Jamaica*, Heinemann. An analysis of the
belief system based on taped discussions.

Patterson, S. (1968) *Immigrants in Industry*,
Oxford University Press. The author
reports on research (1958–60) on the
'absorption' of white and black immigrants into light-engineering firms in the
Croydon area.

Patterson, S. (1969) *Immigration and Race
Relations in Britain 1960–67*, Institute of
Race Relations/OUP. A detailed, general
discussion.

Peach, C. (1968) *West Indian Migration into
Britain: A Social Geography*, Oxford Uni-

versity Press. The author examines the employment distribution of West Indian workers, arguing that they have taken jobs that white workers have moved away from.

Pearson, D. G. (1980) *Race, Class and Political Activism: A Study of West Indians in Britain*, Gower. A comprehensive study of West Indian social organization and political mobilization in Britain and the Caribbean which discusses different patterns of colonial relationship.

Prescod-Roberts, M. and Steele, N. (1980) *Black Women: Bringing it all Back Home*, Falling Wall Press. West Indian women describe the social and emotional costs involved when they left their homes to migrate to Britain, and the problems of coping with a society that is often hostile towards them.

Pryce, K. (1979) *Endless Pressure: A Study of West Indian Life-Styles in Bristol*, Penguin. Based on the St. Pauls area, Bristol, it turned out to be a prophetic book.

Ratcliffe, P. (1981) *Racism and Reaction*, RKP. A study of minorities living in Handsworth, Birmingham, and the racism and conflict many of them experience.

Rehfisch, F. (Ed.) (1975) *Gypsies, Tinkers and Other Travellers*, Academic Press. A comprehensive collection of readings.

Release (1978) *Immigration: How the Law Affects You*, available from Release, 1 Eigin Avenue, London, W9. A short booklet which describes entry regulations for tourists, EEC national and Commonwealth citizens with dependants. It also explains deportation procedures.

Rex, J. (1970) *Race Relations in Sociological Theory*, Weidenfeld and Nicolson. Not an easy book for the non-specialist it provides a theoretical analysis of race and race relations.

Rex, J. (1973) *Race, Colonialism and the City*, RKP. A major sociological text by a respected writer on race relations and racial problems. Here he discusses imperialistic social systems and examines the position of black people at the colonial and metropolitan ends of those systems.

Rex, J. and Moore, R. (1967) *Race, Community and Conflict*, Oxford University Press. This work analyses the tensions existing in a multiracial community in a twilight zone

of Birmingham. The focus is on the struggle for housing.

Rex, J. and Tomlinson, S. (1979) *Colonial Immigrants in a British City*, RKP. A study of race and community relations in a major centre of West Indian and Asian settlement. It extends and supersedes the earlier (1967) study.

Richmond, A. (1973) *Migration and Race Relations in an English City*, Oxford University Press. The author argues that it is not so much actual hardship that leads to racial prejudice and scapegoating on the part of white people as feelings of deprivation and deterioration.

Rimmer, M. (1972) *Race and Industrial Conflict*, Heinemann.

Rogers, J. (1968) *Foreign Places, Foreign Faces*, Penguin. The first part is about the British abroad, the second part about foreigners in Britain. Illustrated with cartoons, newspaper cuttings and photographs it is basically aimed at students in further education.

Rose, E. B. J. (1969) *Colour and Citizenship: A Report on British Race Relations*, Panther. A comprehensive report on the state of race relations in Britain since the 1960s.

Runnymede Trust and the Radical Statistics Group (1980) *Britain's Black Population*, Heinemann. This work provides up-to-date statistical information relating to Britain's black population, coupled with an examination of social policy issues.

Schermerhorn, R. A. (1970) *Comparative Ethnic Relations*, Random House. The author analyses on a comparative basis the ways in which racism manifests itself.

Searle, C. (1979) *Beyond the Skin: How Mozambique is Defeating Racism*, Liberation. An analysis of racism within the context of revolution in Mozambique.

Simons, R. J. and Alstein, M. (1977) *Transracial Adoption*, John Wiley. This looks at the system of adoption across racial lines.

Simpson, G. E. and Yinger, J. M. (1972) *Racial and Cultural Minorities*, Harper and Row, (4th edition). A comprehensive analysis of prejudice in various contexts.

Smith, D. J. (1977) *Racial Disadvantage in Britain*, Penguin. The author gives the results of a survey carried out between 1972 and 1975 and provides information on employment, family structure, housing and official policy responses.

Smith, D. J. (1980) *Overseas Doctors in the National Health Service*, Heinemann. A report on the findings of a detailed study of British and overseas doctors within the NHS. The relative differences between the careers of British- and overseas-qualified doctors are examined.

Tambs-Lyche, H. (1980) *London Patidars*, RKP. A study of Patidars, an Indian land-owning caste, who are heavily involved in business enterprises. The author examines the potential tensions with white people as a result of the Patidars' prosperity.

Tinker, H. (1977) *The Banyan Tree: Overseas Emigrants from India, Pakistan and Bangladesh*, Oxford University Press. This book examines important overseas communities, looking at their culture and relationship with other people.

Triseliotis, J. P. (1972) *Social Work with Coloured Immigrants and their Families*, Oxford University Press.

Twaddle, M. (Ed.) (1975) *Expulsion of a Minority*, Athlone Press. A collection of papers on the Ugandan Asians.

United Kingdom Association for the International Year of the Child (1979) *Immigrant Children*, available from 85 Whitehall, London, SW1. 'A Code for their protection.'

Van den Berghe, P. (1967) *Race and Racism*, Wiley. A general discussion of the topic.

Vesey-Fitzgerald, B. (1973) *Gypsies in Britain*, David and Charles. A study of their history and experiences.

Walin, J. (1973) *Black and White*, Penguin.

Wallman, S. (Ed.) (1979) *Ethnicity at Work*, Macmillan. A collection of papers dealing with the ways in which ethnic identity is used or not used by various groups in an effort to cope with the problems posed by industrial society.

Watson, J. L. (Ed.) (1977) *Between Two Cultures: Migrants and Minorities*, Blackwell. A description of the problems faced in attempting to come to terms with life in another culture.

Wellman, D. T. (1977) *Portraits of White Racism*, Cambridge University Press. Although not about Britain specifically, a relevant analysis by an American sociologist of the meaning of white racism.

Wilson, A. (1978) *Finding a Voice: Asian Women in Britain*, Virago. Written by an Asian, the book examines the life of Asian women living in Britain.

Wilson, A. (1979) *Asian Women Speak Out*, National Extension College, Cambridge. A relatively rare opportunity for Asian women to express themselves.

Wilson, W. J. (1973) *Power, Racism and Privilege*, Macmillan. The author relates racist ideology to the exploitation of black people.

Wright, P. (1968) *The Coloured Worker in British Society*, Oxford University Press. The author reports on research (1961–64) in the Midlands and the North. He stresses the importance of legislation to ensure 'fair' employment of black people, and sees inertia, rather than deep-rooted opposition, as the obstacle.

Zubaida, S. (Ed.) (1970) *Race and Racialism*, Tavistock. A collection of sociological papers which attempts to define theoretical issues and locate race relations situations in the context of the wider social structure and historical development.

SECTION B: EDUCATION

Studies focusing on minority children have been included here, as well as those specifically to do with education.

Bagley, C. (1974) *Race Relations and Education*, RKP. A well-researched examination of the way in which education in Britain treats and damages black children. It includes a discussion on the spurious uses to which IQ tests have been put.

Bagley, C. and Verma, G. K. (1979) *Racial Prejudice, the Individual and Society*, Gower. 'The authors look in detail at the social factors involved between expression of a prejudiced opinion and the actual activity of racism.' Particular attention is paid to the mass media.

Bagley, C. and Verma, G. K. (1979) *Self Esteem and Prejudice,* Gower. A companion volume to the one above.

Banfield, B. (1979) *Black Focus on Multi-Cultural Education.* New York: Edward Blyden Press. A practical guide for teachers on how to develop a racially and sexually positive curriculum.

Bell, R. (1978) *Bilingualism in Lancaster*, Lancaster University. A pilot study analysing the extent and nature of bilingualism in Lancaster, together with the sorts of attitudes in evidence.

Bhatnagar, J. (1970) *Immigrants at School*, Cornmarket Press. A comparison between black children born in Britain and those born in the Caribbean in terms of deviant behaviour.

Bibby, C. (1969) *Race, Prejudice and Education*, Heinemann.

Bogle, D. (1974) *Toms, Coons, Mulattoes, Mammies and Bucks*, Bantam. A history of black people in American films.

Bolton, F. and Laishley, J. (1972) *Education for a Multi-Racial Britain*, Fabian Research Series, 303. The authors concentrate on the need to remove prejudice from the education system and promote a sympathetic, multiracial world. They also suggest ways in which this can be done in schools.

Bowker, G. (1968) *The Education of Coloured Immigrants*, Longman. Most of the material is based on the author's study of West Bromwich. The author looks at the effects of rapid minority student population increases.

Broderick, D. M. (1979) *The Image of the Black in Children's Fiction*, Bowker and Co. This examines British and American books published between 1927 and 1967 and illustrates the condescension that is often present.

Brown, D. (1979) *Mother Tongue to English*, Cambridge University Press. An analysis of the problems faced by young children in multiracial schools in a practical way.

Bullivant, B. (1979) *Pluralism, Teacher Education and Ideology*, Melbourne. An Australian study of the education of minority children.

Burgin, T. and Edson, P. (1967) *Spring Grove: The Education of Immigrant Children*, Oxford University Press.

Burrows, G. (1978) *Bilingualism and Mother Tongue Teaching: A Select Bibliography*, Bedfordshire Education Service Resource Unit. A comprehensive source for those working in this field.

Butterworth, E. and Kinniburgh, E. (1970) *The Social Background of Immigrant Children from India, Pakistan and Cyprus*, Longman. The background material is specifically related to the experience of schooling in Britain.

Coard, B. (1971) *How the West Indian Child is Made Educationally Subnormal in the British School System*, New Beacon Books. The author shows how and why West Indian children typically fare so badly in the British school system.

Cole, W. O. (1973) *The Multi-Faith School*, Bradford Educational Services Committee for Community Relations, obtainable from YCCR, Charlton House, Hunslet Road, Leeds, LS10 1EU. This book provides information, teaching suggestions and materials for use by teachers in multiracial primary and middle schools.

Coventry Community Education Project (1978) *Talkback*, Coventry Department of Education. A range of materials on the theme of English language development.

Derrick, J. (1966) *Teaching English to Immigrants*, Longman. A practical introduction to teaching English as a second language.

Dixon, B. (1977) *Catching Them Young: Sex, Race and Class in Children's Fiction*, Vols. 1 and 2, Pluto Press. Drawing on numerous examples, the author discusses racial and ethnic stereotyping in children's literature. As he points out, many of the books cited are still widely read by children in Britain.

Edwards, V. K. (1979) *The West Indian Language Issue in British Schools: Challenges and Responses*, RKP. An account of the language used by West Indian children—in no way deficient, argues Edwards, to standard English. Written for non-specialists. The author discusses negative attitudes towards West Indian language, and the effects upon children's motivations.

Elkin, J. (1976) *Books for the Multiracial Classroom*, Public Library, Birmingham. A bibliography prepared in collaboration with Birmingham Public Libraries for primary- and secondary-age students.

Gibbes, N. (1980) *West Indian Teachers Speak Out*, from c/o Lewisham Council for Community Relations, 48 Lewisham High Street, London, SE13 5JH. The author discusses the racism met by West Indian teachers in London and how it affects them when applying for jobs and as practising teachers.

Giles, R. H. (Ed.) (1977) *Language, Ethnicity and Intergroup Realtions*, Academic

Press. A comprehensive collection of readings.

Giles, R. H. (1977) *The West Indian Experience in British Schools,* Heinemann. A report by a black American Professor of Education on research into how British teachers perceive the educational needs of West Indian pupils in socially disadvantaged areas. He concludes by stressing the importance of black unity for the development of positive black concepts, of new educational programmes in multiracial schools and the need to distinguish between social class prejudice and racism as factors affecting black children's education disadvantage.

Mary Glasgow Publications Ltd have produced 'Stimulus Units': *Prejudice* (B. Kennedy) and *Immigration* (N. Fromer). Each unit comprises a film strip, sound cassette and pamphlet.

Haringey, London Borough of (1978) *Racialist Activities in Schools*, Haringey Education Service, Somerset Road, Tottenham, London, N17 9EH. A booklet on this theme.

Hartmann, P. and Husband, C. (1974) *Racism and the Mass Media,* Davis-Poynter. An examination of the role of the mass media in the formation/reinforcement of white beliefs and attitudes regarding black people.

Hawkes, N. (1966) *Immigrant Children in British Schools,* Pall Mall Press. The author believes that the solution to educational problems has to be found in the classroom. He emphasizes the importance of English language teaching in this respect.

Haynes, J. M. (1971) *Educational Assessment of Immigrant Pupils,* National Foundation for Educational Research. A search for relatively culture-free tests of ability and potential.

Heinemann Educational Books, *Books for Multicultural Education,* Heinemann.

Hicks, D. (1981) *Minorities: A Teacher's Resource Book for the Multi-Ethnic Classroom*, Heinemann. The author discusses approaches and materials which might be used by teachers in order to introduce children to majority/minority issues in the world today.

Hill, D. (1976) *Teaching in Multi-Racial Schools,* Methuen. A short review of the field, with suggestions on how teachers can contribute to multiracial integration.

Hill, J. (Ed.) (1971) *Books for Children: The Homelands of Immigrants in Britain,* Institute of Race Relations. A classification of children's books in print on the countries from which immigrants have come.

Hobbs, M. (1976) *Teaching in a Multi-Racial Society,* Association of Christian Teachers.

Hoyles, M. (Ed.) (1977) *The Politics of Literacy,* Writers' and Readers' Publishing Cooperative. The book includes chapters on racism.

Husband, C. (Ed.) (1975) *White Media and Black Britain,* Arrow Books. A collection of readings on the theme of how white controlled media present black people.

Inner London Education Authority (1977) *Education Officer's Report on Multi-Ethinic Education*, ILEA.

Jackson, B. and Garvey, A. (1974) *Chinese Children,* available from National Educational Development Trust.

James, A. G. (1973) *Sikh Children In Britain,* Oxford University Press. The author examines the extent to which the traditions of Punjabi villages are maintained in Sikh households in Britain.

Jeffcoate, R. (1979) *Positive Image: Towards a Multi-Racial Curriculum,* Writers' and Readers' Publishing Cooperative/Chameleon Books. Criticizing those who underestimate the problems of racism, the author gives advice on 'positive' action, though stretches the liberal conscience to the point of arguing for the National Front to be allowed into the classroom to put their case.

Jeffcoate, R. and James, A. (Eds.) (1981) *Multicultural Education*, Harper and Row. A collection of readings dealing with multicultural education in British Schools.

Kirp, D. L. (1980) *Doing Good by Doing Little: Race and Schooling in Britain,* Berkeley: University of California Press. An assessment by an American of British social policy—especially in the field of education—*vis à vis* the black population. His conclusion is that there more or less isn't any.

Labov, W. (1977) *Language in the Inner City: Studies in the Black English Vernacular,* Blackwell. Although not specifically about Britain, this book by an influential

American linguist raises important issues in the area of language and deprivation.

Leab, D. J. (1975) *From Sambo To Superspade*, Secker and Warburg. The author discusses the portrayal of black people in films from a historical perspective.

Library Association Youth Libraries Group (1976) *Books for the Multi-Racial Classroom*, Pamphlet No. 17.

Little, A. (1978) *Educational Policies for Multi-Racial Areas*, London University, Goldsmith's College.

Lloyd, G. (1977) *Deprivation and the Bilingual Child*, Blackwell. A Schools Council sponsored study of infant-school children.

Lobo, E. H. de (1978) *Children of Immigrants to Britain: Their Health and Social Problems*, Hodder and Stoughton.

Mapp, E. (1972) *Blacks in American Films Today and Yesterday*, Scarecrow Press. A comprehensive general analysis.

Maynard, R. (1974) *The Black Man on Film: Racial Stereotyping*, New Jersey: Haydon Book Co. The author discusses the part played by the cinema in the perpetuation of such stereotypes.

McNeal, J. and Roger, M. (Eds.) (1971) *The Multi-Racial School*, Penguin. A collection of readings on this theme.

Milner, D. (1975) *Children and Race*, Penguin. A review of psychological aspects of racial attitudes and awareness, with special attention given to children in Britain.

Morrish, I. (1971) *The Background of Immigrant Children*, Allen and Unwin.

National Association of Teachers in Further and Higher Education (1979) *Further and Teacher Education in a Multicultural Society*, NATFHE.

National Union of Students (1979) *Towards a Multi-Cultural Education*, NUS.

National Union of Teachers (1978) *All Our Children*, NUT.

National Union of Teachers (1979) *In Black and White*, NUT. A 12-page pamphlet to help teachers deal with problems of racial stereotyping in school textbooks.

New Beacon Books (1971) *Special Caribbean Booklist for Teachers, Parents and Teenagers*, New Beacon Books.

Noor, N. S. and Khalsa, S. S. (1979) *Survey of Asian Parents in Wolverhampton*, published by the Wolverhampton branch of the Indian Workers' Association. This book is based on a survey of 1000 Asian

parents to find out what they think of the education being provided for their children in the area. The parents are extremely critical.

Oakley, R. (Ed.) (1968) *New Backgrounds: The Immigrant Child at Home and at School*, Oxford University Press. The social and cultural backgrounds of Cypriot, Indian, Pakistani and West Indian immigrants are briefly summarized. The study was carried out under the auspices of the Institute of Race Relations.

Oxford University Press (1979) *Books for Multicultural Education*, Oxford University Press.

Peach, C., Smith, S. and Robinson, V. (Eds.) (1981) *Ethnic Segregation in Cities*, Croom Helm. A collection of papers by sociologists and social geographers presenting a board overview of theoretical thinking and research findings.

Penguin Books, *A Multi-Ethnic Booklist*, Penguin. For children of all ages.

Pines, J. (1975) *Blacks in Films*, Studio Vista. The author discusses racial themes and images in the American film.

Power, J. (1967) *Immigrants in School: A Survey of Administrative Policies*, Councils and Education Press. A look at the way in which multiracial education is organized.

Proctor, C. (1975) *Racist Textbooks*, National Union of Students. The author draws up a list of things to look for in racist textbooks. There is a short summary of obstacles and suggestions on what to do.

Purushothaman, M. (1978) *The Education of Children of Caribbean Origin: Select Research and Bibliography*, Centre for Information and Advice on Educational Disadvantage, Manchester. A comprehensive sourcebook which contains detailed summaries of over 1000 up-to-date reports, many of them unpublished.

Raynor, J. and Harris, E. (Eds.) (1977) *Schooling in the City*, Ward Lock. One of three readers for the Open University course on Education and the Urban Environment. It includes sections on city schools, curriculum, race and teacher–child relationships.

Reiss, C. (1975) *Education of Travelling Children*, Macmillan. A look at the special problems encountered by travelling children.

Rosen, H. and Burgess, T. (1980) *Language and Dialects of London School Children*, Ward Lock.

Searle, C. (1972) *The Forsaken Lover: White Words and Black People*, RKP. A West Indian teacher of English explains the problems of identity encountered by black people in a culture in which white is virtuous and black is associated with evil.

Searle, C. (1978) *The World in a Classroom*, Writers' and Readers' Publishing Co-operative/Chameleon Books. Children's writing on minority experiences of racism and the local community.

Simon, B. (1970) *Intelligence, Psychology and Education*, Lawrence and Wishart. The author has a chapter on 'Intelligence, Race, Class and Education', where he explores the ways in which these elements are interrelated.

Snyder, P. A. and Stone, F. A. (Ed.) (1972) *Minority Education in Global Perspective: Proceedings of the World Education Workshop*, University of Connecticut, School of Education. A collection of papers on the theme of the education of minority group children across the globe.

Stinton, J. (Ed.) (1979) *Racism and Sexism in Children's Books*, Writers' and Readers' Publishing Co-operative. A comprehensive set of readings giving guidelines for teachers.

Stock, A. K. and Howell, D. (Eds.) (1976) *Education for Adult Immigrants,* National Institute of Adult Education. A set of readings dealing with the problems and issues connected with the education of adult immigrants.

Stone, M. (1981) *The Education of the Black Child in Britain,* Fontana. The author attacks liberal assumptions in Britain's education system where 'multicultural education views the child as deprived and lacking in self-esteem'. This will probably be an influential book in the 1980s.

Street-Porter, R. (1978) *Race, Children and Cities*, The Open University. Part of the Open University course on urban education.

Taylor, F. (1974) *Race, School and Community: A Study of Research and Literature*, National Foundation for Educational Research. A detailed summary of a great deal of relevant literature.

Taylor, M. and Hurwitz, K. (1979) *Books for Under-Fives in a Multi-Cultural Society,* Islington Library Service. This lists a large number of books suitable for children in nurseries, pre-school groups and infant classes.

Teachers Action, Issue on *Multi-Racial Education*, No. 9. Distributed by Publications Distribution Co-operative, 27 Clerkenwell Close, London, EC1.

Teaching London Kids (1978) Issue on *Teaching Black Students,* No. 11, available from 79 Ronald Road, London, N5.

Townsend, H. E. R. and Brittan, E. M. (1972) *Organisation in Multi-Racial Schools*, National Foundation for Educational Research. The second part of a NFER project, covering such things as language teaching, assessment of ability and attainment, streaming, home and school co-operation and staffing as practised in the multiracial schools surveyed.

Trudgill, P. (1975) *Accent, Dialect and the School,* Edward Arnold. An overview of socio-linguistics.

Tuck, L. (1979) *The Next Step*, published by the author. This looks at the provision of education in the Inner London area for 16–18-year-olds of low academic achievement.

Verma, G. K. and Bagley, C. (Eds.) (1975) *Race and Education Across Cultures,* Heinemann. Very much an international look at race and education. The fifteen original articles are divided into three sections. The first section exposes the fallacies of scientific racism; the second is largely a social psychological approach to attitudes, personality and behaviour; the third explores the question of curriculum, including the effects of racism, and proposals for reform. There is an extensive bibliography.

Verma, G. K. and Bagley, C. (1979) *Race, Education and Identity,* Macmillan. The authors examine how minority children and adolescents react to racism. The study focuses on attainment, race-relations teaching, identity and self-esteem.

Wainwright, H. and Fraser, M. (1977) *English as a Second Language in Multi-Racial Schools: A Bibliography,* National Book League.

Wight, J. and Norris, R. (1970) *Teaching Eng-*

lish to West Indian Children, Methuen. The authors focus on deviance among West Indian children.

SECTION C: HISTORY

Aptheker, H. (1978) *American Negro Slave Revolts,* International Publishers. He discusses in detail the revolts of Turner, Vesey, Gabriel, Prosser, etc. The book also contains an extensive bibliography.

Ballhatchet, K. (1980) *Race, Sex and Class Under the Raj*, Weidenfeld and Nicolson. A scholarly piece of socio-cultural research. In it the author attempts to situate sexual relations between the rulers and the ruled within the broader social structure of the British Raj.

Blainey, G. (1975) *The Triumph of the Nomads: A History of Ancient Australia,* Macmillan. A detailed discussion of life among the first Australians.

Bolt, C. (1971) *Victorian Attitudes to Race,* RKP. The author discusses the development of white racist attitudes in Britain during the 19th century colonial period.

Brown, D. (1971) *Bury My Heart at Wounded Knee,* Picador. A popular book which documents in graphic style the experiences of the North American Indians during the 19th century.

Cole, H. (1967) *Christophe's King of Haiti,* Eyre and Spottiswoode. A history of late 18th/early 19th century revolution in Haiti.

Crookall, R. E. (1977) *Handbook for History Teachers in Africa,* Ibadan. This book looks at Africa's history and Africa's resistance.

Crowder, M. (Ed.) (1971) *West Indian Resistance,* Hutchinson. The author illustrates the various ways in which black people have resisted the invasions of, and treatment by, Europeans.

Curtin, P. (1969) *The Atlantic Slave Trade,* USA: Madison. A detailed study of the phenomenon of slavery.

Davidson, B. (1978) *Discovering Africa's Past,* Longman. This helps to fill the gap regarding the history of Africa, about which there is widespread ignorance in the West.

Davidson, B. (1978) *Africa in History,* Paladin. An introduction to Africa's real history.

Zimet, S. G. (1976) *Print and Prejudice*, Hodder and Stoughton. An examination of the impact of the printed word.

Elkins, S. M. (1963) *Slavery,* The Universal Library, Grosset and Dunlap. An authoritative examination of the history of slavery.

Fanon, F. (1967) *A Dying Colonialism,* Monthly Review Press.

Fanon, F. (1968) *The Wretched of the Earth,* Monthly Review Press. An influential Caribbean writer focuses on black resistance to colonialism.

File, N. and Power, C. (1981) *Black Settlers in Britain 1555–1958,* Heinemann. A detailed study showing the long history of black migration into Britain and its consequences.

Genovese, E. D. (1971) *In Red and Black: Marxian Explorations in Southern and Afro-American History,* Penguin. Not an easy book for the non-specialist, but it offers an in-depth theoretical discussion of plantation/slave systems.

Genovese, E. D. (1980) *From Rebellion to Revolution,* Louisiana State University Press. A scholarly study of Afro-American slavery showing the development from 'rebellion'—where the aim, in opposition to the growth of European capitalism, was the creation of separate black societies—to 'revolution'—where the aim was the destruction of the slave system itself.

Gibbs, R. M. (1974) *The Aborigines,* Longman. A historical account of Australian Aborigines from the earliest times to the present day.

Grieve, A. M. (1968) *Last Years of the English Slave Trade. Liverpool 1750–1807,* F. Cass. An informative book on the long history of black people in Britain. A reminder that black 'immigration' is not a new thing.

Hemming, J. (1978) *Red Gold: The Conquest of Brazilian Indians,* Macmillan. The author examines the impact of Western intruders on Indian culture.

James, C. L. R. (1963) *The Black Jacobins,* Vintage Books. A classic account of the Haitian revolutions.

Josephy, A. M. (1968) *The Indian Heritage of America*, Penguin. A well researched, informative book and a comprehensive analysis from pre-history to the present day.

Kiernan, V. G. *Lords of Human Kind*, Penguin. An examination of victorian images of subordinate 'races', and the rationalization of colonialism.

Killingray, D. (1973) *A Plague of Europeans: Westerners in Africa Since the Fifteenth Century,* Penguin. The author shows the ways in which the West has intruded into Africa and oppressed the Africans.

Lanning, G. and Mueller, M. (1980) *Africa Undermined: A History of the Mining Companies and the Underdevelopment of Africa,* Penguin. A disturbing book which documents the plunder of Africa's riches by European and American mining companies.

Latham, N. (1977) *Heritage of West Africa,* Hulton. A collection of original documents, beginning with the earliest written evidence of the Niger by Herodotus, going on to extracts of speeches by modern politicians.

Lees, L. H. (1980) *Exiles of Erin: Irish Migrants in Victorian London*, Manchester University Press. A meticulously researched piece of work which analyses the life of first generation immigrants from Ireland.

Lester, J. (1970) *To Be a Slave,* Longman. Aspects of slavery are described in detail by men and women who have themselves been slaves. Reconstructed from their own memories written down both before and after the American Civil War. A suitable book for secondary-school teaching.

Lowenthal, D. (1972) *West Indian Societies,* Oxford University Press/Institute of Race Relations. This provides detailed background reading.

Morris, J. (1968) *Pax Britannica: The Climax of an Empire,* Penguin.

Morris, J. (1973) *Heaven's Command: An Imperial Progress,* Penguin.

Morris, J. (1978) *Farewell the Trumpets: An Imperial Retreat,* Penguin. A trilogy of books providing an in-depth study of Britain's imperial history.

Oliver, R. and Fage, J. D. (1972) *A Short History of Africa,* Penguin. A concise and authoritative history, suitable for sixth-formers.

Pitman, J. (1975) *The Autobiography of Miss Jane Pitman.* Bantam Books. The story of a woman who was born into slavery in America and lived until the 1960s.

Preiswerk, R. and Perrot, D. (1979) *Ethno-Centrism and History: Africa, Asia and Indian America in Western Textbooks,* NOK International. A major review of white, Western perspectives and interpretations.

Roberts, J. (1978) *From Massacres to Mining: The Colonisation of Aboriginal Australia,* available from War on Want, 467 Caledonian Road, London, N7 9BE. A sobering book which discusses the treatment of Australian Aborigines by the colonists. 'This book tells how we stood up to the invasion of our lands and were slaughtered'.

Robinson, C. (1969) *The Fighting Maroons of Jamaica*, Collins. A description of black resistance in Jamaica.

Robinson, F. and York, B. (1977) *The Black Resistance,* Camberwell, Australia: Widescope. An account of Aboriginal struggles against white intruders.

Rodney, W. (1973) *How Europe Underdeveloped Africa*, Bogle-L'Ouverture Publications. A readable account of Europe's role in Africa's poverty—from slavery to the present era.

Rowley, C. D. (1970) *Outcasts in White Australia,* Pelican. The author documents the treatment of Aborigines by white Australians.

Segal, R. (1966) *The Race War*, Cape. A well-respected analysis and a potted history of the viciousness of imperialism.

Spear, P. (1966) *A History of India Vol. II,* Penguin. A companion volume to Thapar (1965).

Sterne, E. G. (1978) *The Long Black Schooner,* Follet. The North Atlantic slave trade: an examination of black slave revolts.

Thapar, R. (1965) *A History of India Vol. I,* Penguin. A concise and detailed study of Indian history.

Tinker, H. (1977) *Race, Conflict and the International Order,* Macmillan. A succinct discussion of colonialism and the ideology of white racism, followed by an analysis of the imperial system and the continuing influence of race on international relations.

Wachtel, N. (1977) *The Vision of the Van-quished: The Spanish Conquest of Peru through Indian Eyes,* Harvester Press. A history from below, for a change.

Walvin, J. (1971) *The Black Presence*, Orbach and Chambers. The author looks at the history of white attitudes to blacks between Elizabethan and Victorian times.

Watson, J. L. (Ed.) (1976) *Asian and African Systems of Slavery,* Blackwell. A collection of readings based on a seminar held at the School of Oriental and African Studies in London in 1976 on the theme of 'The Economics of Slavery'.

Williams, E. (1964) *A History of Trinidad and Tobago,* André Deutsch. Comprehensive background material on the West Indies.

Williams, E. (1964) *Capitalism and Slavery,* André Deutsch. An examination of the contribution made by the slave trade in providing finance for the English Industrial Revolution, and the part played by mature industrial capitalism in subsequently destroying the slave trade.

Wilson, D. (1975) *A Student's Atlas of African History*, University of London Press. This contains detailed and clear maps on many topics in African history from AD 1000 to the present day.

Wilson, J. (1974) *Canada's Indians,* Minority Rights Group, London. The author illustrates the appalling treatment of Indians in Canada.

SECTION D: RACE

This section contains books which address themselves to race as a concept

Baldwin, J. and Mead, M. (1972) *A Rap on Race,* Corgi. A transcript of a discussion on the theme of race.

Banton, M. (1977) *The Idea of Race*, Tavistock. The author analyses the historical process whereby people have come to be classified on the basis of physical characteristics into distinct 'racial' types.

Banton, M. and Harwood, J. (1975) *The Race Concept,* David and Charles. An examination of the way the concept has been and still is used.

Biddliss, M. D. (Ed.) (1979) *Images of Race,* Leicester University Press. A collection of eleven essays, first published between 1864 and 1880, on the theme of race, though, inevitably, the term is not always used consistently. It gives an insight into Victorian views on 'race'.

Billig, M. (1980) *Psychology, Racism and Fascism,* available from A. F. and R. Publications, 21 Great Western Buildings, 6 Livery Street, Birmingham, 3. A short, introductory booklet.

Black, N. and Dworkin, G. (1977) *The I.Q. Controversy,* Quartet.

Burnham, C. (1971) *Race,* Batsford. An introduction to the subject for secondary pupils which includes an analysis of the meaning of race, and examines racism in Nazi Germany, South Africa, America and Britain.

Darlington, C. D. (1969) *The Evolution of Man and Society,* Allen and Unwin. A massive work which examines the concept of race. 'Perhaps this should be compulsory reading for anyone wishing seriously to get to grips with the concepts of race and their implications.' (CRE).

Ehrlich, H. J. (1973) *The Social Psychology of Prejudice,* Wiley. The author examines a vast range of material on the theme of prejudice.

Flynn, J. R. (1980) *Race, I. Q. and Jensen,* RKP. An attempt to answer Jensen's views on race and IQ.

Gillie, O. (1976) *Who Do You Think You Are? Man or Superman: The Genetic Controversy,* Hart Davis McGibbon.

Jencks, C. (1972) *Inequality,* Penguin. A classic American study of the inability of education to achieve egalitarian ideals.

Kamin, L. J. (1977) *The Science and Politics of I.Q.,* Penguin. Though not specifically on race, an illuminating analysis of the political uses to which IQ scores have been put.

Kuper, L. (Eds.) (1975) *Race, Science and Society.* Allen and Unwin. A collection of readings on the theme of how scientists have handled the notion of race.

Lawler, J. (1978) *I.Q., Heritability and Racism,* Lawrence and Wishart. A Marxist critique of Jensenism.

Mead, M. et al (Eds.) (1968) *Science and the Concept of Race,* Columbia University Press. Based on a symposium called by a number of scientific groups in the US, the book is a critical survey of what science has to say about race.

Progressive Labor Party Pamphlet (1974) *Racism, I.Q. and the Class Society,* USA.

Richardson, K. and Spears, D. (Eds.) (1972) *Race, Culture and Intelligence,* Penguin.

Rose, S., Hambley, J. and Haywood, J. (1973) *Science, Racism and Ideology.* In the *Socialist Register,* Milliband, R. and Saville, J. (Eds.). A critical discussion of the issues.

Rose, S. and Richardson, K. (1978) *Race and Intelligence,* free from the Publicity Department, National Union of Teachers, Hamilton House, Mabledon Place, London, WC1. This pamphlet attacks the idea that there are immutable, genetically based differences of character and ability between people of different colour. It should be in every staffroom.

Sherwood, R. (1980) *The Psychodynamics of Race: Vicious and Benign Spirals,* Harvester Press. Based on a study of a multiracial London suburb, the author attempts to unravel the psychological bases of racial conflict.

Smith, A. (1968) *The Body,* Allen and Unwin. A general book on the human body which includes a chapter on race.

Smith, A. (1975) *The Human Pedigree,* Allen and Unwin. This book has a chapter on racial variation, and also discusses the arguments relating to intelligence.

Watson, P. (Ed.) (1973) *Psychology and Race,* Penguin. Cross-cultural studies from a psychological perspective.

A large number of anthropologists have addressed themselves to the question of race. Paul Bohannan, for example, in common with anthropologists in general, stresses the social dimension to racial classification: 'Races are socially recognized categories into which people are thrust on the basis of socially recognized criteria'. (Bohannan, P., 1966 *Social Anthropology,* Holt, Rinehart and Winston, p. 198.)

SECTION E: RACIST PARTIES AND GROUPS

Due to the rather specialist nature of this section we have included some relevant articles.

Benewick, M. (1977) *The Fascist Movement in Britain,* Allen and Unwin. A comprehensive study, though the author makes the debatable suggestion that Britain is somehow immune to right-wing extremism.

Billig, M. (1978) *Fascists,* Academic Press. An examination of National Front membership. The book contains a number of interviews with NF members.

Edgar, D. (1977) *Racism, Fascism and the Politics of the National Front,* Institute of Race Relations. An important booklet.

Fielding, N. G. (1981) *The National Front,* RKP. A participant observation study of the organization and functioning of the National Front.

Walker, M. (1977) *The National Front,* Fontana. An analysis of the National Front and its history by a journalist on The *Guardian.*

Articles

Hanna, M. (1974) The National Front and other right-wing organisations. *New Community,* Vol. iii, 49–55.

Harrop, M. and Zimmerman, G. (1977) The anatomy of the National Front. Mimeograph, Department of Geography, University of Essex.

Husbands, C. T. (1977) The National Front becalmed. *Wiener Library Bulletin,* Vol. XXX, 74–79.

Nugent, N. and King, R. (1979) Ethnic minorities, scapegoating and the extreme right. In Miles, R. and Phizacklea, A. (Eds.) *Racism and Political Action in Britain,* RKP.

Scott, D. (1975) The National Front in local politics: some interpretations. In Crewe, I. (Ed.) *British Political Sociology Yearbook,* Vol. 2, The Politics of Race, Croom Helm.

Taylor, S. (1978) The National Front: backlash or bootboys? *New Society,* 11 August, 283–284.

Taylor, S. (1978) The National Front: a contemporary evaluation. *University of Warwick Occasional Papers,* No. 16.

Taylor, S. (1979) The National Front: anatomy of a political movement. In Miles, R. and Phizacklea, A. (Eds.) *op. cit.*

PART 2: ORGANIZATIONS AND GROUPS

SECTION A: GENERAL

ACTION GROUP ON IMMIGRATION AND NATIONALITY (AGIN)
44 Theobald's Road, London, WC1X 8SP. Tel. 01-405 5527. Examples of publications:
  Immigration Control: How it Works
  Immigration: How the Truth Got Swamped (Criticizes the Select Committee Report and
    Conservative Party proposals.)

ACTION GROUP AGAINST NATIONALITY LAWS
C/O Millar Centre, 59 Trinity Road, London, SW17. Examples of publications:
  Immigration: Where the Debate Goes Wrong (1978)
  The New Immigration Rules (1978)

AMNESTY INTERNATIONAL
Tower House, 8–14 Southampton Street, WC2E 7HF.

THE ANTI-NAZI LEAGUE (ANL)
12 Little Newport Street, London, WC2. Tel. 01-734 5456. A pressure group mobilizing those
who are concerned about the growth of racist parties and groups in Britain.

ANTI-RACIST, ANTI-FASCIST CO-ORDINATING COMMITTEE
C/O All-London Teachers Against Racism and Fascism, 66 Littleton Street, London, SW18.

ANTI-SLAVERY SOCIETY FOR THE PROMOTION OF HUMAN RIGHTS
60 Weymouth Street, London, W1N 4DX. Tel. 01-935 6498.

ASSOCIATION FOR BLACK ETHNIC ADVANCE
7 Auckland Avenue, London, NW10.

ASSOCIATION FOR MULTI-RACIAL SOCIAL WORK
C/O 3 Bowmer Lane, Fritchley, Derbyshire. The association publishes the journal *Multi-Racial
Social Work*.

BLACK PEOPLE'S INFORMATION SERVICE
301 Portobello Road, London, W1. Tel. 01-969 9825. A comprehensive advisory service.

BLACK PEOPLE'S POLITICAL PRESSURE GROUP
78 Becklow Gardens, Shepherd's Bush, London, W12.

BLACK SOCIALIST ALLIANCE
Box 24, 182 Unger Street, London, N1.

BRITISH YOUTH COUNCIL
57 Chalton Street, London, NW1 1HU. Tel. 01-387 7559. The council has produced study
documents and, with the CRE, *Racial Harmony Information Pack*—aimed at youth leaders.

CAMPAIGN AGAINST THE IMMIGRATION LAWS (CAIL)
C/O Lansbury House, Camberwell Grove, London, SE5.

CAMPAIGN AGAINST RACIAL DISCRIMINATION (CARD)
52 Station Road, London, NW10.

CAMPAIGN AGAINST RACIST LAWS (CARL)
PO Box 353, London, NW5 4NH.

CAMPAIGN ON RACISM, I.Q. AND THE CLASS SOCIETY
C/O BSSRS, 9 Poland Street, London, W1.

CENTRE FOR HUMAN RIGHTS AND RESPONSIBILITIES
16 Ponsonby Street, London, SW1. Tel. 01-834 2457.

COLONIALISM AND INDIGENOUS MINORITIES RESEARCH AND ACTION (CIMRA)
92 Plimsoll Road, London, N4. CIMRA produces *Natural People's News*—a newsletter containing information and articles on cultures world wide.

COMMISSION FOR RACIAL EQUALITY (CRE)
Main addresses of the CRE:

London: Elliot House, 10/12 Allington Street, London, SW1E 5EH. Tel. 01-828 7022.
Birmingham: Daimler House, 4th Floor, 33 Paradise Circus, Queensway, Birmingham, B1 2BJ. Tel. 021-643 7525/7526.
Leeds: 133 The Headrow, Leeds, LS1 5Q. Tel. Leeds 34413/4.
Leicester: Haymarket House, 4th Floor, Haymarket Shopping Centre, Leicester, LE1 3YG. Tel. 0533 57852.
Manchester: Maybrook House, 40 Blackfriars Street, Manchester, M3 2EG. Tel. 061-831 7782/8.

The CRE can provide a great deal of help for teachers working in the field of multiracial education, e.g. teaching aids, article reprints, publications, lists of local Community Relations Councils.

The Commission has produced a large number of free and priced publications. Write to the CRE for an up-to-date list. As examples, the following are available free of charge:
   Audio-Visual Aids for Teachers
   Books for Under-Fives in Multi-Racial Britain
   Teaching the History of Africa
   The Multi-Faith School: A Guide for Teachers
   Teaching about the Caribbean
   Teaching about India, Bangladesh and Pakistan
   Teaching about Africa
   Sikh Children in Britain
   Chinese Children in Britain
   Race in the Curriculum (contains a comprehensive resource guide)
   Teaching about Islam
   Racialism and Sexism in Books: A Check List
   Some People Will Believe Anything
   A Bibliography for Teachers
   Ethnic Minorities in Britain: Statistical Background
   Looking for Work: Black and White School Leavers in Lewisham
   Brick Lane and Beyond: An Enquiry into Racial Strife and Violence in Tower Hamlets
   Community and Race Relations. An annotated film catalogue, listing films on prejudice, minorities, employment, Africa, America, Asia, Australasia and the Far East, Commonwealth, Europe, South Africa, West Indies, community action, religions and customs.
Examples of priced publications:
   Education Needs of Children from Minority Groups. Reference Series No. 1 (reprint)
   The Education of Ethnic Minority Children
   In-Service Education of Teachers in Multi-Racial Areas. An evaluation of current practice
   A Second Chance. Further education in multi-racial areas

Meeting Their Needs. An account of language tuition for ethnic minority women
Don't Rush Me. The comic-strip, sex education and a multi-racial society (S. Curtis)
The Employment of Non-English-Speaking Workers. What industry must do. Reference
Series No. 2
World Religions. A handbook for teachers
Home Tutor Kits (reprint)
Ethnic Minorities in the Inner City. The ethnic dimension in urban deprivation in England (C.
Cross)
Urban Deprivation, Racial Inequality and Social Policy. A Report. Reference Series No. 13
(HMSO)
Caring for Under-Fives in a Multi-Racial Society
Fostering Black Children. Reference Series No. 6
Multi-Racial Britain. Social services response
Who Minds? A study of working mothers and childminding in ethnic minority communities
Some of My Best Friends . . . A report on race relations attitudes. Reference Series No. 8
Five Views of Multi-Racial Britain. Talks on race relations broadcast by BBC TV
Between Two Cultures. A study of relationships between generations in the Asian commun-
ity in Britain (M. Anwar). Reference Series No. 12
The Arts Britain Ignores. The arts of ethnic minorities in Britain (N. Khan)
As They See It. A race relations study of three areas from a black viewpoint (L. Morrison).
Reference Series No. 11
Seen But Not Served. Black youth and the Youth Service
East Comes West. Background to Hinduism, Islam and Sikhism (P. Holroyde et al)
Teacher Education For a Multi-Cultural Society
Who's Doing What? A directory of projects and groups involved in race relations
The *Reprints* series (free), e.g. Teaching About Africa, give quite a lot of information regarding
history and culture in addition to providing a resources guide—books, films, posters, etc.—for
teachers.
The CRE will also give financial help to schools which wish to organize a multicultural or
international parents function. It will also fund small-scale research projects initiated by schools.
Periodicals:
New Community. A forum for the discussion of race/ethnic relations. Quarterly.
New Equals. Tabloid format newspaper. Bimonthly (free).
Education Journal. Bimonthly (free).
Employment Report. Quarterly (free).
Network. Bimonthly (free).

COMMONWEALTH INSTITUTE
Kensington High Street, London, W8 6NQ. Tel. 01-602 3252/6. The institute has exhibitions, a
library and special facilities for visits by school parties.

COMMONWEALTH RE-SETTLEMENT ASSOCIATION
9–11 Nicholl Road, London, NW10. Tel. 01-961 0112.

COMMUNITY RELATIONS COUNCILS
These are locally based groups—see the local telephone directory for addresses, or contact the
CRE. *NATIONAL ASSOCIATION OF COMMUNITY RELATIONS COUNCILS*. Mary
Ward House, 5–7 Tavistock Place, London, WC1H 9SS. Tel. 01-388 3368. Main services of
CRCs:
To publish material of use to teachers.
Education Officers visit schools to advise on libraries.
Community Relations Officers work in schools with teachers, and will liaise between school
and the community.
Provide contacts with translators for teachers when there is a need to communicate with
parents.

DEPARTMENT OF EMPLOYMENT RACE RELATIONS ADVISORY SERVICE
Hanway House, Red Lion Square, London, WC1.

EQUAL OPPORTUNITIES COMMISSION
Overseas House, Quay Street, Manchester, M3 3HN. Tel. 061-833 9244.

HARMONY INTER-RACIAL FAMILIES
42 Beech Drive, Borehamwood, Herts, WD6 4QU. Tel. 01-953 8862.

HIGH COMMISSIONS
Apart from being a source of general information about their countries, High Commissions usually have films available on loan.
Bangladesh: 28 Queen's Gate, London, SW7. Tel. 01-584 0081.
Barbados: 6 Upper Belgrave Street, London, SW1. Tel. 01-235 8686.
Botswana: Suite W, 3 Buckingham Palace Gate, London SW1. Tel. 01-730 5216.
China: SACU, 152 Camden High Street, London, NW1. Tel. 01-485 8241.
Eastern Caribbean: King's House, 10 Haymarket, SW1. Tel. 01-930 7902.
Ghana: 13 Belgrave Square, London, SW1. Tel. 01-235 4142.
Guyana: 3 Palace Court, London, W2 4LP. Tel. 01-229 7684.
India: India House, Aldwych, London, WC2. Tel. 01-836 8484.
Ivory Coast Embassy: 190 Piccadilly, London, W1. Tel. 01-235 6991.
Jamaica: 48 Grosvenor Street, London, W1. Tel. 01-499 8600.
Kenya: 45 Portland Place, London, W1. Tel. 01-636 2371.
Malaysia: 43 Belgrave Square, London, SW1. Tel. 01-245 9221.
Mauritius: Mezzanine Suite, Grand Buildings, Trafalgar Square, London, WC2. Tel. 01-581 0294.
Nigeria: 9 Northumberland Avenue, London, WC2. Tel. 01-839 1244.
Pakistan: 35 Lowndes Square, London, SW1. Tel. 01-235 2044.
Swaziland: 58 Pont Street, London, SW1. Tel. 01-584 2159.
Tanzania: Tanzania House, 43 Hertford Street, London, W1. Tel. 01-499 8951.
Trinidad and Tobago: 42 Belgrave Square, London, SW1. Tel. 01-245 9351.
Uganda: Uganda House, Trafalgar Square, London, WC2. Tel. 01-458 9285.
Zambia: 7/11 Cavendish Place, London, W1.

INSTITUTE OF RACE RELATIONS
247–249 Pentonville Road, London, N1 9NG. Tel. 01-837 0041. An established resource centre, providing a library service, bibliographies and various publications, e.g.
Racism, Fascism and the Politics of the National Front (1977), D. Edgar.
The institute publishes the journal *Race and Class* (quarterly) which contains serious articles on race and politics in an international context.

INTERNATIONAL LABOUR ORGANISATION (ILO)
Dolcis House, 87/91 New Bond Street, London, W1Y 9LA.

INTERNATIONAL WORKGROUP FOR INDIGENOUS AFFAIRS
C/O CIMRA (see p. 178).

THE JOINT COUNCIL FOR THE WELFARE OF IMMIGRANTS (JCWI)
44 Theobald's Road, London, WC1X 8SP. Tel. 01-405 5527/8. The council campaigns for non-racist laws relating to immigration and nationality, and assists minorities in claiming their rights. Occasional publication: *Immigrant Voice*. Also publishers booklets, e.g.
The Unpublished Report: The European Commission on Human Rights and British Immigration Policy (1979).

LABOUR PARTY ACTION GROUP
2 Campbell Road, London, E17 6RR. The group occasionally publishes material of interest to those working with ethnic minorities, for example:

Local Authorities: Ethnic Records and Monitoring. A publication which argues that local authorities should keep up-to-date records in respect of ethnic minorities in order to tackle problems of disadvantage more effectively. It criticizes the government's decision not to include questions on ethnic orgins in the 1981 census and to rely only on a sample survey for information.

LEAGUE OF IMMIGRANTS
C/O Cecil Road, Ilford, Essex. Tel. 01-553 5363.

MANCHESTER LAW CENTRE
595 Stockport Road, Longsight, Manchester, 15 5NA. Tel. 061-225 5111. The centre provides legal information on immigration, housing, social services, etc. Publications include:
Handbook No. 5, *The Thin End of the White Wedge* (1981) This discusses the new nationality laws, second-class citizenship and the welfare state.

MARTIN LUTHER KING FOUNDATION
1–3 Hildreth Street, London, SW12 9RQ. Tel. 01-673 6511/6512.

MIGRANT SERVICES UNIT
68 Chalton Street, London, NW1.

MINARET HOUSE
9 Leslie Park Road, Croydon, Surrey. Produces pamphlets, books, charts. A list is available.

MINORITIES ADVISORY SERVICES LTD
8 Halliford Street, London, N1. Tel. 01-359 9291.

MINORITIES ARTS ADVISORY SERVICE
91 Mortimer Street, 2nd Floor, London, W1.

MINORITY RIGHTS GROUP (MRG)
Benjamin Franklin House, 36 Craven Street, London, WC2 5NG. Tel. 01-930 6659. The group publishes reports of discrimination against ethnic, religious and cultural minorities or majorities in all parts of the world. Some selected titles:
No. 13, *East Indians of Trinidad and Guyana*
No. 14, *The Roma: The Gypsies of Europe*
No. 15, *What Future for the Amerindians of South America?*
No. 22, *Race and Law in Britain and the United States*
No. 28, *Western Europe's Migrant Workers*
No. 35, *Australia's Policy towards Aborigines 1967–1977*
No. 38, *The Social Psychology of Minorities*
No. 41, *The International Protection of Minorities*
Also worth reading:
The Roots of Prejudice (M. Jahoda)—a leaflet discussing the psychology of racism. Write to MRG for an up-to-date list of publications.

NATIONAL COUNCIL FOR CIVIL LIBERTIES (NCCL)
186 Kings Cross Road, London, WC1. Tel. 01-278 4675. An organization concerned with the question of civil rights as they affect all groups in society. The council gives practical legal help.

OXFAM
274 Banbury Road, Oxford, OX2 7DZ. The organization publishes a range of educational books and materials on the Third World, e.g. a wallet on India containing photographs, factsheets, games, recipes and a record.

RACE TODAY COLLECTIVE
74 Shakespeare Road, London, SE24 0PT. Tel. 01-737 2268. The collective provides help for black groups in Britain, and publishes the bimonthly magazine *Race Today: an expression of the black experience.*

RESEARCH UNIT ON ETHNIC RELATIONS
8 Priory Road, Bristol. Tel. 0272 311296.

ROCK AGAINST RACISM
14 Whitehall Road, Hanwell, London, W7.

ROYAL ANTHROPOLOGICAL INSTITUTE
56 Queen Anne Street, London, W1M 9LA. Tel. 01-486 6832. A folder is available on resource material, and films are available on loan. An Education Committee will advise teachers.

RUNNYMEDE TRUST
62 Chandos Place, London, WC2N 4HH. Tel. 01-836 3266. The Runnymede Trust was set up as an educational charity to 'provide expert and reliable information on the subject of race relations and immigration.' As well as carrying out its own research, the trust collects and disseminates a wide range of academic research. Services include the following.

Information Office
Statistics, reports, leglislation changes relating to Britain and the EEC are kept on record, as well as a small collection of reference books. The trust also possesses an extensive collection of press cuttings dating from 1968. The library staff are available to help with queries from teachers and others.

Publications
In addition to publishing its own research, the trust occasionally publishes work done independently. Information handbooks on race relations for the general reader are published regularly. The trust also publishes specialized training material relating to the industrial field.

Runnymede Trust Bulletin
This is a monthly summary of current information on race relations and immigration.

Briefing Papers
Occasional briefing papers are prepared by the research staff dealing with various current issues, analyses of statistical information and summaries of important new research.

A full list of publications is available from the trust. The following are some recent examples:
Reports
'Sus'—A Report on the Vagrancy Act 1824 (1978) C. Demuth.
A New Immigration Policy (1978) A. Dummett.
Problems of Asians in Penal Institutions (1978) R. Horabin.
A Review of the Race Relations Act 1976: proceedings of a one-day seminar organized by the Runnymede Trust (1979).
Briefing Papers
Census 1981—Question on Racial and Ethnic Origin (1978) C. Saunders.
Immigration—a brief guide to the numbers game (1978) C. Demuth.
Linguistic Minorities in Britain (1978) K. Campbell-Platt, revised by S. Nicholas.
Language Testing and Indirect Discrimination (1979) S. Grosz.

SCRAP SUS CAMPAIGN
C/O Lambeth Law Centre, 506 Brixton Road, London, SW9. 'Sus'—the offence of being a 'suspected person loitering with intent to commit a felonious offence'—came under the terms of the 1824 Vagrancy Act. The section was replaced in 1981 with the Criminal Attempts Act which Scrap Sus claims is used in the same way by the police.

TAMIL ASSOCIATION
164 Browning Road, Manor Park, London, E12. Tel. 01-552 5827. A charity organization concerned with cultural and linguistic advancement.

THIRD WORLD FIRST (TWF)
232 Cowley Road, Oxford, OX4 1UH. Tel. 0865 45678.

THIRD WORLD PUBLICATIONS LTD
151 Stratford Road, Birmingham, B11 1RD. Tel. 021-773 6572. This organization promotes and distributes a wide range of materials (many designed for teaching purposes) from and about the Third World, for example:
  White Student Black World (1978)—a handbook against racism.

UJAMAA CENTRE LOAN SERVICE
Multi-ethnic Development and Third World Studies Centre, Oxfam Education Department, 14 Brixton Road, London, SW9. Tel. 01-582 2068. A wide range of teaching materials is available from the centre. Write for a complete list.

UNITED KINGDOM IMMIGRANTS ADVISORY SERVICE
Brettenham House, Savoy Street, London, WC2E 7EN. Tel. 01-240 5176. The service gives help with appeals, and information of latest developments and how they affect minority groups.

VOLUNTARY COMMITTEE ON OVERSEAS AID AND DEVELOPMENT
25 Wilton Road, London, SW1. The Education Unit acts to supervise the work of aid agencies such as War on Want and Oxfam. Resources for teaching available on developing nations, for example:
  The Development Puzzle—a sourcebook for teachers.

WAR ON WANT
467 Caledonian Road, London, N7 9BE. Tel. 01-609 0211.

WORLD STUDIES PROJECT
C/O One World Trust, 24 Palace Chambers, Bridge Street, London, SW1. Tel. 01-930 7661. Examples of various publications include:
  Learning for Change in World Society: Reflections, Activities, Resources, (rev. ed., 1979) R. Richardson
  Schools in a World of Change (1979) R. Richardson, M. Flood and S. Fisher.

SECTION B: EDUCATIONAL

ALL LONDON TEACHERS AGAINST RACISM AND FASCISM (ALTARF)
2 Balfour Road, London, SE24.

ASSOCIATION OF TEACHERS OF CULTURAL AND SOCIAL STUDIES
C/O The Coleraine Regional Teachers Centre, Coleraine, County Derry, Northern Ireland. The New University of Ulster in partnership with the Association has linked up with a number of schools to develop a curriculum project dealing with important issues, including minority groups (see below).

ASSOCIATION FOR THE TEACHING OF CARIBBEAN AND AFRICAN LITERATURE
C/O The Commonwealth Institute. 'Aims to make inroads into schools by encouraging teachers to take seriously works of African and West Indian authors, and to teach them in the classroom.'

BANGLADESH EDUCATION CENTRE
1 Wilberforce Road, Finsbury Park, London N4.

CARIBBEAN TEACHERS' ASSOCIATION
44 Waller Road, London, SE14. Tel. 01-639 6599. The association has produced, with Lewisham Council for Community Relations, *Black Teachers Speak Out*.

CENTRE FOR INFORMATION ON LANGUAGE TEACHING AND RESEARCH (CILT)
20 Carlton House Terrace, London, SW1Y 5AP. Tel. 01-839 2626. A number of publications are available, for example:
   Information Guide 1: Languages for Minorities: A Bibliography (1977)
   A Survey of English Courses for Teachers (1970)
   Information Guide 10: Information for Language Teachers (1976)—a list of organizations
      and centres
   Information Guide 13: Teachers Centres with a Special Interest in Language Teaching (1977)
   Teaching Foreign Languages in Great Britain—Why? (1976)
   Modern Languages for the 1980s (1976)
CILT Reports and Papers:
   No. 10: *The Space Between . . . English and Foreign Languages at School* (1974)
   No. 12: *Less Commonly Taught Languages: Resources and Problems* (1975)
   No. 14: *Bilingualism and Education: The Dimensions of Diversity* (1976)
CILT Reading List:
   Applied Linguistics and Language Teaching (1975)

CENTRE FOR SOCIAL EDUCATION
Nansen House, 63 Millbank, London, SW1. Tel. 01-834 6327.

CENTRE FOR URBAN EDUCATIONAL STUDIES (CUES)
34 Aberdeen Park, London, N5 2BL. Tel. 01-226 5437/2922. CUES is a specialist teachers' centre serving all ILEA teachers. Its brief is the exploration of issues in inner-city education with particular emphasis on community education and the role of language in multiracial London.

Community division. School-based curriculum development work, courses, conferences. Emphasis is on community resources for education in a multi-ethnic society and home/school/community links.

Language division. Collaborative curriculum development projects with teachers leading to new materials, courses and conferences.

Library. Display collection of children's books which reflect the ethnic mix in schools, also teacher's books on sociology, education, race, linguistics and language. Selected book lists available. Over 1000 English language books are stocked as well as a small collection of fiction in Greek, Turkish, Arabic, Chinese, Hindi, Punjabi, Gujarati, Bengali and Urdu. There are also non-fiction materials, e.g. on the arts, cookery and literature. Teachers, librarians and others are invited to visit the centre (preferably by appointment) to examine the resources on display.

Projects. A number of projects have been set up at CUES by the ILEA on various aspects of multicultural education. As a result of these projects a range of material for use by teachers has been produced. An up-to-date list may be obtained from the Information Unit at CUES.

Courses. For details of courses available for teachers (ILEA) write to the Information Unit.

Materials. A *resource list*—a single duplicated sheet—is available free (s.a.e.). It deals with resources in the following categories:

Resources for the Multi-Ethnic Society within the ILEA (inspectors/interpreters/advisory
   teachers/projects, etc.)
Resources for the Multi-Ethnic Society: useful addresses
Minority Group Organizations
Education Offices in Borough CRCs
Films for the multi-ethnic society
   The centre produces *occasional papers*. Also available (free) is a booklet giving practical
guidelines for teachers in primary and secondary schools: *Assessing Children's Books for a
Multi-Ethnic Society*.
   The centre has developed a number of language learning packs. Published by the ILEA
Learning Materials Service (LMS), these are available from CUES. For further details see the
LMS Primary and Secondary Catalogues.
   In addition, the centre publishes a newsletter, *Junction*.

CENTRE FOR WORLD DEVELOPMENT EDUCATION
128 Buckingham Palace Road, London, SW1V 1JS. Tel. 01-730 8332/3.

CHILDREN'S RIGHTS WORKSHOP
4 Aldebert Terrace, London, SW8 1BH. Tel. 01-582 4483. The workshop produces a booklist
detailing children's books, and reference works on racism in children's literature. It publishes
Children's Book Bulletin, and has published:
   Racist and Sexist Images in Children's Books
It also distributes:
   Interracial Digest
   Interracial Books for Children

CHRISTIAN AID EDUCATION DEPARTMENT
PO Box 1, London, SW9. Tel. 01-733 5500.

COMMISSION FOR BLACK STUDIES
63 Napier Court, London, SW6. A number of publications are available, for example:
A Treatise on Black Studies (1973) S. Morris. A book which discusses what 'black studies'
   means and outlines 36 lessons aimed at middle and upper secondary children.

COMMONWEALTH STUDENTS CHILDREN'S SOCIETY
4 Cambridge Terrace, London, NW1. Tel. 01-487 3444. The society gives help and advice to
Commonwealth students with children.

COUNCIL FOR EDUCATION IN WORLD CITIZENSHIP
43 Russell Square, London, WC1. Tel. 01-637 8321. Available from the council:
   World Studies: Resource Guide (1977)

COUNCIL ON INTERRACIAL BOOKS FOR CHILDREN (CIBC)
CIBC Resource Centre, Room 300, 1841 Broadway, New York, NY 10023, USA. A group
formed in the United States 'to initiate much needed change in the all-white world of children's
publishing and to promote a literature for children that better reflects the aspirations of a
multi-racial, multi-cultural society.'
   Produced in the US but available in the UK are teaching packs based on sound-colour film
strips:
   From Racism to Pluralism
   Understanding American Indian Stereotypes
   Understanding Institutional Racism
Write to CIBC for catalogue.

CROWN STREET LANGUAGE CENTRE
Crown Street, Liverpool, 8. Various publications useful for teachers are available:
  Teaching English as a Second Language (shortened version without bibliography, free)
  Bibliography of Textbooks (free)
  English Language Difficulties for Chinese Speakers (shortened version, free)
  Aspects of Chinese Culture—background information for teachers (history, religion, festivals, etc.)
  Information for Teachers of Chinese Children (free)

DEPARTMENT OF EDUCATION AND SCIENCE (DES)
Elizabeth House, York Road, London, SE1 7PH. Tel. 01-928 9222. The DES occasionally publishes material on the theme of race/ethnicity and education. For example:
  Education Survey 10: *Potential and Progress in a Second Culture* (1971) HMSO
  Education Survey 13: *The Education of Immigrants* (1971) HMSO
  Education Survey 14: *The Continuing Needs of Immigrants* (1972) HMSO
  Education Survey 15: *Educational Needs of Children from Minority Groups* (1974) HMSO
  Educational disadvantage and the educational needs of immigrants—*Observations on the Report on Education of the Select Committee on Race Relations and Immigration.* (Cmnd. 5720) (1974) HMSO

EDUCATION FOR PEACE GROUP
Peace Pledge Union, 6 Endsleigh Street, London, WC1H 0DX.

ETHNIC MINORITIES ADVISORY COMMITTEE ON EDUCATION
C/O Education Offices, Somerset Road, London, N17. Tel. 01-808 3251.

INNER LONDON EDUCATION AUTHORITY
County Hall, London, SE1. A number of projects and organizations are run under the auspices of the ILEA.
  Multi-Ethnic Inspectorate: Room 465, County Hall, London, SE1. Tel. 01-633 8551.
  Secondary Curriculum Development Unit: Based at the Centre for Learning Resources. Tel. 01-582 4509.
  Senior Liaison Officer CRE/ILEA: Room 465, County Hall. Tel. 01-633 8977.
  Translators and Interpreters: For details of translators and interpreters covering a range of mother tongues telephone 01-633 1448.
  English as a Second Language in Further Education: The co-ordinator is based in Room 437, County Hall. Tel. 01-633 8979.
  Lambeth Whole School Project: Aspen House, Christchurch Road, London, SW2 3ES. Tel. 01-674 3179. The project is based on five schools in Lambeth, and the aim is 'to identify processes by which schools can review the requirements of their multi-ethnic populations in all respects of their life and work and develop appropriate responses.'
  Afro-Caribbean Education Resources Project: Based at the Centre for Learning Resources. Tel. 01-582 9027. The project focuses on collecting resources and information and developing Afro-Caribbean materials for use in primary and secondary schools. Trial materials are available for teachers.
  East London Whole School Project and Asian Resource Project: Based at Room 465, County Hall.

  The following are not exclusively concerned with multi-ethnic education, though much of their work is in this field.
  Centre for Learning Resources: 275 Kennington Lane, London, SE11. The reference library of all books and audio-visual aids is on Tel. 01-735 8202. The loans library is on Tel. 01-735 1338.
  Teacher's Centres: These give courses and can arrange courses on request on aspects of multi-ethnic education. A full list will be found in 'ILEA Resources for Teachers', available from the ILEA Learning Materials Service and CUES.

Learning Materials Service: The service lists learning materials developed in the Authority
   for London schools—free from LMS (Tel. 01-226 9143).
Education Library: Situated on the 4th floor, County Hall. Tel. 01-633 6990.
Centre for Language in Primary Education: Ebury Bridge, Victoria, London, SW1. Tel.
   01-834 0476. The library has a large reference collection of reading schemes and
   readers for mother-tongue English and English as a foreign language children. There is
   also a collection of fiction books.
The English Centre: Ebury Bridge, Victoria, London, SW1. Tel. 01-828 4906. The centre
   provides various teaching materials. Its publications include *The English Magazine*,
   which contains writings by ILEA pupils from a variety of backgrounds.
Centre for Urban Educational Studies: (See page 184).

MEDIA RESOURCES CENTRE
Highbury Station Road, London, N1 1SB. Tel. 01-226 0041. The centre produces material useful
for teachers working in multi-ethnic schools. In particular:
   Drop in on Some London Families. A set of broadsheets illustrating the lifestyles of some
      recently settled families in London. For secondary schools.
   Caribbean Lifestyles 1 and 2
   Lifestyles of Cyprus
   Some Lifestyles of India, Pakistan and Bangladesh
   Some Lifestyles of Chinese People from Hong Kong and Singapore

NATIONAL ASSOCIATION FOR MULTI-RACIAL EDUCATION (NAME)
86 Station Road, Mickleover, Derby, DE3 5FP. Tel. 0283 511751. The association has produced a
number of publications, for example:
   West Indian Language: Attitudes of the School (1967) V. Edwards
   Deciding What to Teach (1978) G. Ward
   New Approaches in Multiracial Education is the official journal which is produced termly
The London branch of NAME also produces a twice termly newsletter: *Issues in Race and
Education.* This is available from 11 Carelton Gardens, Brecknock Road, London, N19. Details
of the Exhibition on Racial Bias in Learning Materials may be obtained from 150 Weston Park,
London, N8. Tel. 01-340 0961.

NATIONAL ASSOCIATION FOR RACE RELATIONS TEACHING AND ACTION RESEARCH (NARTAR)
C/O Centre for Applied Research in Education, University of East Anglia, Norwich, NR4 7TJ.
NARTAR is an association of teachers concerned with teaching about race relations. Various
materials are available. An example of publications:
   Teaching About Race Relations (1979) P. J. Sykes (Ed.)
   Also at the university is a project on problems and effects of teaching about race relations. This
is carried out under the supervision of Lawrence Stenhouse, and is about to be published.

NATIONAL COMMITTEE ON RACISM IN CHILDREN'S BOOKS (NCRCB)
The Methodist Church, 240 Lancaster Road, London, W11. The committee publishes *Dragon's
Teeth* (quarterly), which contains articles on the theme of racism in children's literature. For
subscriptions write to the Treasurer, NCRCB, 46 High Street, Southall, Middlesex, NB1 3DB.
NCRCB organized the campaign against the Golliwog in general and Robertson's Golly in
particular.

NATIONAL EDUCATIONAL DEVELOPMENT TRUST (formerly the Advisory Centre for Education)
32 Trumpington Street, Cambridge.

NATIONAL EXTENSION COLLEGE
18 Brooklands Avenue, Cambridge, CB2 2HN. The college has produced a set of four, eight-

page comics, each with a double-page factsheet, all enclosed in a wallet. Written for young people, the aim is to link up colonialism with current immigration.

NATIONAL FOUNDATION FOR EDUCATIONAL RESEARCH (NFER)
The NFER has published quite a lot of material on multiracial education. The following is a selection.
> *Educational Assessment of Immigrant Pupils* (1971) J. M. Haynes
> *Immigrant Pupils in England: The L.E.A. Response* (1971) H. E. R. Townsend
> *Organisation in Multi-racial Schools* (1972) H. E. R. Townsend and E. M. Brittan
> *Race, School and Community* (1974) F. Taylor
> *The Immigrant School Learner: A Study of Pakistani Pupils in Glasgow* (1975) L. Dickinson et al
> *Language Proficiency in the Multi-Racial Junior School* (1975) E. C. McEwan, C. V. Cripps and R. Sumner
> *The Half-Way Generation: A Study of Asian Youths in Newcastle-upon-Tyne* (1976) J. H. Taylor
> *The Cultural Context of Thinking: A Comparative Study of Punjabi and English Boys* (1976) P. A. S. Ghuman
> *Able to Learn?: The Pursuit of Culture-Fair Assessment* (1978) S. Hegarty and D. Lucas

THE NETHERLANDS INSTITUTE FOR PEACE AND SECURITY
Nederlands Instituut voor Vredesvraagstukken, Alexanderstraat 7, P.O. Box 1781, 's Gravenhage, Netherlands. The Peace Education Group at the institute has developed various materials on the theme of teaching about minorities.

RACISM/SEXISM RESOURCE CENTRE
1841 Broadway, New York, NY 10023, USA. The centre has published *Racism in the English Language,* and other materials. Write for complete list.

SCHOOLS COUNCIL
160 Great Portland Street, London, W1N 6LL. Tel. 01-580 0352.
> Regional: 129 Cathedral Road, Cardiff, CF1 9SX. Tel. 0222 44946/7.
> Pendower Hall, West Road, Newcastle-upon-Tyne, NE15 6PP. Tel. 0632 743620.
> (Library Headquarters) Balne Lane, Wakefield, WF2 0DQ. Tel. 0924 71231, ext. 41.
'The Council sponsors research leading to improved teaching methods and changes in the curriculum in schools. It also monitors and makes recommendations on examinations.'
   The council has sponsored around 200 projects leading to published material for use by pupils. Some of this is related to multiracial education, for example:
> *English for Immigrant Children (5–16)* EN 05 01
> *Teaching English to West Indian Children (7–9)* EN 07 01
   A range of teaching material is available published by various publishers in the UK. As examples:
> *English for Immigrant Children Project (5–16+):* SCOPE, Stage 1 pupil material and teacher's book (2nd edition)
> *Scope Plays and Dialogues* (1978) *Scope Storybook,* Stage 2 pupil material and teacher's book, and Senior Course (14+) pupil material and teacher's books 1969–75; three teacher's handbooks 1976–78. Published by Longman.
   The council has also published a number of Working Papers, for example:
> *Teaching English to West Indian Children,* J. Wight (1971) Schools Council Working Paper 29, Evans Methuen Educational
> *Immigrant Children in Infant Schools,* Schools Council Working Paper 31 (1970) Evans Methuen Educational
> *Multi-Racial Education: Needs and Innovation,* H. E. R. Townsend, (1973) Schools Council Working Paper 50, Evans Methuen Educational

A pamphlet series is also available, for example:
   Multi-Ethnic Education: The Way Forward—Pamplet 18—A. Little and R. Willey (1981)

SCHOOLS CULTURAL STUDIES PROJECT
The New University of Ulster, Coleraine, BT52 1SA, Northern Ireland. Materials developed by SCSP are available from the Association of Teachers of Cultural and Social Studies (see above).

SCHOOL KIDS AGAINST THE NAZIS (SKAN)
12 Little Newport Street, London, WC2. Tel. 01-734 5456.

SCHOOL OF ORIENTAL AND AFRICAN STUDIES
University of London, Extra Mural Division, Malet Street, London, WC1 7HP. Tel. 01-837 7651. The Extra Mural Studies Division provides lectures on Asian and African history, art, etc., for schools and colleges of further education. They also run a teachers' resource centre, and can organize conferences. Booklists and information sheets are available free. Some of the publications available are:
   Teachers' Handbook on Resources on Asia and Africa, M. Killingray and W. B. Mason
   The World of Islam: A Teachers' Handbook, R. Tames
   Africa: A Teachers' Handbook, M. Killingray
   Perspectives on World Religions: A Handbook for Teachers, R. Jackson (Ed.)

SIKH STUDENT FEDERATION
C/O 46 High Street, Southall, Middlesex.

TEACHERS AGAINST THE NAZIS (TAN)
12 Little Newport Street, London, WC2. Tel. 01-734 5456.
Available from TAN are *Tankits*, a series of teaching packs:

1. Secondary Kit—*Nazism in Germany and the National Front in Britain.*
2. Junior Kit—*Multiracial Stories and Rhymes*
3. *Women and the Nazis* (Secondary)
4. *John Bull* (Junior)—a poem on British racism
5. *The Roots of Racism* (Junior/Secondary)

UNIVERSITY OF LONDON INSTITUTE OF EDUCATION
Centre for Multicultural Education, Bedford Way, London, WC1H 0A1. Tel. 01-636 1500. The centre produces Occasional Papers:
   Occasional Papers No. 1—*Racism in Society and Schools: History, Policy and Practice,*
      (1980) C. Mullard.

WEST INDIAN STUDENTS UNION
122 Fernlea Road, London, SW12.

WEST INDIAN STUDENTS CENTRE
1 Collingham Gardens, London. Tel. 01-373 6838.

WORLD STUDIES TEACHER—EDUCATION NETWORK
27 Queens Road, Hertford, SG13 8AZ. Tel. 0992 57639.

SECTION C: MINORITY

AFRICA CENTRE
38 King Street, London, WC2. Tel. 01-836 1973.

AFRO-CARIBBEAN ASSOCIATION
13 Rideout Street, London, SE18. Tel. 01-855 2920.

AKLOWA: CENTRE FOR TRADITIONAL AFRICAN DRUMMING AND DANCING
Takeley House, Brewers End, Takeley, Essex, CM22 6QJ. Tel. 0279 871062.

AMALGAMATED AFRO-CARIBBEAN COUNCIL
19 Milton Road, London, W7.

AMERICAN-INDIAN MOVEMENT (AIM)
UK Committee, 6 Woodland Road, Birmingham 31. Tel. 021-476 7003.

ASIAN COMMUNITY ACTION GROUP
15 Bedford Road, London, SW4. Tel. 01-733 7494. The group has produced a *Maternity Rights Handbook,* originally published in English by NCCL, now in Gujarati for Asian women. Also available: *Sheltered Housing and the Asian Elderly*—a brief report on a sheltered housing project in Wandsworth, London. This was the first of such schemes when it was set up three years ago.

ASIAN WELFARE SOCIETY
41 Montbelle Road, Eltham, London, SE9.

ASIAN YOUTH MOVEMENT
226 Lumb Lane, Bradford 8, West Yorkshire.

ASIAN YOUTH CIRCLE
229 Seven Sisters Road, London. Tel. 01-272 1442.

ASSOCIATION OF CEYLONESE IN THE U.K.
15 Macfarlane Road, London, W12. Tel. 01-749 4532.

ASSOCIATION OF JAMAICANS
102 Marlborough Hill, Harrow. Tel. 01-427 0971.

BANGLADESH YOUTH FRONT
Polner Street, London. Tel. 01-481 1166.

BANGLADESH YOUTH LEAGUE
Toynbee Hall, Commercial Street, London, E1.

BANGLADESH CENTRE
24 Penbridge Gardens, London. Tel. 01-229 9404.

BENGALI INSTITUTE
12 Elsham Road, London, W14. Tel. 01-723 4520.

BENGALI WORKERS' ACTION GROUP
C/O 39 Tottenham Street, London, W1. Tel. 01-580 4576.

BHARATIYA VIDYA BHAVAN (U.K. CENTRE) INSTITUTE OF INDIAN CULTURE
4A Castletown Road, London W14 9HQ. Tel. 01-381 3086.

BRITISH CARIBBEAN ASSOCIATION
15 Brockwell Gardens, London SE24.

CARIBBEAN AND COMMONWEALTH MULTI-RACIAL ASSOCIATION
86 Abbeville Road, London, SW4. Tel. 01-622 8404.

CARIBBEAN OVERSEAS ASSOCIATION
3 Ormiston Grove, Shepherd's Bush, London, W12.

CHINESE ACTION GROUP
The Basement, 11 Gerrard Street, London, W1.

CO-ORDINATING COMMITTEE OF SRI LANKA ORGANISATION U.K.
Flat 24, Devonport, Sussex Gardens, London, W2. Tel. 01-402 9065.

CYPRIOT CENTRE
15 Hercules Street, London, N7. Tel. 01-272 4142.

EAST AFRICAN ASIAN ASSOCIATION
34 Cavendish Road, London, N4.

FEDERAL COUNCIL OF INDIAN ORGANISATIONS
36 Hereford Road, London, W9.

FEDERATION OF BANGLADESHI ORGANISATIONS
2 Marchwood Road, Sheffield, 6.

GOAN OVERSEAS ASSOCIATION
36 Errington Road, London, W9.

HINDU CENTRE LONDON
39 Grafton Terrace, London, NW5. Tel. 01-567 9340.

HONG KONG GOVERNMENT LIAISON OFFICE
6 Grafton Street, London, W1X 3LB. Tel. 01-499 4701. Leaflets and pamphlets with up-to-date information on Hong Kong are available. This is also a free film/filmstrip hire service for schools.

INDIAN NATIONAL ASSOCIATION (GB)
10 Woodlands Road, Southall, Middlesex.

INDIAN WORKERS' ASSOCIATION
18 Featherstone Road, Southall, Middlesex.

LONDON/CHINA CHINESE ASSOCIATION
C/O Hong Kong and Shanghai Ranking Compilation, 17 Gerrard Street, London, W1.

MONTSERRAT OVERSEAS BLACK PROGRESSIVE ALLIANCE
46A Lydford Road, London, W9.

MOROCCAN WORKERS ACTION GROUP
Paddington Advice and Law Centre, 441 Harrow Road, London, W9. Tel. 01-960 4481.

NATIONAL ASSOCIATION OF ASIAN YOUTH
46 High Street, Southall, Middlesex. The association aims to help Asian youth in Britain by advising youth workers and setting up its own projects. It has published *Which Half Decides?* dealing with sex discrimination, British nationality and immigration laws.

NATIONAL GYPSY COUNCIL
61 Blenheim Crescent, London, W11 2EG. Tel. 01-727 2916.

ONAWAY TRUST
275 Main Street, Shadwell Leeds, West Yorkshire, LS17 8LH. Tel. 0532 659 611. The trust

concerns itself with the preservation of minority cultures around the world, especially native American.

PAKISTAN MUSLIM WELFARE ASSOCIATION
184 Charlton Lane, Charlton, London, SE7. Tel. 01-853 3415.

PAKISTAN WELFARE ASSOCIATION
86 Oakleigh Road, London, N11.

PAKISTAN WORKERS' ASSOCIATION
24 Buckley Road, London, NW10.

PAN-AFRICAN PEOPLE'S ORGANISATION
4 Dalston Lane, London, E8.

SIKH CULTURAL SOCIETY OF G.B.
88 Mollison Way, Edgware, Middlesex.

SURVIVAL INTERNATIONAL
36 Craven Street, London, WC2N 5NG. Tel. 01-839 3267. This organization is concerned with small-scale societies and their survival in a modern world.

UNITED ANGLO-CARIBBEAN SOCIETY
19 Adelaide Road, West Ealing, London, W13 9ED.

WEST INDIAN STANDING CONFERENCE
46A Lydford Road, London, W9.

WEST INDIAN WELFARE ASSOCIATION
Flat 5, The Poplars. 152 Queens Drive, London, N14.

SECTION D: RELIGIOUS

ALL FAITHS FOR ONE RACE
1 Finch Road, Lozells, Birmingham, B19 1HS. Tel. 021-523 8076. A number of booklets are available:
   So What Are You Going to Do About the National Front?, T. Holden
   Christianity and Race, J. Hick
   The New Nazism of the National Front, J. Hick

BAPTIST UNION OF GREAT BRITAIN AND IRELAND: COMMUNITY RELATIONS COMMITTEE
4 Southampton Row, London, WC1. Tel. 01-405 9803.

BRADFORD COUNCIL OF CHURCHES RACIAL HARMONY GROUP
20 Moorside Gardens, Bradford, West Yorkshire, BD1 1BA. The council has produced (in association with Leeds Diocesan Justice and Peace Commission) a *Race Pack* based on discussion/action papers for use in groups of up to ten. The aim is to get people to face up to the issue of racism.

BRITISH COUNCIL OF CHURCHES: RACE RELATIONS UNIT
2 Easton Gate, London, SW1W 98T. Tel. 01-730 9611. The council has a full-time staff and produces various publications and study material. A catalogue gives details of publications, and a

list of grants made available to groups. A regular newsletter gives details of policies. Examples of publications:

> *The Place of Imagination in Religious Education*, J. Prickett—teaching RE in a multiracial society.
> *Christian Witness in a Plural Society,* Bishop L. Newbigin
> *A New Threshold,* Bishop D. Brown—concerned with Muslims in Britain.
> *Combating Racism,* K. Sansbury
> *Resources for a Plural Society*—a comprehensive bibliography

CATHOLIC COMMISSION FOR RACIAL JUSTICE
1 Amwell Street, London, EC1R 1UL. Tel. 01-278 5880.

CENTRE FOR THE STUDY OF ISLAM AND CHRISTIAN–MUSLIM RELATIONS
Selly Oak Colleges, Birmingham, B29 6LE. Tel. 021-472 4321.

CHRISTIAN ACTION
43 Holywell Hill, St. Albans, Herts, AL1 1HE. Tel. 0727 54832.

CHRISTIANS AGAINST RACISM AND FASCISM
1 Finch Road, Lozells, Birmingham, B19 1HS. Tel. 021-523 8076. 'This is a movement of Christians committed to opposing these two evils in all their forms and to working for the benefits of a multi-racial society. It tries to look critically at the racial scene and invites membership from both individuals and Christian groups.' The organization produces leaflets regularly.

CHURCHES COMMITTEE ON MIGRANT WORKERS IN EUROPE
Avenue d'Auderghem 23, B—1040 Brussels, Belgium. Tel. 02-734-18-09.

CHURCH OF ENGLAND: BOARD OF SOCIAL RESPONSIBILITY
Church House, Westminster, London, SW1P 3NZ. Tel. 01-22 9011.

EVANGELICAL RACE RELATIONS GROUP
19 Draycott Place, London, SW3 2SJ. Tel. 01-581 0051.

FEDERATION OF STUDENTS' ISLAMIC SOCIETIES IN THE UNITED KINGDOM AND EIRE
38 Mapesbury Road, London, NW2 4JD.

FRIENDS COMMUNITY RELATIONS COMMITTEE
Friends House, Euston Road, London, NW1 2BJ. Tel. 01-387 3601.

ISLAMIC COUNCIL OF EUROPE
18 Northumberland Avenue, London, WC2. Tel. 01-930 7209.

ISLAMIC CULTURAL CENTRE
The Mosque, 146 Park Road, London, NW8. Tel. 01-723 7611.

THE ISLAMIC FOUNDATION
223 London Road, Stoneygate, Leicester, LE2 1ZE. Tel. 0533 700725.

METHODIST CHURCH: DIVISION OF SOCIAL RESPONSIBILITY
Central Buildings, London, SW1 9NH. Tel. 01-930 2638.

MUSLIM PARENTS' ASSOCIATION
550 Manchester Road, Bradford 5, West Yorkshire. Tel. 0274 493753.

SCOTTISH CHURCHES COUNCIL COMMUNITY AND RACE RELATIONS GROUP
41 George IV Bridge, Edinburgh, EH1 1E1. Tel. 031-225 1772. An advisory group to the
Scottish Council of Churches which is involved with permanent and student minority groups in
Scotland.

SIKH MISSIONARY SOCIETY (U.K.)
27 Pier Road, Gravesend, Kent.

UNION OF MUSLIM ORGANISATIONS OF THE U.K. AND EIRE
109 Campden Road, London W1. Tel. 01-229 0539. The union has produced a number of
publications, for example:
    Guidelines and Syllabus on Islamic Education (1978)
    Islamic Education and Single Sex Schools (1975)

WORLD COUNCIL OF CHURCHES: MIGRATION DESK
150 Route de Ferney, 1211 Geneva 20, Switzerland. Tel. Geneva 989400.

WORLD COUNCIL OF CHURCHES: PROGRAMME TO COMBAT RACISM
2 Eaton Gate, London, SW1 9BT. Established in 1969 to fight racism, the WCC organizes
international seminars. An assessment of the first five years is in the leaflet *A Small Beginning*. A
leaflet is also available explaining the programme. A useful study guide for teachers is:
    Racism in Children's and School Textbooks

SECTION E: WOMEN

AWAZ ASIAN WOMEN'S GROUP
C/O 41 Stockwell Green, Richmond, London, SW9.

BANGLADESH WOMEN'S ASSOCIATION
38 Umfreville Road, London, N4.

BLACK WOMEN'S GROUP
C/O 41a Stockwell Green, Richmond, London, SW9.

CYPRIOT WOMEN'S LEAGUE
96 Palmerston Road, London, N22.

ORGANISATION OF WOMEN OF ASIAN AND AFRICAN DESCENT
C/O 41a Stockwell Green, Richmond, London, SW9.

PAKISTAN WOMEN'S MOVEMENT
81 The Vale, London, NW11 8TJ.

SANGAM—ASIAN WOMEN'S ORGANISATION
235/237 West Hendon Broadway, London, NW9.

SRI LANKA WOMEN'S ASSOCIATION
194 Woolwich Road, London, SE10.

UNITED BLACK WOMEN'S ACTION GROUP
C/O 2 Chasewater House, Bryton Road, London, N8.

WOMEN INDIA ASSOCIATION
6 East Close, Ealing, London, W5.

PART 3: PERIODICALS

Where a periodical has already been mentioned under *Organizations*, only the name of the organization will be given here.

Africa (Quarterly)
International African Institute, 210 High Holborn, London, WC1V 7BW.

Africa Annual
59 Paddington Street, London, W1.

Africa Centrepoint (Monthly)
Published by the Africa Centre. For members only.

Africa Confidential (Fortnightly)
Flat 5, 33 Rutland Gate, London, SW7.

Africa Currents (Quarterly)
Africa Publications Trust, 48 Grafton Way, London, W1P 5LB.

Africa Guide (Annually)
World of Information, 21 Gold Street, Saffron Walden, Essex, CW10 1EJ.

Africa Magazine (Monthly)
Africa Journal Ltd, 54a Tottenham Court Road, London, W1P 0BT.

Africa South of the Sahara (Annually)
Europa Publications Ltd, 18 Bedford Square, London, WC1B 3JN.

Africa Woman (Alternate months)
Africa Journal Ltd—see above.

African Affairs (Quarterly)
Royal African Society, 18 Northumberland Avenue, London, WC2N 5BJ.

African Development
African Buyer and Trader (Publications) Ltd, Wheatsheaf House, Carmelite Street, London, EC4Y 0AX.

African Research and Documentation (3 per year)
ASAUK, Centre of West African Studies, University of Birmingham, P.O. Box 363, B15 2TT.

African Social Research (2 per year)
Manchester University Press, Oxford Road, Manchester, M13 9PL.

The Afro-Caribbean Post (Weekly)
5 Grantham Road, London, SW9 9DP.

The Asian (Monthly)
101 Praed Street, London, W21NT.

Asian Affairs (2 per year)
Journal of the Royal Asiatic Society of Great Britain and Ireland, 56 Queen Anne Street, London, W1M 9LA.

The Asian Express (Monthly)
1a Poppleton Road, London, E11.

The Asian Observer
47 Marlborough Drive, Clayhill, Ilford, Essex, IG5 0JW.

Black Liberator (Occasional)
Publications Distribution Co-operative, 27 Clerkenwell Close, London, EC1R.

Caribbean Chronicle (Bimonthly)
48 Albemarle Street, London, W1X 4AR.

Children's Book Bulletin
From Children's Rights Workshop.

Community and Race Relations Unit Newsletter
From the British Council of Churches Community and Race Relations Unit.

Dragon's Teeth (Quarterly)
Bulletin of the National Committee on Racism in Children's Books.

Educational Journal (Bimonthly)
Free from the Commission for Racial Equality.

Employment Report (Quarterly)
Free from the Commission for Racial Equality.

English Language Teaching (Quarterly)
Oxford University Press, Journals Department, Press Road, Neasden, London NW10 0DD.

Ethnic Groups (4 issues per volume)
Gordon and Breach Science Publishers Ltd, 41–42 William IV Street, London, WC2N 4DE.

Ethnic and Racial Studies (Quarterly)
Goldsmith College, University of London. Published by RKP.

India Weekly
Wheatsheaf House, Carmelite Street, London, EC4Y 0AX.

ILEA Multi-Ethnic Newsletter
From the ILEA.

Institute of Race Relations Newsletter
From the institute.

Interracial Digest
From the Council on Interracial Books for Children.

Issues in Race and Education
From the London branch of the National Association for Multi-Racial Education.

Jamaican Weekly Gleaner
International Press Centre, Suite 511, 76 Shoe Lane, London, EC4.

Junction
Newsletter of the Centre for Urban Educational Studies.

Language Learning (2 per year)
    5714, University Hospital, University of
    Michigan, Ann Arbor, Michigan 48109,
    USA.
Language Matters
    From the Centre for Learning in Primary
    Education.
Language in Society (3 per year)
    Cambridge University Press, P.O. Box
    110, Cambridge, CB2 3LR.
Language Teaching and Linguistic Abstract
    (Quarterly)
    Cambridge University Press, P.O. Box
    110, Cambridge, CB2 3LR.
Multicultural Education Abstracts (Quarterly)
    Up-to-date information regarding develop-
    ments in this field. International Centre
    for Multicultural Education, City of
    Birmingham Polytechnic, 9 Westbourne
    Road, Edgbaston, Birmingham B15
    3TN.
Multi-Racial Social Work
    Journal of the Association for Multi-
    Racial Social Work.
National Foundation for Educational Research:
    Research News
    From NFER.
Natural People's News
    Newsletter of Colonialism and Indigenous
    Minorities Research and Action.
Network (Bi-monthly)
    Free from the Commission for Racial
    Equality.
New Approaches in Multiracial Education
    (Termly)
    Journal of the National Association for
    Multiracial Education.
New Community (Quarterly)
    From the Commission for Racial Equal-
    ity.
New Equals (Bimonthly)
    Free from the Commission for Racial
    Equality.

New Era (6 per year)
    18 Campden Grove, London, W8 4JG.
New Internationalist (Monthly)
    Montague House, High Street, Hunting-
    don, PE18 6EP.
One World (Monthly)
    World Council of Churches, 150 Route de
    Ferney, P.O. Box 66, 1211, Geneva, Swit-
    zerland.
Patterns of Prejudice
    Published by the Institute of Jewish
    Affairs.
Race and Class (Quarterly)
    Journal of the Institute of Race Relations.
Race Relations Abstracts (Quarterly)
    Department of Applied Social Studies,
    Sheffield City Polytechnic, Sheffield S10.
Race Today (Monthly)
    Published by the Race Today Collective.
Rights (Bimonthly)
    From the National Council for Civil Liber-
    ties.
Root
    6 Queen Street, Mayfair, London, W1.
Runnymede Trust: The Bulletin (Monthly)
    See the Runnymede Trust.
Schools Council Newsletter
    From the Council.
Sikh Courier (Quarterly)
    88 Mollison Way, Edgware, Middlesex,
    HA8 5QN.
Tesol Quarterly
    School of Language and Linguistics,
    Georgetown University, Washington DC,
    USA.
West Africa (Weekly)
    West African Publishing Co. Ltd, 53 Hol-
    born Viaduct, London, EC1A 2FD.
West Indian Digest
    122 Shaftesbury Avenue, London, W1V
    8HA.
West Indian World (Weekly)
    111 Mathias Road, London, N16.

PART 4: BOOKSHOPS

Arthur Probsthain, 41 Great Russell Street,
    London, WC1.
Bogle L' Ouverture, 5a Chigwell Place, Ealing,
    London, W13. Tel. 01-579 4920. Afro-
    Caribbean Material.
Books from India, 69 Great Russell Street,
    London, WC1.
The Bookplace, 13 Peckham High Street, Lon-
    don, SE15. Tel. 01-701 1757.

Bread and Roses Bookshop, 316 Upper Street,
    London, N1. Tel. 01-226 9483.
Campaign Books, 9 Rupert Street, London,
    W1. Tel. 01-493 8233.
Centerprise Bookshop, 136–138 Kingsland
    High Street, Hackney, London, E8. Tel.
    01-254 9632.
Grass Roots, 61 Goldbourne Road, London,
    W10. Tel. 01-969 0687.

Harriet Tubman Books, 27/29 Grove Lane, Birmingham, B21 9ES. Afro-Caribbean historical and political material, plus children's books.

Headstart Bookshop, 25 West Green Road, Seven Sisters, London, N15. Tel. 01-802 2838.

Islamic Book Centre, 148 Liverpool Road, London, N1.

Luzac and Co. Ltd, 46 Great Russell Street, London WC1.

New Beacon Books, 76 Stroud Green Road, London, N4. Tel. 01-271 4889. Africa and the Caribbean, including children's books.

Pam's Sikh Bookshop, 17 Abbotshall Road, London, SE6.

The Sabarr Bookshop, 121 Railton Road, Brixton, London, SE24. Tel. 01-274 6785.

Shakti, 46 High Street, Southall, Middlesex. Tel. 01-574 1325.

Soma Books, 38 Kennington Lane, London, SE11. Tel. 01-735 2102. Largest distributor of children's books on Indian and Islamic culture.

Third World Books, 28 Sackville Street, London, W1. Tel. 01-734 0481.

Third World Publications, 151 Stratford Road, Birmingham, B11 1RD. Tel. 021-773 6572. Import many books covering a wide range of subjects and issues from the Third World. Special packs are available for schools.

The World of Islam Publishing Co. Ltd, 85 Cromwell Road, London, SW7.

PART 5: FILM DISTRIBUTORS

Blacks Britannica Defence Committee, 4 Perrins Lane, London, NW3. *Blacks Britannica* is a film which looks at the situation of black people in Britain today. There have been many attempts to have the film suppressed.

British Broadcasting Corporation, Film Hire, Woodston House, Oundle Road, Peterborough, PE2 9PZ. Tel. 0733 52257/8.

British Film Institute, 81 Dean Street, London, W1. Tel. 01-437 4355.

Central Film Library, Government Buildings, Bromyard Avenue, London, W3 7JB. Tel. 01-743 5555.

Cinema Action, 35a Winchester Road, London, NW3. Tel. 01-586 2762.

Columbia-Warner, 135 Wardour Street, London, W1. Tel. 01-439 7621.

Commission for Racial Equality, (See under *Organizations.*) Film catalogue: *Community and Race Relations.*

Concord Film Council, 201 Felixstowe Road, Ipswich, Suffolk, 1P3 9BJ. Tel. 0473 76012.

Concordia Films, 117 Golden Lane, London, EC1Y 0TL.

Contemporary Films, 55 Greek Street, London, W1. Tel. 01-734 4901.

Educational Foundation for Visual Aids, Film Library, Paxton Place, London, SE27. Tel. 01-670 4247.

Edward Patterson Associates, 68 Copers Cope, Beckenham, Kent.

Fair Enterprises, 5 Park Village, London, NW1. Tel. 01-387 3230.

Gateway Film Hire Library, 15 Beaconsfield Road, London, NW10 2LE. Tel. 01-451 1127.

Guild Sound and Vision, Woodston House, Oundle Road, Peterborough, PE2 9PZ. Tel. 0733 52257/8. Deals in all Open University productions.

High Commissions, These often have films available—see under *Organizations.*

Independent Broadcasting Authority, Contact individual television companies.

ILEA Educational T.V. Centre, Thackery Road, London, SW8.

Knight Film Distributors, 53 Brewer Street, London, W1. Tel. 01-437 6487.

Liberation Films, 6 Bramshill Gardens, London, NW5 1JH. Tel. 01-450 7855

The Other Cinema, Little Newport Street, London, WC2. Tel. 01-734 8508/4131/ 7410.

Religious Films Ltd, Foundation House, Walton Road, Bushey, Watford, WD2 2JF. Tel. 923 5444

Voluntary Committee on Overseas Aid and Development, Parnell House, Wilton Road, London, SW1.

Name Index

199

Subject Index